The study of the work of Christ under the headings of Prophet, Priest, and King has a venerable history reaching back to the careful analysis of John Calvin and even before him. But, I venture that it has never been done like this study, which employs a sound method of biblical theology. Edgren takes the widest possible biblical context for the Old Testament themes that lead us to Christ; he begins with the initial promise in Genesis that generates hope for a fallen race. This work is a refreshing, and non-technical, approach to the fulfilment of the offices of the Israelite mediators of God's word, redemption, and rule. It will repay the reader with many insights into how the discipline of biblical theology works and what its benefits are. It will also enrich you with a deeper understanding of the gospel of what God has done for us in Christ.

—**Graeme Goldsworthy, PhD**, author and former lecturer at Moore Theological College, Sydney

Scott Edgren's independent study has given new insights into the Scriptures. Especially significant in this regard are chapter 2 ("Toledot: A New Generation") and chapters 6 and 7 ("Dueling Serpents" and "Discerning Good and Evil," respectively). Readers will grow in their appreciation of the riches in the Bible as they read *Hope Begins*.

It was my privilege to have Scott as a student when I taught at Grace University in Omaha, Nebraska. I have followed his ministry in Ecuador and am now especially pleased to recommend his book, *Hope Begins*. As the Apostle John wrote, "I have no greater joy than to hear that my children walk in truth" (3 John 1:4).

—**Harold J. Berry, ThM, DD**, author and former professor at Grace University, Omaha, Nebraska

Many readers of the Scriptures have no idea of the larger Story Line of the Bible—they are not able to see the forest for all the trees! Edgren's book is a wonderful aid for helping readers to see the Bible's Big Picture. It brims with insights and wonderful illustrations from the author's own experience which help to make sense of many of the fascinating details of biblical revelation. It is communicated with a passion by someone whose exploration of the many trees of Holy Scripture has led him to a mountain peak, where he has seen the astonishing vista of the forest!

—**Stephen G. Dempster, PhD**, author and professor
at Crandall University, Moncton, New Brunswick

Hope Fulfilled
Tracing Themes in Biblical Theology

Hope Begins

Scott Edgren

CHRIST TRUTH
Newton, Kansas

Hope Begins, Book 1
Hope Fulfilled: Tracing Themes in Biblical Theology Series

Published in the United States of America by CHRISTtruth Publishing
www.CHRISTtruthPublishing.com

Version 1.2

Paperback ISBN: 978-0-9988696-2-9

Library of Congress Control Number: 2017905244

To the most important people in my life:

Kristi

David

Shelby

Joel

Luke

Lindsey

With sincere gratefulness to:

Amy Simpson for her invaluable editing

My parents, John and Marlene Edgren, for instilling in me a love for God's Word

Brent Becker and Phil Holcomb for their encouragement and stimulating conversations about the beauty of Scripture

My many students who have given me feedback and additional observations that are interspersed throughout this book

Contents

Introduction

We slowly crept forward, peering through the branches of the cottonwood tree and across the motionless water in the direction of our unseen enemy. I motioned to my younger sisters to leave our bikes under the tree and follow me toward the jumble of branches and brush at the edge of the water. We began to make our way across the mass of logs that stretched across to the other side of the pond—a dam that had been built and rebuilt by beavers to create the habitat necessary to support their lodge in the small body of water. When we reached the center of the dam—the lowest spot, where water was slowly trickling over the sticks under our feet—the exaggerated danger of falling off one side or the other of our walkway nearly eclipsed the threat we felt from our imaginary foes across the way. Finally, after assuring ourselves that things were under control on the other side of the creek, we made our way home for dinner, content with the hours of exploration and playing Nancy Drew and The Hardy Boys.

As a young man growing up in rural Nebraska, I lived about a mile and a half from that very small creek. Although I didn't know it at the time, that little stream eventually flowed into a larger one called North Dry Creek. The creek by our house was the source of a lot of fun for a handful of kids. We were attracted to one specific spot where a beaver dam formed a small pond that was the source of hours of entertainment for active minds and bodies. In spite of all the joy we got from playing at the beaver dam, there was something missing that could have made it even better. Our concept of the beaver dam lacked perspective.

Another waterway that deeply fascinated me in those years was the Platte River, located several miles away from our house. The Platte, very important to Nebraska's history, is an interesting river. It's called a braided stream because of its many channels that join and then later separate again with small islands in between. It has sometimes been described as being a mile wide and only an inch deep, which is only a slight exaggeration.

At the time, I didn't have a very good perspective of these two bodies of water. It never really occurred to me to consider how they were related. But in fact, as I confirmed this morning with Google Maps, North Dry Creek is a tributary of the Platte River. They always seemed like such different entities. Not only that, but to my limited perspective, the creek by our house didn't really feel like it could be any longer than maybe about a mile. That's because I knew only one little part of it, almost just one spot—the beaver dam. If I could have backed up to get a different perspective—zoomed out, so to speak, on Google Maps—I would have seen how the details related to the whole.

This book is a little about Bible interpretation and a lot about biblical perspective. We're going to take several steps backward and look at the Bible from a different perspective than what you might be used to. Instead of focusing on details, we'll try to see the big picture those details work together to paint. It's not that we won't notice the details; that's where our interpretation will play a big part. Rather, we'll selectively choose the details that most help us with the bigger picture, and that latter perspective is our ultimate goal.

We often approach the Bible the way I did our little creek. We visit different parts of the Bible as if they were each little beaver dams with only what they have to offer us on their own. That kind of attention to detail is important, and it's right for us to spend hours and even days enjoying our visits to those ponds. But sometimes what is missing—at least speaking from my own experience—is attention to the linear progression of Scripture. We play at the beaver dam with hardly even an awareness of the Platte River to which it connects. If you will join me in the next pages, I think you'll find a new perspective in one way or another. I am enjoying a new way of looking at God's Word, and I'd love to share it with you. Each little pond at the beaver dams of the Bible is important, but if we stop there, we're missing that which is of greatest significance. The most important things God has given us in the Bible are the mighty rivers of truth. Let's follow them and see where they take us.

My task in this book is to help you see more connections between different texts of the Bible than what you might be accustomed to observing. My hope is that you'll gain new insights into God's Word by studying broad themes that can be truly appreciated only by backing up and seeing the whole. If applied well, these themes will in turn help you with a deeper understanding of the detail of every individual passage you study.

My approach to Scripture has undergone a fundamental change in the last ten years. It's not that my theological beliefs have changed in any significant way. Rather, I have seen Scripture come alive in a whole new way as I notice exactly *how* it presents the most foundational truths of the Christian faith. When I learned to look for the overarching theological connections in the Bible, God's Word became even more exciting to read. I started to notice allusions and artistry in Scripture that seemed almost too fanciful to be real. At first I was skeptical, but as I cautiously looked for clues to the authors' intended meaning, I found there are too many such clues to deny their existence. Their abundance precludes the possibility of being coincidental. I learned to give the benefit of the doubt to God and to his Word—to assume that the Bible is much more complex than I might at first expect. I learned to give more credit to the theological message presented in the Old Testament concerning Christ before he even came; and I learned to look with more care at the New Testament to see how it bases the presentation of its truth on all that came before. In short, I learned to ask how each component, every detail, of the Bible fits with God's overall plan in redemption history. My new assumption is that every single word of Scripture in some way supports that overarching plan.

Reading the Bible has now taken on a whole new level of excitement! I anticipate the discovery of a whole new "hidden meaning" behind every text. I don't mean the meaning is hidden in the sense that it's unclear and it can't be discovered from a plain interpretation of Scripture. I mean the deepest theology presented in the Bible is often cleverly and artistically presented in a way that is less than immediately obvious. Much of the Bible's message is put on a slightly higher shelf, and the diligent seeker will find his or her effort rewarded. Finding a hidden meaning is much more exciting than reading a list of facts. I believe God purposefully made Bible study challenging so we can enjoy the fruit of our labor that much more. And what I am finding lately has definitely been rewarding me!

What makes this search even more exciting is that every quest ends in finding the same treasure; sooner or later, every theme of the Bible ends up pointing to Christ. Over and over, I end up finding him. Finding Christ in each theme then serves as a confirmation that the assumptions I have made about the Bible's artistry are correct. Even more important, when I see Christ magnified in this way it multiplies my love for him. As I approach Scripture, there is nothing more thrilling than when I find my Savior in yet another passage. I am more convinced than ever that revealing Christ is the main purpose behind all of God's Word.

The entire Bible shares the same purpose that John had for writing his gospel, which was patently written so that we "may believe that Jesus is the Christ, the Son of God, and that by believing [we] may have life in his name" (John 20:31). (See also John 5:46 and Luke 24:27.) Although I have been a follower of Christ for many years, I am finding more recently that my faith contains new dimensions. My belief in Christ is accompanied by a level of passion I previously did not know. I want it to keep increasing, and I want to invite my readers to move in the same direction I am. Let's fan the flames of our passion for Jesus with the bellows he gave us for that very purpose—the Bible.

Seeing the broader picture of the message of the Bible instills in us a greater confidence about who God is and what he is doing in the history of the world. We believe God offers salvation as the perfect solution to the problem of humanity. We also believe God is infinitely powerful; he can accomplish what he wants exactly when he wants to. Why, then, does it take him so long to save his people? The Bible is one long, continuous story of God at work throughout history, rescuing humanity from their broken relationship with Him and providing a way of reconciliation. Sin enters the world as early as the third chapter, and it isn't fully defeated until Revelation 20. Everything in between is part of the slow progression of redemption history. We might be tempted to think the world would have been much more perfect if God would have built into it a certain impossibility for sin. Or at the very least, could he not have redeemed Adam and Eve immediately after the fall, restoring creation to its original state, or even wiping things clean and starting all over? I believe all these possibilities were real options for God, but for his own reasons he chose not to act on them. There is something about the long progression of redemptive history that brings God more glory. The more we observe what the Bible teaches us about this process, and the more we reflect on that message, the more we will marvel at God's greatness. Writing this book has given me a lot of time to do just that. I hope I can inspire some of the same wonder in you as you consider the redemptive historical themes in the following pages.

In a broader sense, this kind of study of redemptive historical themes is often called biblical theology. By this term I don't mean theology that is not unbiblical. Rather, I am referring to a branch of theology that is distinct from systematic theology. D. A. Carson has done a great job of defining the two concepts:

> Systematic Theology...looks at theological topics logically and atemporally. That is, how they fit together taken as a whole, without a lot of consideration given to how they've been revealed across time.... So it asks questions like, "Who is God?" "What is sin?" "What does the cross achieve?" "What is the person and work of Jesus Christ?" And so on. You see, all of these questions are questions that are addressing the whole field from a particular

topical perspective.... Biblical Theology is more interested in the temporal development of theological themes across the sweep of redemptive history.[1]

One particular kind of biblical theology is "the examination of certain themes that run right through the entire canon where you're keeping an eye on the temporal development."[2] That is exactly the kind of biblical theology we will be pursuing in these pages.

Any careful and responsible attention to the theology of the entire Bible will reveal that all its important themes point to Christ. When we look at individual passages of Scripture—the little ponds in the Bible—we sometimes miss this fact. The great rivers of Scripture, however, all point ultimately to Christ and his ministry. The farther back we step, the easier it is to see our Lord. Even Jesus himself was aware of this fact. I would have loved to hear him explain much of it on the road to Emmaus: "And beginning with Moses and all the Prophets, he interpreted to them in all the Scriptures the things concerning himself" (Luke 24:27).

If you are familiar with the concept of typology in biblical interpretation, you will likely recognize its implementation in much of this book. Typology is the establishment in Scripture of historical connections between specific people, events, objects, or institutions of the Old Testament and their counterparts in the New Testament. The Old Testament entity is referred to as the type; its corresponding entity in the New Testament is the antitype. The antitype is always Christ or some aspect of his ministry. The study of themes in biblical theology relies heavily on the use of typology in some instances, and in others simply operates in a very similar way. The main difference is that types of Christ are usually quite well defined and studied more rigidly. The discipline of biblical theology, on the other hand, recognizes that even when there may not be a formal typological comparison present, the authors of Scripture sometimes leave clues that they are intending to make connections between the Old and New Testaments.

In order to trace the development of themes through the whole length of the Bible, one needs to make certain assumptions about the unity of its message. Centuries ago there was a general understanding that the Bible was one book with a unified message. Its interpreters clearly recognized that

---

[1] D. A. Carson, 'Introduction to Biblical Theology.' *The Gospel Coalition*. The Gospel Coalition's 2014 National Women's Conference. Audio. 29 June 2014. Web. http://resources.thegospelcoalition.org/library/introduction-to-biblical-theology. Accessed 28 July 2015.

[2] Ibid.

in spite of the number and variety of human authors, the Bible also had one divine author who oversaw the entire process. A proper view of the inspiration of Scripture confirms this creative cooperation between the human and divine authors. With the rise of modern critical approaches to biblical studies, however, the conservative respect for God's Word has been under attack for several decades. This attack has made us a little gun-shy, and probably somewhat unconsciously, we have slowly changed our perspective of the Bible. In the following quote Stephen G. Dempster describes the faulty perspective that sometimes characterizes our study. He discusses the conclusion of some who believe the Bible is just "an interesting, eclectic collection of ancient texts...[which] contain no storyline, coherence or unity — and, in the judgment of many, any unity that might exist would be strictly artificial."[3]

> At first sight this conclusion seems to result from looking objectively at the literary character of the Bible, but in my judgment it is the consequence not only of getting lost in the massive variety of literary material which is the Bible, but also and particularly of the hermeneutical myopia of the last few centuries of biblical scholarship, which has used presuppositions that magnify the texts and minimize the Text. One of the philosophical assumptions that has produced this situation has been a diminution in the belief that the Bible is the Word of God: to expect authorial unity is simply too much to ask and must be given up as an outmoded view from a precritical era. This particular theological judgment has gone hand in hand with an enchantment with the minute details of the biblical text rather than with its more global features, which *ipso facto* cannot exist.[4]

Even among well-meaning conservative scholars, the result has sometimes been an undue emphasis on the separate study of each individual book of the Bible and how its message stands alone. Such a study is not without merit, for it was definitely intended by the biblical authors. Nevertheless, it should be practiced alongside a concerted effort to see the Bible as also being a veritable one-volume treatise crafted by God. He was at work in the entire process to communicate rivers of glorious teachings about Jesus Christ. Since this book attempts to understand the big picture of the Bible, its focus will be slightly more concentrated on the divine author of Scripture than on its human authors. The result will be an increased effort to notice patterns

---

[3] Stephen G. Dempster, *Dominion and Dynasty: A Biblical Theology of the Hebrew Bible* (Downers Grove, IL: Intervarsity Press, 2003), 26-7.

[4] Ibid., 28.

that lead to an understanding of God's main message. I want us to get better at reading the Bible the way Stephen G. Dempster describes:

> It will be seen as a book and not as a ragbag, 'a well-made omelette indeed.' As Alter acknowledges, the premodern tradition was better able to see the pattern because it assumed that the text was an interconnected unity rather than a collage of diverse documents.[5]

I openly acknowledge a presupposition in this book that the Bible is God's authoritative, inspired, and inerrant Word. I maintain the highest respect for Scripture. I place very low value on modern, critical methods of the study of God's Word, except to the extent that they help us notice and analyze details in the text that we might not otherwise see—a service that is somewhat contrary to the intents of critical scholars. In the practice of biblical theology such presuppositions are necessary to arrive at an understanding of the unified message of the Bible. This is the same approach described in the *New Dictionary of Biblical Theology*:

> To do biblical theology, then, is to read the Bible as a Christian, someone who welcomes the witness of Scripture to what God was and is doing in Christ, which is 'according to the Scriptures.' The biblical theologian makes no apology for his or her explicitly theological assumptions about the nature and identity of God.[6]

In order to perceive the deepest messages of the Bible, we need to be especially aware of the literary techniques its authors used. A literary interpretation of the Bible requires one to approach it as prose or poetry and according to the more specific genre it was intended to be. This means sometimes we should be a lot better at reading it as if it were a novel or a poem (which it is in some places). Novels and poems utilize artistic techniques to carry the meaning meant to be conveyed. Too often we find ourselves reading the Bible as if it were a dry newspaper report instead, and we miss the most important details. Much of what I share in the following chapters will require an openness to viewing the Bible in this more artistic sense.

The truths in these chapters should inspire in us a tremendous awe as we notice the beauty built in to the literary shape of the Scriptures. We can see the hand of our creator as he designed his Word to include details at the lowest levels of the text, which point to his most passionate proclamations.

---

[5] Ibid., 30.

[6] T. Desmond Alexander and Brian S. Rosner, ed., *New Dictionary of Biblical Theology*, electronic ed. (Downers Grove, IL: InterVarsity Press, 2000).

The Bible really is a piece of artistry, carefully crafted to capture our attention and share what God wants us to know, believe, and feel. We should approach the analysis of Scripture in the same way we would our favorite movie, novel, or poem. There is a place for left-brained systematic analysis of the Bible, but we should also use our right brains at times to catch other details we might otherwise miss.

By nature I am very detail oriented and I sometimes miss the big picture. Through the grace of God I have been increasingly learning to see the big-picture view of his Word. I used to read the Bible more like a newspaper—seeking to get the facts. Now with more attention to the big picture, I am learning to read it somewhat like a love letter—looking for the message between the lines, the meaning that all the facts point to. The result is often a great impetus for worship in my life.

With greater frequency I find my heart leaping to a joyful response to truth shared by word or music in a worship service. At times a line in a song catches my attention in a whole new way. Although I'm singing a truth about Christ that I have believed for years, my mind will suddenly make several connections to passages that show how that truth develops through redemption history. My heart responds by singing the truth of the song with renewed vigor. Sometimes I get so excited that I almost have to restrain myself from immediately stopping the worship service and ensuring that everyone else understands the truth of what we are singing. I want to say, "I know you believe this already, but look at the overwhelming evidence in Scripture that this is a core part of God's message to us!" My desire in the present work is to spark some of the same excitement in you as we study the Bible together. This book is my platform to share in appropriate ways what I sometimes want to express indecorously in a moment of elation.

When we view Scripture in larger chunks, the perspective we gain helps us notice things in the text that God intended for a purpose. Remember my experience with North Dry Creek? If I would have had the right perspective on that water, my mind would have been open to seeing significant connections. North Dry Creek connects to the Platte River, which empties into the Missouri River, which in turn feeds the great Mississippi. If I had followed all those streams of water to their end, I would have arrived at the Gulf of Mexico. As a youth, the gulf wasn't even on my radar; I was missing a perspective that could have expanded my horizons considerably. I'm quite sure I never would have personally attempted the trip, but I'm also sure I would have enjoyed imagining it, or at least throwing in a stick to make the trip as my proxy!

Reading God's Word in the right way gives us the perspective we need to grow a boundless hope in God and his promises. The themes that run along the whole length of Scripture are all related to Christ and his work on our behalf. Some of the themes I present in this book will be quite familiar. Others are original to me. That is, as far as I know they haven't been presented anywhere else. In every case I plan to challenge your thinking to include an awareness of textual details that you've likely previously overlooked. In this book I trace a handful of themes to show how the details can be connected to the whole. As we navigate these streams the answers to the following questions, among others, should become much more clear:

- How is the Pentateuch foundational for the message of the Bible?
- What is the purpose of the book of Kings?
- If the Bible is mostly about God's Son, what is its message about us, and how does that connect with Christ?
- What should come to mind nearly every time we see the word *snake* in Scripture?
- Which characters in the Old Testament present the greatest typological connection with Christ?
- In what ways does Jesus beat Satan at his own game?
- What is the one question that the entire book of Genesis seeks to address?
- If Jesus is so important, why do we read of so many other heroes in Scripture?
- What makes it so amazing to learn that Jesus is prophet, priest, and king?

As we learn to give due emphasis to the rivers of Scripture instead of just stop at the ponds, our focus will be drawn increasingly to Christ, our eternal hope. All those rivers pull together to one final end. The "gulf" of the Bible is yet future, but it is described throughout the text of God's Word. Our "gulf" is real, and we will arrive there some day; we will see Jesus' kingdom fully consummated in all his glory. Join with me in seeing and appreciating the rivers. Doing so will only increase our present hope. When we arrive at the end we will find our *hope fulfilled!*

1
A Seed of Hope

When was the last time you thought carefully about the wonder of a seed? A seed is a marvelous thing, even though it's nothing more than a relatively small piece of a plant. Sometimes it's all that remains of an old, dead plant, but it contains all it needs to start a new plant that fully thrives. The tiny embryo inside a seed can stay alive for a very long time if the conditions are right. The longest documented case is of a Judean date palm seed that was found in Israel and successfully germinated in 2005.[1] The seed was carbon-dated at 2000 years old, and although that species of tree had been extinct for 1800 years, it is currently thriving and may produce fruit by 2022.[2]

Because seeds are so important, we currently have about 1400 seed banks all over the world. These banks save seeds in case of a natural disaster or another problem that causes a plant or a certain strain of plant to become extinct. People have even successfully reintroduced plants into their habitats when otherwise they would have become extinct.

Seeds are a good picture of biblical hope. Just as the survival of any species of plant depends on the seeds it produces, so God's Word describes for us a hope that is based on the production of a different kind of seed—a specific descendant of Eve who would prove to be the solution to some very deep problems. As believers who live in the church age, we know who the seed proved to be. If, however, we fail to notice how pervasive this biblical theme is, how long the wait for the descendant's arrival was, or how hopeless the survival of the seed seemed to be, we won't appreciate the full joy of noticing its fulfillment in the New Testament. Let's look at some biblical texts about the descendant of Eve who would prove to be the promised seed. Because of the message of hope these texts originally gave to God's people, they still serve as signposts of hope when we understand the sense of perspective they are meant to give.

---

[1] National Geographic. '2,000-Year-Old Seed Sprouts, Sapling Is Thriving.' N.p., 22 November 2005. Web. Accessed 13 May 2016. http://news.nationalgeographic.com/news/051122-old-plant-seed-food/

[2] Green Prophet: Sustainable News for the Middle East. '2000-Year-Old Date Pit Sprouts In Israel.' N.p., 25 March 2012. Web. Accessed 13 May 2016. http://www.greenprophet.com/2012/03/2000-year-old-date-pit-sprouts-in-israel/

A Seed Promised

This theme of promised seed was introduced almost at the very beginning of the existence of humankind. We find the first biblical reference to seed in the third chapter of Genesis. Genesis teaches us about the beginning of everything, including the way sin came into the world. Read Genesis chapter 3 to remind yourself of the details of this story.

Now look more carefully at verse 15:

> **Genesis 3:15**
> "I will put enmity between you and the woman,
>   and between your offspring and her offspring;
> he shall bruise your head,
>   and you shall bruise his heel."

The Lord is describing in turn the punishment he would mete out for the serpent, for Eve, and for Adam, and this verse is in the section that applies to the serpent. He was talking directly to the serpent and told him there would be enmity between him and Eve. I'm sure it's true that whenever Eve saw the serpent after that day she was reminded of the fatal decision she made and the role the serpent played, and I doubt if she ever again had good feelings for the serpent. Her probable hatred toward the serpent partially fulfilled this verse.

But this verse has a significance that goes way beyond Eve and a single snake. The second line of the poem mentions the offspring of each of them. The Hebrew word used here is often translated into English as either "seed" or "offspring." It means "seed, semen, offspring, descendants, origin, or descent."[3] (In this chapter I will use "seed" and "offspring" interchangeably.) According to this verse, both Eve and the serpent would have offspring, and God is saying these children would continue in an enemy relationship with each other. In the second line of the verse he is talking about the descendants of Eve (all mankind) and the descendants of the serpent (every snake everywhere). Speaking in a general way, throughout history people probably have always had a deep hatred of snakes. Not too many people like snakes, and those who do like them still need to be careful to handle them correctly—avoiding risks that could result in a dangerous bite.

The third and fourth lines of the poem extend the meaning even further. We can interpret these lines better by asking ourselves who is meant by each

---

[3] William Lee Holladay and Ludwig Köhler, *A Concise Hebrew and Aramaic Lexicon of the Old Testament* (Leiden, Netherlands: Brill, 2000), 92-93.

Offspring of the Serpent   **Offspring of the Woman**

Figure 1: showing descendants and lines of conflict

of the pronouns. The word *he* obviously refers to the offspring of the woman, but it's interesting that the pronoun is singular, even though we know the descendants of Eve are very numerous. The word *you* also comes as a surprise, since the parallel for the offspring of the woman would be the offspring of the serpent. Instead, here the Lord is speaking of a conflict between one particular descendant of Eve and the original serpent in the garden. For that reason we should see that the serpent mentioned here is more than a common reptile. Rather, here we are dealing with Satan, who has either embodied a serpent or emulated one in appearance.

The promise given in this verse is that there would be one special descendant of Eve who would struggle with Satan. Even though Satan would give him an injury, the injury he would deal out to Satan would be much more severe. A bite on the heel is insignificant compared to the life-threatening potential of an injury to the head. Therefore, this verse teaches that one day there would come a descendant of Eve who would act as a "savior" to defeat Satan and solve the problem of sin he had introduced in chapter 3 of Genesis. This is one of the biggest themes in the remainder of the book. Moses (the probable author of Genesis) wrote to help answer the question of who would be the descendant of Eve that was promised, or at least to show from whose genealogical line he would come. In addition, all the rest of Scripture really is founded on the fact that hope exists only because of the seed promised to the woman in Genesis 3.

Just as a plant species can be maintained only through its production of seed, so the human race was now dependent on the seed God promised. The consequence of sin was death and God recognized that, left to itself, all humankind was now in that hopeless condition. The promise of seed meant a small grain of hope was left as long as the seed remained. The seed gave hope for future life.

The First Seed

Let's look at Genesis 4 to see how this theme begins to impact the interpretation of succeeding passages.

> **Genesis 4:1–2**—Now Adam knew Eve his wife, and she conceived and bore Cain, saying, "I have gotten a man with the help of the LORD." And again, she bore his brother Abel. Now Abel was a keeper of sheep, and Cain a worker of the ground.

In verses 1 and 2, we find that two boys are born to Eve. Have you ever wondered what it was like for her to give birth to another human being for the very first time in history? If birth had never before been witnessed, just imagine the amazement she and Adam felt. I was overwhelmed by the birth of my children even when I knew more or less what to expect. But to see a child emerge from the womb for the very first time in human history must have been incredible. Besides being amazed by the very experience of birth, what do you think she thought about the significance of the birth of her sons? Remember what she had been promised in the previous chapter? Now at the very moment her offspring arrived, I'm sure God's promise of seed must have been uppermost in her mind. I think her default assumption must have been that her current offspring would be the person who would fulfill God's promise by crushing the head of the serpent. Why wouldn't she think that?

We really aren't told many details about Cain and Abel. We don't have any clues that lead us to believe what Eve might have thought about the potential of each one and who could end up being the promised seed. Either Cain was older, or they were twins. Whichever the case, it seems likely Eve didn't know which of the two would be the one. And it probably was just as well, because as the story turns out, it was neither. As you know, Cain killed Abel. The two serve as a demonstration, on a small scale, of the enmity God promised between the offspring of the woman and the offspring of the serpent. Although Cain was a child of Eve, he showed he was at the core an offspring of Satan. Although Abel was a child of Eve, he couldn't completely fulfill the promise of God because he was defenseless as he confronted the enmity of Satan. So as it turns out, neither was a good candidate to save the world from sin. For his part, Abel was definitely out of the picture. And on the other hand, instead of crushing the head of the serpent, Cain crushed his brother.[4] Furthermore, I think it's clear that Cain never repented of his sin; he remained rebellious. In fact, it looks as if his whole line of descendants were rebellious people; look at verses 23–24:

> **Genesis 4:23–24**
> Lamech said to his wives:
> "Adah and Zillah, hear my voice;
>   you wives of Lamech, listen to what I say:
> I have killed a man for wounding me,
>   a young man for striking me.
> If Cain's revenge is sevenfold,
>   then Lamech's is seventy-sevenfold."

One of Cain's descendants, Lamech, followed in the footsteps of his ancestor. The striking thing about his crime is that he boasted about it and even went so far as to claim God's protection for himself. Since he knew God protected Cain from those who might have wished to deal him retribution, Lamech demanded an even greater measure of God's protection. This kind of boastful rebellion was not becoming of one who would be a righteous offspring to carry out God's will. Therefore, the big question still hangs in the air: who will fulfill the promise of seed for Eve?

The Line Is Selected

This question is apparently uppermost in the mind of Moses as he writes, for he answers it in the following verses. Read Genesis 4:25–26:

> **Genesis 4:25–26**—And Adam knew his wife again, and she bore a son and called his name Seth, for she said, "God has appointed for me *another offspring* instead of Abel, for Cain killed him." To Seth also a son was born, and he called his name Enosh. At that time people began to call upon the name of the LORD (emphasis added).

---

[4] Len Kinzel, Sermon. English Fellowship Church, 24 March 2013.

Once again we see that God gave a son to Eve. This time Eve used the term "offspring" to describe her gift from God. In Hebrew, this is the same word used for "seed" in 3:15. Thus, Eve made clear that Seth's birth restored in her a new hope for what God could do through him. The communication of Eve's hope is intensified by the statement at the end of verse 26. Moses makes sure we know that at that time people began to call on the name of the Lord. It's hard to say what significance this statement would have apart from the contrast implied between the line of Cain and the line of Seth.

Another intended contrast between Cain and Seth is in chapter 5, where we have a genealogy of Seth with a different outcome than Cain's in chapter 4. Instead of ending in a person who boasts in his sin, this genealogy ends with Noah, the most righteous man of his generation. When Noah was born, his father gave a significant prophecy:

> **Genesis 5:29** — …and called his name Noah, saying, "Out of the ground that the LORD has cursed, this one shall bring us relief from our work and from the painful toil of our hands."

So we see that Cain's line only brings more sin while Seth's line gives hope for relief from the curse that was introduced by sin.

But as you know, Seth didn't really personally do anything to fulfill the promise to defeat the serpent. Seth's important contribution was simply to be a channel through which Noah was brought in to the world. Noah had a much greater role. In fact, we will see that there is a certain tension in the text as to whether Noah actually fulfilled the promise of chapter 3.

Eve celebrated Seth's arrival, and the author makes it a point to make us aware of that fact. In this Seth illustrates a principle that will resonate through much of the rest of the Bible. That is, the birth of Seth partially fulfilled the hope Adam and Eve had for the promised seed, but he wasn't its final fulfillment. Seth was, after all, a descendant of Eve just like the Ultimate Seed would be. And in contrast to Cain, Seth apparently was a righteous man who had the potential to be the right one for the job if God so chose. Nevertheless, the real reason Seth is so important is not that he was in the fullest sense of the word a savior, but rather that he would ultimately prove to be instrumental in producing the True Savior of the world. Apparently, we are to understand that one way for faithful biblical characters to defeat the serpent is to engender someone else who will carry out the task. Even a small task in faithfully carrying out God's plan is of great value. This pattern repeats itself over and over throughout Scripture in people who carry some sense of fulfillment of the prophecy of seed but do not ultimately satisfy all the terms of fulfillment. Each of these characters points forward to Someone who will ultimately prove to be the object of our hope.

When we see the partial fulfillments of the provision of seed, our response should be one of praise to God. We can be excited because they show us God has not forgotten his promise, God is indeed able to carry through on what he has said, and God knows what is needed to provide a complete fulfillment. What's more, our hope is, in a sense, increased even more when we realize the partial fulfillment fell short of satisfaction because then we have confidence that something even greater is on its way — Someone who will prove to be all we hope for and even more. Therefore, when we see characters in Scripture who are precursors to Jesus Christ, even faint shadows of who our true Savior is, our faith and hope should be strengthened. It should cause us to praise God for his wonderful plan, for knowing exactly what we need, and for not withholding the best he could offer (which is Jesus himself). And it should produce in us a sense of marvel as we consider that as of now we have not yet experienced the full benefit of all the spiritual blessings Jesus will one day give us. We still hold hope that Jesus' final victory in our lives and in the world as a whole will be glorious beyond our wildest expectations and dreams! Our greatest contribution comes through emulating the biblical characters by similarly pointing forward to Christ as the ultimate hope for the world around us.

A "Savior" Arrives

In the midst of a corrupt world where things had only gone from bad to worse, we find Noah. God had determined to destroy the entire world, but wanted to use Noah to save a remnant of righteous people who could be God's own. Because Noah found favor in God's eyes he was chosen for this special task:

> **Genesis 6:17–18** — For behold, I will bring a flood of waters upon the earth to destroy all flesh in which is the breath of life under heaven. Everything that is on the earth shall die. But I will establish my covenant with you, and you shall come into the ark, you, your sons, your wife, and your sons' wives with you.

For the first time in the Bible we see God promise to establish his covenant with someone, and the purpose is so that person can be a source of blessing to others. Noah, as a seed of the woman and as part of the righteous line that Moses has been following, deals a blow to Satan. The careful reader of the text will ask himself whether this is the crushing of the head of the serpent which was promised in chapter 3. In fact, Noah was the key human player in God's judgment, which wiped out all of sinful mankind—definitely a blow to the serpent. One could even say he was a "savior" whom God used to provide salvation in the ark for every righteous person who simply chose to escape God's judgment.

Everything seems to be going well and Noah seems to be the perfect solution to the problem of sin—until we find a problem at the end of chapter 9. The root of the problem is in the fact that Noah himself is sinful. We can see that, as things turn out, not all of sinful humanity has been wiped out after all. The account of what first happened after the flood demonstrates that even Noah and his son are prone to sin:

> **Genesis 9:20–23**—Then Noah began farming and planted a vineyard. He drank of the wine and became drunk, and uncovered himself inside his tent. Ham, the father of Canaan, saw the nakedness of his father, and told his two brothers outside. But Shem and Japheth took a garment and laid it upon both their shoulders and walked backward and covered the nakedness of their father; and their faces were turned away, so that they did not see their father's nakedness (NASB).

A lot can be said about these verses, but the main point is how the author of the Pentateuch (the first five books of the Bible) would evaluate them. Leviticus 18:6, among other verses, uses some of the same words to characterize what happened here as contrary to the law of God.

> **Leviticus 18:6**—"None of you shall approach any one of his close relatives to uncover nakedness. I am the LORD.

The Hebrew text of Genesis 9:21 tells us literally that Noah uncovered himself. Noah was guilty for uncovering his own nakedness. When Ham saw it, he apparently told his brothers with the wrong attitude, thereby sharing in his father's guilt. Both Noah and Ham violated God's guidelines for righteousness. Therefore, although Noah partially fulfilled the promise of 3:15, it was only in an imperfect way. If the serpent's head had been truly crushed, we would expect the effects of the sin he introduced to be completely removed. Instead, it is ironic that the savior who supposedly brought victory over sin was himself overcome by sin. "...Like the first Adam, he ends up as a disobedient son whose nakedness reveals shame rather than full integrity."[5] Noah *almost* defeated the serpent. In so many ways he was exactly what was needed; but there were some key ways in which he fell short. And in matters like this, being *almost* the perfect savior is infinitely distant from being the Perfect Savior!

Other Contrasting Lines in Genesis
After the flood, very few descendants of Eve were left from whom to choose The Offspring to solve the problem of sin, but that didn't matter. God had Noah, who would serve as his seed bank. Even though Noah wasn't The True Seed, God would use him to continue the line from which The True Seed would come. That's why in chapter 10, Moses continues his account by tracing the genealogies of the sons of Noah—Japheth, Shem, and Ham. Here he continues the pattern he established with Cain and Seth—first mentioning the unrighteous line and later tracing the seed through the chosen line. He deals in a general way with the two sons of Noah who were not chosen. After getting those details out of the way, he can then focus more specifically on Shem, the seed of the woman (11:10ff). This is a pattern he uses in most of the rest of Genesis.

Chapters	The Line Not Chosen	The Chosen Line
4–5	Cain, Abel (somewhat neutral)	Seth
6:1–9:17		Noah
9:18–11:26	Ham (Canaan), Japheth (somewhat neutral)	Shem
11:27–15:21	Lot	Abraham
16–24	Ishmael	Isaac
25–29	Esau	Jacob
30–50	Joseph	Judah

In the final division, special emphasis is on two of Jacob's twelve sons—Judah and Joseph. In this long, climactic section of the book of Genesis we are supposed to read the narrative with a great amount of tension as we seek to discover which of these two tribes will prove to be the source of the promised offspring. Each of the other ten sons of Judah has been eliminated as a

---

[5] Peter John Gentry and Stephen J. Wellum, *Kingdom Through Covenant: A Biblical-Theological Understanding of the Covenants* (Wheaton, IL: Crossway, 2012), Kindle version, chapter 5, location 4065.

possibility for various reasons. In the end, we find in chapter 49 that although Joseph is worthy of much honor for having saved the fledgling nation of Israel from famine, Judah becomes prominent. Joseph was a "savior" in the short term, but Judah will produce the True Savior who will have a much more important mission. Israel prophesies that Judah will have a transcendent importance when his future descendant defeats his enemies and leads the other eleven tribes as king. (See Genesis 49:8–12 and chapter 5, "The Perfect King.") Thus, by the end of Genesis we have a partial answer to the identity of the snake crusher in Genesis 3:15.

The Seed Becomes a Nation

Now we need to back up just a little and focus on the central character of the book of Genesis. Abraham is the one around whom the entire book turns. God made a covenant with him, and not surprisingly, his descendants are one of the key components of the covenant. The Hebrew word for "seed" is an important part of the promises God gave to Abraham in these chapters. In chapter 12 when the Lord first speaks of his blessings on Abraham, he makes it clear that Abraham's seed will include an entire nation:

> **Genesis 12:2** — And I will make of you a great nation, and I will bless you and make your name great, so that you will be a blessing.

And in verse 7 he mentions the offspring of Abraham, using the same word used to speak of the seed of Eve:

> **Genesis 12:7** — Then the LORD appeared to Abram and said, "To your *offspring* I will give this land." So he built there an altar to the LORD, who had appeared to him (emphasis added).

Later he told Abraham his offspring would be as numerous as both the dust of the earth and the stars of the sky (Genesis 13:15–16; 15:5). For the first time, the promise of seed takes on the concept of a corporate seed which will be specially blessed by God. The nation of Israel would eventually be the fulfillment of this promise to Abraham. And yet, after the nation comes into being at the end of Genesis, it is made clear that there will still be one special Seed who rises to prominence as the promised one of chapter 3 (see again Genesis 49:8–12).

The corporate and individual natures of the seed promise are demonstrated very clearly in one single verse. Look at what we see in Genesis 22 after Abraham displays his faithfulness through his willingness to sacrifice Isaac:

> **Genesis 22:17–18**—I will surely bless you, and I will surely multiply your offspring as the stars of heaven and as the sand that is on the seashore. And your offspring shall possess the gate of his enemies, and in your offspring shall all the nations of the earth be blessed, because you have obeyed my voice."

Verse 17 is especially interesting in its grammatical choices. It's clear that in the first part of the verse God is talking about a plurality of descendants. Abraham's offspring will be as numerous as the stars and the sand. The second sentence in this verse, however, is talking of one individual. Although not all translations capture the grammar, both the verb for "possess" and the pronoun "his" are singular. God is speaking of the seed of Abraham in a way that includes a corporate and an individual sense. In verse 18, therefore, the word *offspring* contains a hint of ambiguity. Does it refer to plural or singular offspring? Although it is true that all nations have been blessed in one way or another by the nation of Israel, the world has received a much greater set of blessings through one specific descendant of Abraham, Jesus Christ. At the end of verse 18, God attributes this blessing to the obedience of Abraham. We have a lot of respect for Abraham, but the Bible presents him as a human just as weak as the rest of us. It would seem God's means of blessing the world would rest on a very weak pedestal were it not for the fact that our Sovereign Lord always maintains control, even in the weakest of circumstances.

The Seed in Danger
As we follow the theme of seed through Scripture, we see there were moments in history when there was a significant possibility of failure in regard to the arrival of the promised seed. Although theologically we know the Lord can and will fulfill his promises without any shadow of a doubt, in a literary sense at times the Bible allows a certain tension about whether God will truly be able to come through on what he has said. In at least four major passages, the line which is to produce the seed is in jeopardy of dying out. In each case, a woman is potentially unable to bear children for one reason or another. The first of these is Sarah, but she also sets the stage for the stories of Tamar, Ruth, and Hannah. Let's look a little at each of these in turn.

Sarah
The story of Abraham and Sarah is very familiar. Even though God had promised them a son, they didn't see how it could ever be. At the time of the first promise they were already too old, humanly speaking. Even though

nothing was happening for several years, the Lord continued to assure them they could maintain their hope in what he had said. On separate occasions both Abraham and Sarah found reason to laugh in the face of God's promise. They even tried to offer God alternative ways to prove his faithfulness, but look at how he responded in Genesis 17:19:

> **Genesis 17:19**—God said, "No, but Sarah your wife shall bear you a son, and you shall call his name Isaac. I will establish my covenant with him as an everlasting covenant for his offspring after him."

Not only could Abraham and Sarah maintain confidence in God's provision of an offspring, but he even promised that more offspring would come from that offspring. The name Isaac means "laughter," and God wanted to teach them (and us) to have the right kind of laughter. Instead of a laugh of doubt in the face of God's impossible task, those who have faith in him can laugh with joy over the fulfillment of the hope he gives!

> **Genesis 21:5–7**—Abraham was a hundred years old when his son Isaac was born to him. And Sarah said, "God has made laughter for me; everyone who hears will laugh over me." And she said, "Who would have said to Abraham that Sarah would nurse children? Yet I have borne him a son in his old age."

The pattern has been established. This is not the last time God's promise of a seed will be threatened by the lack of a child to carry on the line. But to God that doesn't seem to matter. Rather, he seems to delight in meeting challenges over and over! He wants to strengthen our faith by repeatedly fulfilling our hope, no matter how small it seems! God's supernatural intervention to face each threat to the line of the seed also prefigures his future supernatural intervention in the life of a virgin to produce the True Seed. The Bible shows us that no circumstance, no difficulty, and no enemy of God could ever have prevented him from fulfilling his promise in Jesus Christ!

Tamar

The story of Tamar in Genesis 38 plays a big part in our analysis of Judah and whether he will be the one to carry forward the line of the seed. This chapter is not a very familiar one to us; we tend to shy away from it because of intimate details about Judah's sin. Read Genesis 38 to familiarize yourself with the story.

The main plot rivals daytime television in its seedy details of the way all the men of this family are intimate with one woman, but the overarching positive theme is the desire to provide descendants for the tribe of Judah. Judah had three sons and took a wife, Tamar, for the oldest of them. After his oldest son died as a result of God's judgment (we are told only in general terms that it was because of his wickedness), he gave his second son, Onan, to Tamar to produce offspring (literally, "seed"). This was the customary way of providing descendants for his dead brother. Onan refused to share his semen (literally, "seed") with Tamar because of pure selfishness, knowing that any child to be born would not really be his. Therefore, God also took Onan's life because of his sin. Having seen his two older sons die after marrying Tamar, Judah was more than reluctant to allow his third son to experience the same fate, again a demonstration of sinful selfishness on his part. Tamar, as a result, was a helpless widow without hope for a child. The reader should identify with her with the knowledge that all hope for the True Seed also rests in her fate. Tamar took matters into her own hands by pretending to be a prostitute and tricking Judah himself into fathering a child by her, probably in reality motivated by her own selfishness, though perhaps partially rationalized by her desperate circumstances in a society that did not favor women in her position.

The most important verse in this chapter is verse 26, in which Judah gave his evaluation of the events after he was confronted with his sin:

> Genesis 38:26 — "She is more righteous than I, since I did not give her to my son Shelah." And he did not know her again.

He recognized and confessed his own sin, stating at the same time that Tamar's actions were righteous in comparison. This statement shouldn't be taken in the full sense as God's evaluation of the things Tamar did; he would want us to know she sinned in several ways. Nevertheless, Moses allows the statement to stand as his own personal evaluation of the events recounted in the passage. As the narrator, his whole purpose is to show how the seed was almost lost and indeed would have been if not for the actions of Tamar and God working through her. Moses is choosing to tell us that the seed is so important in God's eyes, God can use individual sinful acts to actually fulfill his righteous purpose if they help preserve the promised seed.

Ruth

The book of Ruth is a beautiful short story with many details that would be great to include in this study. Unfortunately our present task does not include digging into all the riches in this book, but I do want to briefly point out the main themes and how they relate to the subject of seed. The main message in the book of Ruth is that God is faithful to continue the line of the seed of the woman (Genesis 3:15) through the lovingkindness of his faithful people.

We can see the purpose of Ruth by looking at the genealogy with which it concludes (4:18–22). The fact that it is at the end of the book shows us the author has been driving to this point throughout the rest of the story. In addition, the principal characters of the genealogy show us it is none other than the genealogical history of King David, one of the most important fulfillments of the promise of seed. The genealogy shows the family relationship between Perez, the seed of Judah through Tamar, and David. The reader is intended to realize that if it were not for the events of this story, the line of the seed once again would have been jeopardized.

The seed was again in danger of dying off because of a string of events in Naomi's life. Elimelech and Naomi left the land of Israel because of famine and went to Moab. Elimelech and their two sons died in that land, but not before the sons had a chance to marry Moabite women. The main part of the story opens with Naomi and her deceased husband hopeless of having any offspring. Naomi probably was too old to have children, and if one of her daughter-in-law widows were to do so, the child likely would belong to the genealogical line of the father—by all expectations, a Moabite.

What makes this story so precious is the repeated theme of lovingkindness demonstrated by the characters, one for another. First Ruth went beyond the call of duty by committing herself to stay with Naomi in spite of the bleak prospects this gave her. Ruth accompanied Naomi back to the land of Israel, and in chapter 2 we see she was even willing to go and glean in the fields to provide for her mother-in-law. This demonstration of love for Naomi was really just a small indication of the lengths she was willing to go to in her provision, for we will see that she eventually provided much more—a seed for Naomi and her family. Through Ruth, Naomi's hope was kept alive against all odds.

When Ruth gleaned barley she ended up in a field belonging to Boaz. We are intended to read of God's providence between the lines of chapter 2, for no other man would have been likely to care for Ruth the way he did. Moreover, Boaz was a kinsman redeemer, meaning he was perfectly suited, culturally speaking, to care for these widows by providing the land and descendants they were lacking. In other words, as kinsman redeemer, he was the only solution to the need for seed. Boaz's generous display of love toward Ruth in the field was, therefore, a precursor to the greater love he would show by the end of the book.

Naomi sent Ruth to Boaz in chapter 3 with an altogether different purpose: apparently she was thinking unselfishly of Ruth's need for a husband. It is significant that she didn't give Ruth instructions about asking Boaz to exercise his redeemer role. Instead it was Ruth's initiative on the threshing floor that set that plan in motion. That was where Ruth's love for Naomi reached its highest point—taking steps to provide offspring for Naomi that would fill the need for seed. So Naomi and Ruth were both thinking most highly of the needs of the other, and Boaz was going to be the instrument to fulfill each of them.

Boaz did his greatest loving deeds in chapter 4, where he artfully and tactfully dealt with the closer relative. He was not afraid of making sacrifices to fulfill his redeemer role and even seemed to manipulate things to make that outcome more likely—all because of his love for Ruth and even Naomi. As someone who foreshadowed Christ in many ways, he proved he was a deserving candidate to provide the seed which would eventually bring Jesus into this world.

The other kinsman made a decision that reminds us a little bit of Onan in Genesis 38. The reader is led to sympathize with him, understanding that his choices were to be expected given his situation. Nevertheless, we recognize he was primarily concerned about his own property and descendants. In 4:5–6, he stated that providing a descendant for the family would jeopardize the inheritance of his own children. His "selfish" choices serve to highlight the selfless lovingkindness of Boaz.

Chapter 4 verse 11 begins the conclusion of the book. When Boaz completed his legal transaction committing to be the redeemer for Ruth and Naomi, the people who witnessed it pronounced a very significant blessing which ended like this:

> Ruth 4:12—"And may your house be like the house of Perez, whom Tamar bore to Judah, because of the *offspring* that the LORD will give you by this young woman" (emphasis added).

This is the only occurrence of the word for "seed" in the entire book, but it shows what the whole plot has been driving toward. And from here the theology only deepens.

The child who was later born to Ruth has incredible significance at the end of the story. In verse 17 of chapter 4, the women of the neighborhood went so far as to say that "a son has been born to *Naomi*" (emphasis added).[6] The irony of this statement is that they attributed the role of motherhood to Naomi instead of to Ruth. The women recognized that the birth of this boy had significance for the existence of a seed that far transcended the immediate circumstances of the mother/son relationship. They were declaring his importance in continuing the line of the offspring who would *redeem* all mankind. This point is further clarified by another twist of irony in their statement of verses 14 and 15:

> **Ruth 4:14–15**—Then the women said to Naomi, "Blessed be the LORD, who has not left you this day without a redeemer, and may his name be renowned in Israel! He shall be to you a restorer of life and a nourisher of your old age, for your daughter-in-law who loves you, who is more to you than seven sons, has given birth to him."

When they mention the provision of a redeemer, at first we might think they are talking about Boaz, who redeemed Naomi's land and provided offspring. But when we get to the end of verse 15, we are told that Ruth has given birth to the redeemer! Since Ruth obviously didn't give birth to Boaz, the only possible interpretation here is that the baby boy is also presented as Naomi's redeemer! This ironic statement eventually leads us to admit that "redeemer" is indeed an appropriate title for one who ultimately would be an ancestor of the greatest Redeemer—one who would offer redemption not only to Naomi, but to the entire world! The book of Ruth shows how God, working through the loving actions of his people, provided a seed when its existence was once again in jeopardy. Furthermore, it heightens our expectation that the Ultimate Seed will be a redeemer even greater than Boaz!

Hannah

The third story I want to include here is that of Hannah, another woman who was childless. Although the son who would be born to her is not directly in the line of the promised seed, he played a very crucial role in that line. In 1 Samuel chapter 1, Hannah prayed in the temple for a baby boy:

> **1 Samuel 1:11**—And she vowed a vow and said, "O LORD of hosts, if you will indeed look on the affliction of your servant and remember me and not forget your servant, but will give to your servant a *son*, then I will give him

---

[6] *The Holy Bible: English Standard Version* (Wheaton, IL: Standard Bible Society, 2001), Ru 4:15-17.

to the LORD all the days of his life, and no razor shall touch his head" (emphasis added).

The phrase that is translated "son" literally means "seed of men," or "male seed." Although she could have more naturally pronounced her desire for a child or even a son, she asked for "seed"—a clue that this passage is meant to contain a theological message related to the promise of Genesis 3:15. The part that her son, Samuel, played in the provision of seed was not that of literally producing a descendant who would be included in the physical lineage of seed; but rather one of recognizing and anointing one of the most important descendants in the line—David himself. Samuel played the role of kingmaker—a crucial role in the life of David who would be a serpent crusher. The importance of this role multiplies in light of God's revelation that the Ultimate Seed would be a royal son of David.

Chapter 2 contains her prayer of thanksgiving after Samuel's birth. It is significant that the reversal of her personal misery is found in the birth of a child. This same child turns out to be the key to the reversal of Israel's present situation and really to that of the entire world. This prayer has themes that are picked up several times over from this point forward, especially in the life of King David. 1 Samuel opens with the desperate prayer of Hannah, followed by her song of thanksgiving (1 Samuel 1–2). Second Samuel closes with "David's song of thanksgiving after he had been delivered from all his enemies (2 Samuel 22:2–51)," followed by his desperate prayer that God would save Jerusalem from his sin (2 Samuel 24).[7] I am indebted to Stephen G. Dempster for pointing out these connections; he does a good job of explaining their significance in the following quotation:

> These two figures, Hannah and David, are crucially important for understanding the book. Hannah's song looks to the future for the overthrow of a tyrannical dominion that will be replaced by a just king, a Messiah, who will bring justice beyond Israel to the ends of the earth (1 Sam. 2:10). David looks back and sees how God has delivered him from all his enemies. David smote them until they fell under his feet (2 Sam. 22:39–40). God gave him the neck of his enemies (22:41), and this becomes the pledge of a future in which God will magnify his salvation to this king and extend covenant loyalty to his Messiah, to David and his seed for ever (22:51).[8]

---

[7] Dempster, *Dominion and Dynasty*, 134.
[8] Ibid.

Many of the images in the poetry of 1 Samuel 2:1–10 show us that God opposes the proud but lifts up the humble. Hannah's song is the first to accompany the announcement of a birth, but it is not the last. Mary's song in Luke 1:45–55 reflects very clearly the concepts first presented by Hannah. Look, for example, at how they each start:

> Hannah: My heart exults in the Lord;
> Mary: My soul magnifies the Lord,

Both songs describe how God has taken somebody humble and lifted her up. Both songs teach that the proud and strong are humbled by God. Both songs rejoice in the fact that God takes away from those who have much and feeds the hungry.

David

Probably the best-known story of David is that in which he faces Goliath. Less familiar is the way in which the story connects to the promise of seed. In this passage both David and his enemy wear armor. As it turns out, David doesn't like his and takes it off. Goliath, on the other hand, keeps his, and it plays an important part in communicating the message of the chapter. His armor is literally described as an armor of scales.

> **1 Samuel 17:5** — He had a bronze helmet on his head, and he was clothed with scale-armor which weighed five thousand shekels of bronze (NASB).

The Hebrew word for "scales" is used 8 times in the Bible and this is the only occurrence that does not literally describe the covering of an animal. The author is intentionally describing Goliath in terms that cause us to recall the serpent in the Garden of Eden. The original serpent has figuratively reappeared as Goliath, and David is determined to do something about it. As you know he ends up killing Goliath by "crushing" his forehead with a rock and then cutting off his head with a sword. We are intended to notice that David has crushed the head of the serpent.

A Son of David

Another passage of huge significance in this theme of seed comes in 2 Samuel 7 during one of the key moments in David's life. In this chapter God makes amazing and monumental promises to David. There are several important themes to study in this passage, but they all revolve around the one found in verse 12:

2 Samuel 7:12—When your days are fulfilled and you lie down with your fathers, I will raise up your offspring after you, who shall come from your body, and I will establish his kingdom.

It's interesting that this passage is really introduced by a complication: 2 Samuel 6:23 states that the queen, David's wife, was barren. By now we shouldn't be surprised that God once again chose a hard circumstance in which to make his glory known. What we do learn is that the source of the seed has been narrowed; instead of generally from Israel or from the tribe of Judah, now we are told he would come specifically from the family of David. Beyond that, the kingly attributes of the seed are amplified in a way they haven't been up to this point. God once again solved the problem of barrenness in a surprising way. He could have given David offspring through his legitimate wife, but instead he chose to work through David's sinful actions—providing an heir to the throne through Bathsheba. Solomon, her son, became an amazing fulfillment of much of what was promised to David; in many ways his glorious kingdom came close to being all that was hoped for. Yet in other ways it fell far short of the perfection God had in mind, which can be fulfilled only through his son, Jesus Christ.

Much of the rest of the history in the Old Testament is written in light of the hope for the Son of David who was promised. Each of the kings of Judah is evaluated with respect to whether he could be the true King. We'll leave the details of this search for when we focus on the theme of a King. (See chapter 5, "The Perfect King.")

New Testament

In its very first verse, the New Testament opens with an affirmation that Jesus is the Seed that was promised. Read chapter 2, "Toledot: A New Generation," for an explanation of how Matthew 1:1 communicates this truth. Now, however, let's jump ahead to Luke 1 and look more closely at Mary's song, in which she uses the Greek term corresponding to "seed." Just as we saw in the case of Hebrew, the Greek word translated "offspring" literally means "seed," and it is related to our word *sperm*.

Luke 1:54–55
He has helped his servant Israel,
in remembrance of his mercy,
as he spoke to our fathers,
to Abraham and to his *offspring* forever" (emphasis added).

In the previous verses, Mary received the news that she would be the mother of the Messiah and she rejoiced over the announcement together with Elizabeth. In verse 54 Mary noted that God was helping his people by giving them the person for whom they had long been waiting. She apparently understood the Old Testament in the way we are reading it here; she recognized there were both corporate and individual components of the promise of seed to Abraham. Mary's words in verse 55 make clear that she was recalling the promises God made to the patriarchs. But how should we understand the second line of this verse? At first glance it might seem natural to read "to Abraham" as a parallel repetition of "to our fathers." What I mean is that it would be tempting to think she was restating the end of line 1 as Hebrew poetry so often does, but that doesn't make sense of the phrase "to his offspring forever." That is, it doesn't make much sense to say God "spoke to Abraham and his offspring forever." Instead, we should understand line 2 as the *content* of what God spoke to the patriarchs. That is, God said several things about the various covenants he was making with Israel, and in Mary's mind they could all be summed up in the phrase "to Abraham and to his offspring forever." Mary is considering all the blessings God said he would give Abraham and his offspring in several parts of the Old Testament. The phrasing she used was actually quite similar to that of Genesis 13:15, to give one example:

> **Genesis 13:15**—For all the land that you see I will give to you and to your offspring forever.

In this verse God was speaking directly to Abraham, and Mary simply restated that last half, replacing the second-person pronouns with the name *Abraham* and a third-person pronoun. Genesis 13:15 refers to God's gift of land, but the context also includes his gift of seed. For Mary, the content of blessing probably included concepts from other passages as well, like Genesis 17:7 and 22:17. Mary was lumping together the whole package and seeing how it all culminated in the gift of the son she would soon bring into the world. One of the most significant parts of her proclamation is that the corporate seed of Abraham would receive its blessing through the arrival of the individual seed of Abraham, Jesus Christ. It's no wonder she would be full of enough joy to break out in song, rejoicing that all God's promises were finally coming into focus at the birth of her son! It makes me want to sing the song with her and celebrate how the Lord chose to bless his people with his precious gift!

In the very next chapter of Luke is another significant passage in this regard. It doesn't use the word *seed*, but when read in the light of the promise of seed, it takes on a richer meaning.

> **Luke 2:25–35**—Now there was a man in Jerusalem, whose name was Simeon, and this man was righteous and devout, waiting for the consolation of Israel, and the Holy Spirit was upon him. And it had been revealed to him by the Holy Spirit that he would not see death before he had seen the Lord's Christ. And he came in the Spirit into the temple, and when the parents brought in the child Jesus, to do for him according to the custom of the Law, he took him up in his arms and blessed God and said, "Lord, now you are letting your servant depart in peace, according to your word; for my eyes have seen your salvation that you have prepared in the presence of all peoples, a light for revelation to the Gentiles, and for glory to your people Israel." And his father and his mother marveled at what was said about him. And Simeon blessed them and said to Mary his mother, "Behold, this child is appointed for the fall and rising of many in Israel, and for a sign that is opposed (and a sword will pierce through your own soul also), so that thoughts from many hearts may be revealed."

There are two indications here of what Simeon had been waiting for. Verse 25 says he had been waiting for the consolation of Israel—a term used in the first line of Isaiah 40 to give immeasurable hope. In Isaiah 40 the ESV translates it "comfort." Read the entire chapter and notice especially its exalted view of our Savior. Simeon seems to have applied all of it to Jesus!

The other indication is in Luke 2:26, where Simeon says he knew he would be able to see the Lord's Christ, the anointed one that had been promised. Even without the word *seed* the concept is clearly present, since the Old Testament promises about the Christ have their roots in the theme of seed—the hope given to Adam and Eve from the beginning. Simeon rejoiced to see Jesus and took him in his arms because he knew Jesus would fulfill all his deepest hopes.

In verses 34 and 35 Simeon confirmed the connection with Genesis 3:15 by referring to Jesus' future. He said in verse 35 that a sword would pierce through Mary's heart—apparently because of pain in Jesus' life. That is, at the cross the serpent would bite Jesus on the heel, and this certainly would be a piercing emotional experience in the life of Mary. Thankfully, though, this would not happen without Jesus causing the rise and fall of many in Israel. The word for "rise" means "resurrection," and all other 41 instances in New Testament clearly use it in that sense. Here too, therefore, it most likely refers to resurrection and, by extension, salvation. The word for "fall" has a broader range of meaning, but it should be understood as perishing spiritually (which is one possible connotation) because of its juxtaposition with "rise." Therefore, Simeon's message is that Jesus is the hinge on which the eternal destiny of others depends: salvation for those who believe in him and damnation for those who reject him. This rise and fall truly would be a crushing blow to the head of the serpent since it is exactly contrary to his every objective.

The gospel of John also has a passage which references seed. In it, Jesus made some pretty provocative statements regarding the assumptions of the Jewish leaders.

> **John 8:33–37** — They answered him, "We are offspring of Abraham and have never been enslaved to anyone. How is it that you say, 'You will become free'?" Jesus answered them, "Truly, truly, I say to you, everyone who practices sin is a slave to sin. The slave does not remain in the house forever; the son remains forever. So if the Son sets you free, you will be free indeed. I know that you are offspring of Abraham; yet you seek to kill me because my word finds no place in you.

The leaders of the Jews claimed to be the offspring of Abraham, but they didn't even know how far they fell short. They assumed they were fine because they were not slaves, as previous generations had been in Egypt. Jesus said they were indeed spiritual slaves — to sin. In verse 35 he set up a contrast between them as the corporate seed of Abraham and himself as the individual seed. He was hinting that the corporate seed needed something from the individual seed in order to fully arrive at the freedom God provides. Interestingly, in verse 38 and following he taught that although they were seed of Abraham, they had the devil for their true father. Thus, speaking in terms of Genesis, they belonged to the ungodly line of Cain, and Jesus was claiming they really were not in the line of the seed after all! The true Seed was about to offer the solution to all spiritual slavery, and it was going to involve a conflict of cosmic proportions.

Crucifixion

Sometimes when we think and teach about Jesus' death on the cross, we focus on how great his suffering was — and rightly so, for Jesus showed he was willing to go to extreme lengths to win our salvation. Yet in light of Genesis 3:15, sometimes our focus should be on how easy it was for Jesus to overcome Satan's attack. The worst Satan could throw at him that day — mock trials, flogging, crucifixion, and even death itself — should be interpreted as nothing more than a bite on the heel! God predicted it in the beginning, when he cursed the serpent in the garden. A Seed was to come who would be at enmity with the serpent.

We've seen a lot of seed come and go through the pages of Scripture, but this Seed is a special one. This seed carries his conflict with the serpent to epic proportions. This seed has a conflict that engages his heel with the head of the serpent. Jesus overcame his passion by rising from the dead; his suffering ultimately produced nothing worse than a few scars—as if it were a bite on his heel. On the other hand, the day of his crucifixion was also the day when he crushed the head of Satan. It's ironic that Satan's futile attack on Jesus was what ultimately led to his own mortal wound. Our God is a god of reversals, and he turned Jesus' apparent defeat into a great victory! He also orchestrated what is perhaps the greatest reversal of all time: making Satan's apparent victory ultimately end in his utter defeat. We live right now in an age when the reversal has not yet been fully completed. Since Jesus' resurrection we know that Satan *already* has been defeated, but there is also a sense in which it is *not yet* fully realized. When the Lord removes us from this world and places us in the new creation, we will finally enjoy all the benefits of Jesus' victory on the cross!

Paul

The Bible teaches us that there are very clear benefits for us as a result of what Jesus has achieved as the promised seed. That is, identifying ourselves with Christ implies we partake with him in some of the important components of the theme of seed in the Old Testament. The Greek word for "seed" shows up again in Galatians, where Paul is clearly returning to this theme.

> Galatians 3:19—Why then the law? It was added because of transgressions, until the *offspring* should come to whom the promise had been made (emphasis added).

Verse 16 clarifies for us that Paul is talking about Christ—the principal offspring among many who were promised to Abraham.

> Galatians 3:16—Now the promises were made to Abraham and to his offspring. It does not say, "And to offsprings," referring to many, but referring to one, "And to your offspring," who is Christ.

Clearly, the promises made to Abraham were in one sense given in regard to an incredibly large number of descendants who would be his offspring. Yet Paul was reading the texts about seed in the Old Testament in the same way we are: although there would be many, one special descendant would fulfill all the promises in an exceptional way. As part of his message, Paul was teaching in verse 19 that the law was only a temporary measure, and Jesus Christ proved to be the final, permanent solution.

Paul applied this principle to us in a very practical way a few verses later in the chapter:

> **Galatians 3:28–29**—There is neither Jew nor Greek, there is neither slave nor free, there is no male and female, for you are all one in Christ Jesus. And if you are Christ's, then you are Abraham's offspring, heirs according to promise.

Since Christ is the principal offspring of Abraham, all his followers belong to Abraham as well. In other words, our Lord Jesus is forming a family. All his followers are children of God and therefore brothers and sisters of Christ. If we are his spiritual siblings, it logically follows that we are also spiritual offspring of Abraham. (I'll include a whole chapter on Father Abraham in a future book.) It no longer matters whether we are physical descendants of Abraham; every one of us has an equal right to be his seed and an equal right to share in the benefits of being his heirs! Earlier, in Galatians 3:6–9, Paul explains that our principle inheritance is justification by faith because that's how Abraham was justified. Paul's argument here would be impossible if it weren't for the fact that the Old Testament constantly switches between the plural and singular focus on the promised seed. Jesus is the One Seed who enables us to be part of the multitude of seed. Praise God he made it possible for you and me to share in these great truths!

As members of Jesus' family we also have the privilege of sharing with him in his work of crushing Satan's head. Look at what else Paul writes in Romans:

> **Romans 16:20**—The God of peace will soon crush Satan under your feet.

It's amazing to realize that God sees fit to use our spiritual feet to defeat his and our enemy! We have no power to do it on our own, for God is the one who does it. Obviously it's possible only through the already completed work of Jesus' defeat of Satan on the cross. This verse refers to God's current progressive work to fully realize this defeat. It will be fully consummated in the future victorious reign of Christ. In the meantime, I want to make myself increasingly available to our Savior for use in his defeat of Satan!

John

As the writer of Revelation, the last book of the Bible, the apostle John assumes the important responsibility of wrapping up this very prominent theme in the Bible. He does a masterful job of summarizing it in chapter 12 and relating how it will all come to a climax in the future. I recommend you read Revelation 12 before proceeding. This chapter contains many details about both Satan and an unnamed woman, who are presented in a timeless kind of way. It's a description of what has been happening since the beginning of time, in many ways throughout history, and of what will ultimately happen to bring this struggle to a conclusion.

Look with me at the text of Revelation 12 to analyze some of the symbolism John uses. First, who do you think the woman represents? In verse 17, John uses the word *offspring* or *seed*, which makes a connection that really goes all the way back to Eve, who was given the first promise of seed. That promise was picked up numerous times through the Old Testament and applied to Israel—the nation which produced the Messiah. She is described as clothed in the sun, moon, and twelve stars—a statement that should remind us of Joseph's dream in Genesis 37:9. The symbolism in this dream points to the entire family of Israel before it had officially become a nation. By extension, the woman of Revelation 12 also applies to Mary, who directly gave birth to Jesus in the flesh. So we can see that the woman in this passage shares symbolism on many different levels with the nation of Israel—she should really make us think of all women in the Messianic line who played a part to enable the arrival of Jesus Christ in the flesh.

Here we also have the dragon, who symbolizes Satan. It is not an accident that a dragon is similar in many ways to a serpent—the animal chosen to represent him in Genesis 3. Verse 9 tells us the dragon is in fact "that ancient serpent, who is called the devil and Satan, the deceiver of the whole world."

The conflict between Satan and the seed of the woman is evident. When the dragon is unable to directly defeat the seed of the woman, he seeks to indirectly cause him harm by focusing his schemes against the woman and later against the rest of her offspring. Revelation 12 is a description of the cosmic struggle between Satan and Jesus. It seems to be a composite description of many events—past, present, and future. In the coming chapters, John describes the future and final defeat of the serpent.

Before we see the last conflict, in Revelation 13 the enemy makes one final effort at escaping the end he knows is coming. In this chapter, Satan shows his tendency to imitate God's glorious plans in his own twisted way.

> **Revelation 13:1–3**—And I saw a beast rising out of the sea, with ten horns and seven heads, with ten diadems on its horns and blasphemous names on its heads. And the beast that I saw was like a leopard; its feet were like a bear's, and its mouth was like a lion's mouth. And to it the dragon gave his power and his throne and great authority. One of its heads seemed to have a mortal wound, but its mortal wound was healed, and the whole earth marveled as they followed the beast.

In verse 2 we learn that the beast described in verse 1 proceeds from the dragon; he sounds like he is an offspring—a seed, almost as if the dragon is attempting to save himself using God's own methods. In verse 3 we learn that one of his heads has a mortal wound, obviously the wound that was predicted in Genesis 3:15. Apparently the offspring of the woman has already crushed the head of the serpent. This wound was dealt out at Calvary, at the very same moment Christ was bitten on the heel. The fact that Satan wants to imitate God prompts him to make the dragon appear as if the wound was healed. So in this chapter Satan also produces an offspring who seems to rival Jesus Christ in victorious power, glorifying himself and attracting followers.

Thankfully we know the final outcome; we can read about our future hope in Revelation 20. As is true for much of Revelation, even though it describes future events, this chapter is written in past tense—giving us a sense of complete confidence, knowing the defeat of Satan is as good as done.

> **Revelation 20:2**—And he seized the dragon, that ancient serpent, who is the devil and Satan, and bound him for a thousand years.

This sounds like a pretty definitive victory, but once again it is only a partial victory, for he is later released for a short time. Consummated victory isn't seen until a few verses later:

> **Revelation 20:10**—And the devil who had deceived them was thrown into the lake of fire and sulfur where the beast and the false prophet were, and they will be tormented day and night forever and ever.

This is where Satan receives a final crushing blow to the head, from which he will never, ever recover. There is no greater victory that could be described for our Savior—the offspring of the woman will, without any doubt, gain an uncontested victory in the end.

Remember how Jesus questioned the Jewish leaders' lineage in the book of John? Whether they were truly part of the seed was in doubt because of their conduct. John taught more about this in his first epistle. Look at 1 John 3:8–15.

> **1 John 3:8–9**—Whoever makes a practice of sinning is of the devil, for the devil has been sinning from the beginning. The reason the Son of God appeared was to destroy the works of the devil. No one born of God makes a practice of sinning, for God's seed abides in him, and he cannot keep on sinning because he has been born of God.

This is where the theme gets even more practical for us. Here John teaches us that those who belong to God cannot continually practice sin, and it's interesting to see the reason he gives us. John tells us that "whoever makes a practice of sinning is of the devil," but those who are born of God cannot keep on sinning "because God's seed abides in him." Without understanding the meaning of seed in the Old Testament, John's statement would be somewhat confusing. We can be sure, however, that John is declaring Jesus to be the promised seed, and his presence in the lives of his followers keeps them from practicing the deeds of his archenemy—whose head he must crush. It's impossible for one person to serve both the serpent and the serpent crusher.[9] That which is true for the whole universe is also true in our own individual lives. That is, in one sense the victory has been won, and in another sense we're waiting to see its consummation. Although sin has been defeated in each of us who follow him, we are still awaiting our glorification—that moment when we will be fully freed from the power of sin.

The most amazing part of this passage is in the following verses, where we see that having God's seed living in us makes us also offspring of God.

> **1 John 3:10–15**—By this it is evident who are the children of God, and who are the children of the devil: whoever does not practice righteousness is not of God, nor is the one who does not love his brother. For this is the message that you have heard from the beginning, that we should love one another. We should not be like Cain, who was of the evil one and murdered his brother. And why did he murder him? Because his own deeds were evil and his brother's righteous. Do not be surprised, brothers, that the world hates you. We know that we have passed out of death into life, because we love the brothers. Whoever does not love abides in death. Everyone who hates his brother is a murderer, and you know that no murderer has eternal life abiding in him.

---

[9] I borrowed the term "Serpent Crusher" from Carrie Sandom, *The Gospel Coalition Podcast*, February 13, 2015.

In Genesis the line of the seed always pointed forward to the coming of the true and final seed; now that Jesus has come, he is powerful enough to make *anyone else* part of the same line! I was nobody special, but now that God's seed abides in me, I have also been converted to seed. John speaks of the possibility of being like Cain—someone who proved himself not to be in the line of the seed by hating his brother. Instead, according to John we have the chance to prove we do belong to the seed by loving our brothers.

Conclusion

From the very beginning of history, the promise of seed gave us hope. Jesus is the seed who was promised long ago, the one who defeated the serpent and solved the problem of sin for humankind. He is the only one who can give us hope on an individual level as well—giving new life to his followers and making them part of the family of the seed. Do you sometimes feel hopeless in your struggle against sin? Does it seem like this world will never overcome the ways of human corruption? Have hope. No matter how dead things may seem, a seed always gives hope for new life. God seeks to glorify himself by producing life where the least amount of hope exists, even where there actually is no hope apart from the hope he alone gives. As in the case of Abraham, so for all of us, he "gives life to the dead and calls into existence the things that do not exist" (Romans 4:17).

Passages for further study:

Most include the word *seed* and can be understood to a whole new depth with the context of this study.

Genesis 9:9	Psalm 37:25–29
Genesis 22:9–18	Psalm 89:4, 29, 36
Genesis 26:1–5, 24	Psalm 105:6
Genesis 28:4, 13–14	Proverbs 11:21
1 Samuel 20:42	Isaiah 6:13
1 Samuel 24:21	Isaiah 41:8–10
1 Kings 11:39	Isaiah 48:19
2 Kings 11:1–3	Isaiah 53:10
Esther 6:13 ("Jewish people" = lit-	Isaiah 54:3
erally, Jewish seed)	Isaiah 66:22
Job 5:25	Jeremiah 22:30
Job 21:8	Jeremiah 30:10
Psalm 25:13	Jeremiah 33:22

Ezekiel 29:1-5
Acts 13
Romans 4:16–25
Romans 9:6–8
2 Corinthians 11:22

2

Toledot: A New Generation

Understanding the themes of the Bible is indispensable for even the slightest understanding of the overarching message of the Bible.

Someone might ask me, "Do you know anything about the water bodies of the central United States?" Based on what I wrote in the introduction to this book, imagine how I might have answered several years ago: "Ummm...yeah, yesterday I saw the beaver pond close to my house; and last week I crossed the Platte River on the way to Kearney. Do you want me to describe them to you?" Although I might have thought my knowledge about those two specific places was pretty impressive, even the way I answered the question revealed my lack of understanding. On the other hand, I could have responded by saying, "The entire central United States is part of the Mississippi water basin. Rainfall from thirty-one states and two Canadian provinces contributes to the river as it drains all the land from New York to Montana."[1] This second answer would demonstrate a true understanding of the subject. Instead of answering with a couple of detailed descriptions of water bodies, I would be showing I see the big picture—I know how these water bodies all fit together. Likewise, if I claim to understand the message of the Bible, my claim is valid only to the extent that I can relate the individual parts to the whole.

This is not to say the details of Scripture are unimportant. It is only through the details of Scripture that we can observe the message of the Bible. Ironically, however, we can't interpret the details correctly without knowing how to fit them into the overall message. This may seem like a hopeless circular dilemma, but much of life follows this same pattern. I need to observe the small streams of the United States in order to even know of the existence of the Mississippi River Basin, yet I will not truly understand the function of each of those streams without a perspective of the basin as a whole. The particulars clarify the generalities, and the generalities clarify the particulars. A proper study of Scripture will always involve a reciprocating interpretation between the two extremes. As students of the Bible we must keep our feet firmly planted in both levels of perspective.

---

[1] "Mississippi River Basin." Greatriverspartnership.org. N.p., 2012. Web. Accessed 17 May 2016. http://www.greatriverspartnership.org/en-us/northamerica/mississippi/pages/default.aspx

Our study in the last chapter is quite possibly the most important general theme for a proper understanding of God's Word. I would be willing to argue that it is the most foundational concept for understanding the message of the Bible. If the term "seed" is not in itself a crucial key for interpretation, at least the more general concept behind it is. One does not understand the Bible without capturing the idea that from the beginning someone was expected who would solve the sin problem introduced in Genesis. The use of the term "seed" in many places throughout the text is a detail used to present the general concept. I will have accomplished nothing with this book if it does not serve to reinforce for all of us a more conscious awareness of the way every passage of the Bible is somehow connected to the concept of an expected deliverer from the effects of Genesis 3.

This chapter is both an application and a reinforcement of the theme discussed in chapter 1. It does not present a new theme to our study. Rather, I want to demonstrate how to apply the perspective of a large theme to the understanding of a specific passage—in this case, one short verse. At the same time, I hope to increase our understanding of the "seed" theme by observing some additional details that support it. Specifically, we will observe one Hebrew word, *toledot*, and the role it plays in the structure of the Bible, working in concert with the term "seed" to heighten our expectation of a deliverer.

In 2002 a long-expected day finally arrived for my wife and me. We had been planning a move to Ecuador for several years. In some way or another, since 1988 when we decided to serve as missionaries in Ecuador, every day of the past fourteen years had something to do with moving us closer to our goal. What's more, we believed (and still do) that God had been preparing us over the course of our lifetime for whatever ministry lay ahead of us. As I poured myself a cup of coffee and got ready to eat breakfast amid twelve large suitcases on the floor, I felt they were somehow representative of the years of preparation for this moment. In a few short minutes we would be in the car and headed for the airport. As I reflected on the significance of this day, it seemed so enormous that I could hardly believe it had arrived. How is it that a lifetime can be spent in planning and then one day, a day that is simply twenty-four hours just like any other day, is the one that fulfills all the hopes and dreams of the rest? If I could measure the importance of my days in a scale, in my mind this day probably would have tipped the scale against the weight of my previous thirty-five years combined.

The opening verse of the entire New Testament is kind of like that; it is the description of a long-anticipated day. Although Matthew 1:1 seems pretty basic at first glance, the words used here are rich in meaning because of some foundations set for us in the book of Genesis:

> **Matthew 1:1**—The book of the genealogy of Jesus Christ, the son of David, the son of Abraham.

Let's understand what Matthew was really expressing as he sat down and began to write the opening lines of his gospel. We're going to see in a whole new way that Jesus Christ is the fulfillment of all our hopes and dreams—past, present, and future. In this chapter I will show that with this verse Matthew was purposefully connecting his gospel with the book of Genesis. He used a Greek word meant to be a very literal translation of an important word in Genesis, and the phrases that accompany it all connect with the theme of seed.

We need to start with the book of Genesis and see what Moses taught there about the hope of the world. In the previous chapter we saw how God promised that an offspring of the woman would be provided to defeat Satan and solve the problem of sin in the world. This promise was given early in the book of Genesis in chapter 3, verse 15. That verse is the foundation for one of the biggest themes in the remainder of the book—one purpose behind Genesis is to tell us who the seed of the woman is. Let's look more closely at one of the techniques the writer used to communicate his message. He used a word in concert with the word *seed* to point to the fulfillment of the promise for a seed.

Moses left clues in the book of Genesis that help us identify the beginning of each new section in his book. There are twelve divisions in Genesis, and every one, except the first (which starts at Genesis 1:1), begins with a phrase that contains the Hebrew word *toledot*. This word means "generation, genealogy, or history." It is especially used in genealogies to give an account of a man and his descendants.[2] When the Old Testament was translated into Greek (the Septuagint) about 250 years before Jesus' birth, the translators chose to use the Greek word *genesis* to convey the meaning of *toledot*. *Genesis* means "birth" or "lineage,"[3] obviously similar to the word *toledot*. The title we use for the book of Genesis comes from the name it was given in the

---

[2] Francis Brown, Samuel Rolles Driver and Charles Augustus Briggs, *Enhanced Brown-Driver-Briggs Hebrew and English Lexicon*, electronic ed. (Oak Harbor, WA: Logos Research Systems, 2000), 410.

[3] Barclay M. Newman, Jr., *A Concise Greek-English Dictionary of the New Testament* (Stuttgart, Germany: Deutsche Bibelgesellschaft; United Bible Societies, 1993), 36.

Septuagint. It's appropriate that they chose to name it after the word used to display the structure of the divisions within the book.

As we read through the book of Genesis, Moses meant for us to ask ourselves whether the descendants described in each section could possibly include the One Descendant that was promised to Eve in chapter 3. Here is a table that lists the first verse of each section of the book. Except for 1:1, these are the verses that contain the word *toledot*.

Divisions of Genesis	
Verse	Descendants of:
1:1	
2:4	Heavens and Earth
5:1	Adam
6:9	Noah
10:1	Shem, Ham and Japheth
11:10	Shem
11:27	Terah
25:12	Ishmael
25:19	Isaac
36:1	Esau (that is, Edom)
36:9	Esau
37:2	Jacob

Now read the actual text of some of these verses to get a sense of how they flow:

Genesis 1:1—In the beginning, God created the heavens and the earth.

Genesis 2:4—These are the generations of the heavens and the earth when they were created, in the day that the LORD God made the earth and the heavens.

Genesis 5:1—This is the book of the generations of Adam. When God created man, he made him in the likeness of God.

Genesis 6:9—These are the generations of Noah. Noah was a righteous man, blameless in his generation. Noah walked with God.

Allow me to make some observation about these sections:

- Generally speaking, each section deals with the descendants of the primary character from the previous section. Notice, for example, that Adam is the primary character of the second section, so we are told of his descendants in the third section.

- Genesis 1:1 does not contain the word *toledot* simply because there was no previous character to deal with. This section describes the origin of the heavens and the earth, and they are not the descendants of anybody.

- Genesis 2:4 does use the word *toledot* describing the descendants of the heavens and the earth. Most of our Bibles don't translate the word very literally because it sounds awkward to say: "These are the generations (or descendants) of the heavens and the earth." In what sense can the universe have children? Nevertheless, in section 2 Moses is describing the primary result of the creation of the heavens and the earth, which is the appearance on earth of people—the crowning glory of God's creation. Furthermore, that is probably the point of 2:7—that God intervened to make the earth produce a man. Notice that Adam comes from the ground.

  > **Genesis 2:7**—Then the LORD God formed the man of dust from the ground and breathed into his nostrils the breath of life, and the man became a living creature.

  The relationship between Adam and ground becomes even more clear when one understands the play on words utilized in the Hebrew text. The word for "man" is 'adam (not necessarily a proper noun), and the word for "ground" is 'adamah. We are told that 'adam was formed from the 'adamah. So textually speaking, Adam is, after all, a descendant of the earth.

- Notice that the structure provided by the word *toledot* matches our analysis of the theme introduced by the word *seed*. The big question in the second *toledot* section of the book of Genesis is who the important descendant will be. We already saw that Genesis 4:25 gives us the answer through the words of Eve when she calls Seth "another offspring." The fact that this is at the conclusion of the *toledot* section is another clue that it is one of its main considerations.

- As we noted in chapter 1, Noah is a seed who dealt a major blow to Satan and sin as a sort of savior. He is the main character in the third section of Genesis—the first section to follow the entrance of sin. The reader's expectations are high that he could be the promised solution. We will see below that this is key to understanding Matthew 1:1.

- In chapter 10, Moses established a pattern by dealing first in a general way with the two sons of Noah who were not going to be the source of the true offspring of the woman. After getting those details out of the way, he could then focus more specifically on Shem, the righteous line.
- At Genesis 11:27 we have arrived at the halfway point of the book. Even though several chapters remain, we have seen six divisions set apart by *toledot*, and six are remaining. I believe Moses purposefully placed the next main character at this crucial halfway point to show that Abraham is the central figure of the entire book of Genesis. Furthermore, he is in the seventh section; the number 7 often stands for perfection. Abraham obviously was not perfect in the sense of sinless, but he is intended to be the character most emphasized in Genesis.
- Following his previous pattern, Moses dealt first with Ishmael and Esau, two sons who proved not to be the source of the long-awaited offspring of Eve.
- Moses wouldn't have had to include the descendants of Esau twice in two successive sections, but he repeated Esau with a different twist the second time. Maybe part of the reason he did this was to make sure he had twelve divisions, allowing Abraham to occupy the important position he has. This number is also important to him because it matches the number of Jacob's sons listed in the final division, thus correlating with the twelve tribes of Israel.

As we can see, the matter of Eve's offspring is a huge issue that really is the overarching theme of Genesis. In the last chapter we saw that "seed" is a very important theme in Genesis. When we observe the use of the term *toledot* we realize the very structure of Genesis is built around communication of that theme. A proper reading of Genesis requires us to search for the promised seed in each of its twelve sections. Moses not only introduced the Pentateuch with a search for the seed (in Genesis), but because the Pentateuch is the beginning of the Old Testament, the entire biblical canon is introduced with the problem of sin and the question of who will be the solution. Much of the Old Testament was written to heighten our expectation of someone who would come and mend our relationship with God, but even Genesis all by itself is a wealth of messianic material.

With this basic understanding of Genesis as a background, we are now ready to look at Matthew 1:1. Matthew was living in a context in which most

Israelites were waiting in hope that someday the special offspring of Eve promised in Genesis would come to Israel. We don't know much about Matthew himself before he met Jesus, besides the fact that he was a tax collector. Did he care about the coming Messiah? Did he still hold on to hope that God would send him? What we do know is that when someone special did come, Matthew became his follower and eventually wrote a gospel to tell the rest of us who he really is. If we read it without the context of *toledot* in Genesis, we are liable to miss part of his message.

Matthew's opening verse is short and sweet, but it hits us with an amazing set of phrases in light of the message of Genesis:

> **Matthew 1:1**—The book of the genealogy of Jesus Christ, the son of David, the son of Abraham.

To understand more deeply what he is affirming here, let's compare it with Moses' introduction to the third section in his book:

> **Genesis 5:1**—This is the book of the generations of Adam. When God created man, he made him in the likeness of God.

Matthew copied, almost word for word, the same formula Moses used to introduce each section of Genesis, especially the way it is found in his third section. Compare with me the first part of these two verses. Genesis 5:1 is the only instance of *toledot* where Moses uses the word *book*, and Matthew has emulated it here to start his gospel. At first glance in our English Bibles, we might think there is a difference between the words *generations* and *genealogy,* but these are both valid English translations of *toledot* in Genesis 5:1. Not only that, but Matthew used exactly the same Greek word that was in his Greek translation of Genesis 5:1: the word *genesis*. It is obvious that Matthew had read Genesis and was influenced by it, even to the point of his word choice.

I believe Matthew wrote his gospel to tie in closely with the message of Genesis. In no uncertain terms he proclaimed he had decided to pick up the theme where Moses left off. He saw that no one in the book of Genesis, or in the entire Old Testament for that matter, perfectly fulfilled the promise of Genesis 3:15. Matthew was 100 percent confident, however, that Jesus is the promised offspring of the woman at the beginning of Genesis. He wanted to give us the account of how Jesus crushed the serpent's head, so his desire was to start his account with another instance of the word *toledot*. Since he was writing in Greek, however, he used *genesis* instead! It's as if he was claiming to write the thirteenth section of the book of Genesis!

Now we must ask ourselves another question in this regard. Of all twelve sections in the book of Genesis, why does Matthew's introduction most resemble the third? What is special about Genesis 5:1 as compared to the other verses which have *toledot*? The answer comes in noticing who the main character is in the third section of Genesis. Genesis 5:1 tells us it is the account of the generations of Adam, but as we discussed above, its main character is Noah. Matthew knew Noah actually came kind of close to being the promised offspring. Noah saved the entire world of his day from God's judgment because of a corrupt and sinful society. Peter also recognized a connection between Noah and Jesus:

> **1 Peter 3:18–21** — For Christ also suffered once for sins, the righteous for the unrighteous, that he might bring us to God, being put to death in the flesh but made alive in the spirit, in which he went and proclaimed to the spirits in prison, because they formerly did not obey, when God's patience waited in the days of Noah, while the ark was being prepared, in which a few, that is, eight persons, were brought safely through water. Baptism, which corresponds to this, now saves you, not as a removal of dirt from the body but as an appeal to God for a good conscience, through the resurrection of Jesus Christ.

Peter tells us Noah's ministry was less than fully effective because the people of his day "did not obey." The waters of the flood were not sufficient, but the waters of baptism are. (I'll deal more with the subject of baptism in a future book.) Even though Noah came close, close is infinitely far from the infinitely complete work of our Savior. Matthew is preparing to tell us about the true and perfect seed of the woman, who completely saved the world from sin. For that reason he chose to emulate Moses' introduction of Noah in his own introduction of Jesus Christ.

Just to make sure we wouldn't miss his point, Matthew added a couple of phrases to help us make the connection. Look again:

> **Matthew 1:1** — The book of the genealogy of Jesus Christ, the son of David, the son of Abraham.

He tells us Jesus is the son of David who was in turn the son of Abraham. In this way he reminds us of Abraham, who was the central figure in all the *toledot* sections of Genesis. In Genesis 12:1–3 Abraham was told he would be blessed by God in several ways, not the least of which was that in him "all the families of the earth shall be blessed." Matthew wants us to know that through his line came Jesus Christ, who would indeed be the greatest source of blessing to all the families of the earth. Abraham was also told that God would make of him "a great nation." His physical offspring are the source of several nations today, including Israel. Jesus Christ, the central figure of the New Testament, is also the father of a great *spiritual* nation (1 Peter 2:9; 1 John 3:1). (I'll deal with this more in a future book.)

Matthew also saw the importance of informing us even more specifically that Jesus is part of the lineage of David. In Genesis 49:10, Judah received a promise that he would be the source of kings for Israel. The greatest of these kings was David, a man after God's own heart (1 Samuel 13:14; Acts 13:22). Later David was also promised he would have a descendant who would reign eternally:

> **2 Samuel 7:12–13** — When your days are fulfilled and you lie down with your fathers, I will raise up your *offspring* after you, who shall come from your body, and I will establish his kingdom. He shall build a house for my name, and I will establish the throne of his kingdom forever (emphasis added).

And now Matthew would have us know that Jesus is the royal offspring promised not only to Eve and Abraham, but to David as well. Matthew doesn't say that Jesus is the seed, but he doesn't have to. By choosing to begin his gospel with the Greek word equivalent to *toledot*, he implies that Jesus has to be the seed that all sections of Genesis fell short of describing. Careful attention to the themes of Scripture can be key to capturing the full meaning of some of its individual parts. An awareness of how Moses introduces the entire Bible is crucial for understanding Matthew's introduction to the New Testament. On its own, Matthew 1:1 seems like a bland way to start an important book. On the contrary, when read in the light of biblical theology, it is connected to one of the Bible's greatest rivers of theological truth. We need to approach all the individual parts of Scripture as links in the chain of its greatest themes.

Matthew continues to emphasize the Davidic aspect of Jesus' genealogy in the rest of chapter 1. After tracing his genealogy in a detailed way, he summarizes it in verse 17:

> **Matthew 1:17** — So all the generations from Abraham to David were fourteen generations, and from David to the deportation to Babylon fourteen generations, and from the deportation to Babylon to the Christ fourteen generations.

If we analyze the genealogy more closely, we realize he manipulated the facts a little in order to be able to make this statement. But by doing so, he was making David the central figure of the entire genealogy. Not only that, but he also emphasized the person of David by mentioning the number fourteen. In Hebrew each letter of the alphabet had a numerical value, and it was common to make significant statements using the value of a word. Adding the value of the letters in David's name produces a sum of fourteen. So Matthew was claiming there is nobody better suited to fulfill the Davidic promises of the Old Testament than Jesus Christ. Read the rest of Matthew 1 and see if you can find further emphasis on Jesus' connection with David.

However, Matthew was not simply claiming that Jesus is great in the same way David was great; he was, in fact, affirming that Jesus supersedes the greatness of David. Matthew included three groups of fourteen intentionally. If we analyze the genealogy in terms of groups of seven, we see something even more significant. Matthew's three groups of fourteen can be divided into groups of seven instead. Since three times fourteen is the same as six times seven, Jesus' birth actually inaugurated the seventh seven since Abraham. For a Jew like Matthew, there could be no number more complete and more perfect than seven. Ever since Genesis chapter 1, when God created the world in six days and rested on the seventh, special focus has been given to that number. "The generation of the Messiah represents the seventh seven, thereby showing that it is He who inaugurates the ultimate Sabbath rest for the people of God, the eschatological age."[4] Matthew was claiming that Jesus fulfills everything ever promised to Abraham and to David about God's solution for the problems of humanity. The *toledot* sections of Genesis built with increasing intensity toward the seed who was never found within its chapters. Genesis mentions some pretty good saviors, but it ends without reaching the heights of our full expectation. Matthew adds one final *toledot* with the perfect seed, who ends up being the climax of our hope.

It is absolutely amazing that Matthew would be bold enough to make these statements. For the knowledgeable student of the Old Testament in his day, there could be no mistaking the deep theological truths he was proclaiming. At times I have wondered whether the biblical authors had any knowledge that what they were writing would later become part of the canon or whether they just wrote something ultimately recognized as valuable and added to the Bible. I think in this case it is clear that Matthew had no doubt of the importance of his gospel. In fact, I think he was making a statement that his book was intended to be taken on the same authoritative

[4] David G. Hagopian, ed. *The Genesis Debate: Three Views On the Days of Creation* (Mission Viejo, CA: Crux Press, Inc. 2001), 226.

level as Genesis. Up to this point there was no New Testament; all that existed was the Tanak, which we currently call the Old Testament. And Matthew was claiming that it was incomplete because there was never a definitive answer to who was the offspring of Eve so long awaited. Matthew, through the inspiration of the Holy Spirit, was bold enough to complete the lacking details!

Matthew couldn't use the word *toledot* since he was writing in Greek. Could it be a coincidence that instead he used its Greek translation, *genesis*? It can't be an accident that the first verse of the New Testament contains the same formula found several times throughout the first book of the Old Testament. At some point when the early church was choosing the order of the New Testament canon, either someone noticed that Matthew would be a good introduction to the entire New Testament or God providentially arranged for it to be so.

Just as moving to a new country is more significant than a whole bunch of days leading up to it, so Matthew's bombshell statement at the beginning of his gospel outweighs the entire book of Genesis. Genesis is a beautiful book, and our understanding of the gospel would be incomplete without it. It is so full of hope regarding the coming Messiah, we should want to read it over and over. Yet some key information is missing. With the text of Genesis as background, we can open the New Testament and get blown away by the impact of Matthew's opening statement regarding the fulfillment of the hope outlined for us in Genesis. As we read any part of the New Testament one of the questions we should be asking is: "How does this passage connect to the themes introduced in the Old Testament?"

Jesus truly is the fulfillment of all our hopes and dreams—past, present, and future. No matter the changes in our lives, no matter the significant days that roll our way, even after moving day, one thing remains—Jesus Christ is our hope. Jesus Christ, the long–awaited Messiah, has come and gained victory over the serpent of Genesis 3.

3
The Perfect Prophet

When the White House press secretary steps to the microphone, the world listens. Probably no other "secretary" commands a more captive audience. The White House press secretary usually is a person with high credentials, but the attention he or she receives has very little to do with personal qualifications. Instead it has to do with whom the secretary represents. Speaking at a press conference, he or she is giving the official administrative position on the topics discussed. Every word is carefully crafted to best convey the relevant message to the public. For this reason, the words are taken with the same weight as if they had come from the president himself. Stephen Early, who served under Franklin D. Roosevelt, is considered the first modern press secretary. Early's position was so important that President Roosevelt did not allow the press to directly quote him unless Early specifically distributed the quoted material in writing.[1]

Figure 2: Three Offices

The next three chapters will deal with a triad of offices in the Old Testament which Jesus Christ fulfills perfectly. The three offices—prophet, priest, and king—were each established by the Father to provide what people needed from God. Jesus, being God himself, is able to fill these roles in a way no one else can. Adam, Abraham, Moses, and Melchizedek were four other people in the Bible who in some sense carried all three titles, but they pale in comparison to our Lord. The title "Christ" (which means "anointed one") by itself implies he is specifically designated to fulfill each of these roles that are so necessary to us.

---

[1] Michael Nelson, *Guide to the Presidency* (New York, NY: Routledge, 2015), p. 853.

The first of the three offices is that of prophet. Our modern concept of a prophet is slightly skewed. While we tend to think of one who predicts the future, the Israelite idea of a prophet was much broader. In the biblical sense, a prophet spoke in the same way as the press secretary of the President of the United States of America, only the prophet communicated words from God himself that the people desperately needed to hear. And whether they wanted to or not, they needed to listen closely. Telling the future was sometimes included, but the prophet's job was more generally to simply declare God's message to his people. One of a prophet's most common phrases was "Thus says the Lord." Therefore, in the Old Testament a prophet was a person who expressed God's Word in either spoken or written form.

Jesus is the prophet who perfectly reveals God's message. Although all prophets in the Bible were important for what they accomplished in their time, another important aspect of their ministry was that they prefigured the greatest prophet of all time. Let's look at what the Bible has to say about prophets and allow it to lead us to Christ.

Adam

In this chapter and the following two, I want to demonstrate that Adam carried a responsibility to fulfill all three of the principle offices. We shouldn't be surprised he carries the same responsibility as Jesus in light of the following verse:

> **1 Corinthians 15:45** — Thus it is written, "The first man Adam became a living being"; the last Adam became a life-giving spirit.

Paul compares and contrasts Christ and Adam, and the similarities are many. (For more, see Chapter 7, "Discerning Good and Evil.") In every possible way, Jesus completes what was lacking in Adam's failures. For now, let's focus only on the fact that Adam was a prophet.

Adam was the very first person to receive God's Word and proclaim it to someone else. After God created Adam and placed him in the garden, God communicated something very important to him:

> **Genesis 2:16–17** — And the LORD God commanded the man, saying, "You may surely eat of every tree of the garden, but of the tree of the knowledge of good and evil you shall not eat, for in the day that you eat of it you shall surely die."

The very next verse describes the search for a helper for Adam, which ultimately terminated in God forming Eve. The Hebrew construction of verse

18 points clearly to a consecutive event, showing that God gave this command before Eve was created. Apparently God did not see the need to repeat the command to Eve but expected Adam to communicate the message to his wife. Adam should have performed the task of a true prophet, just as Moses did after receiving God's commands on Mount Sinai:

> Exodus 19:7—So Moses came and called the elders of the people and set before them all these words that the LORD had commanded him.

When we read chapter 3 of Genesis we are expected to analyze the effectiveness of Adam's communication as a prophet. In verse 3 we find he had indeed communicated with Eve in regard to this matter. Look at what she said to the serpent:

> Genesis 3:3—But God said, "You shall not eat of the fruit of the tree that is in the midst of the garden, neither shall you touch it, lest you die."

Eve had heard the Lord's commandment and understood it—mostly. Unfortunately, she had an additional phrase included in her quotation—"neither shall you touch it." At first glance this may not seem like a big deal. In fact, we might be likely to think she was better off to stay as far away from the tree as possible. On the contrary, however, what we have here is a kind of legalism that the serpent was able to take advantage of in his strategy to tempt Eve. His next move was to make her doubt the goodness of God, and he was able to do it all the more easily because her understanding of the command was more strict than was ever intended. Satan was able to paint God as someone who sought to kill her joy. As in every case of sharing God's Word, both adding and subtracting from the message are fatal mistakes that make us more prone to sin. One of the components in the fall was a lack of communication of God's Word, and Adam as the prophet in charge held full responsibility for this failure.

Later in the chapter, God's analysis of the root problem becomes another clue that Adam failed as a prophet. When God cursed the ground in verse 17 he said it was "because you have listened to the voice of your wife and have eaten of the tree of which I commanded you, 'You shall not eat of it,'" Many times over in Scripture, the people were commanded to listen to the prophets (see for example Deuteronomy 18:18–19 and Jeremiah 37:2). The problem in Eden was that instead of being listened to, the prophet listened to Eve.

Abraham

Another early passage in the Bible that deals with prophetic ministry is Genesis 15. If you're like me, you've read this passage before without realizing a prophet is here. Look at verse 1:

> **Genesis 15:1**—After these things the word of the LORD came to Abram in a vision: "Fear not, Abram, I am your shield; your reward shall be very great."

The introduction to God's statement to Abram is a phrase that should sound familiar to us: "The word of the Lord came to...." This formula is used in the Bible when God is giving his message to a prophet. (Compare 1 Samuel 3:1; 2 Samuel 24:11; 1 Kings 18:1; 2 Kings 20:4; Jeremiah 1:2; and other passages.) "This is a formula for revelation characteristic of the Prophetic books, not of the Patriarchal Tales."[2] What's more, "The night-vision (*mahazeh*) invoked here is also a prophet mode of experience."[3] Here, however, the formula seems to be out of place: not only does Abram not fit who we think of as a prophet, but the message God gave him in this chapter was really intended only for him, not for others. It's clear the author was taking special pains to present Abram as a prophet; the fact that the phrase is out of place makes his intentions even more obvious. One of the key messages in the Pentateuch is to make a comparison at certain points between Moses and Abraham, showing how Moses was a failure compared to Abraham.[4] Thus Abram is presented as a prophet just so he can be more readily compared; his status as prophet is somewhat artificially inflated. Nevertheless, he is the prototype prophet God has presented to us in Scripture.

Genesis 20:1–7 even more clearly states that Abraham occupied the office of prophet. This is the second of two instances when Abraham lied about his wife, saying she was his sister. Verse 3 tells us God came to King Abimelech in a dream to warn him. In verse 7 God told him Abraham was a prophet, apparently all the more reason for returning Sarah and a relief to Abimelech, who would benefit from Abraham's prayers on his behalf. The ironic part about the whole story is that the problem here found its root in Abraham himself, who concocted the idea for the deception in the first place. Although Abraham might have been the very first prophet, it is clear he was

---

[2] Robert Alter, *The Five Books of Moses: A Translation with Commentary* (New York: W. W. Norton & Company, 2004), 73.

[3] Ibid.

[4] John H. Sailhamer, *The Meaning of the Pentateuch: Revelation, Composition and Interpretation* (Downers Grove, IL: InterVarsity Press, 2009), 13-14.

a very imperfect one. If God's people were depending on this prophet for their spiritual needs, they would fall far short of the intimate relationship God expected with them.

The point of presenting Abraham as a prophet was to show that Abraham was the prophet who believed (had faith). He may have been far from a perfect prophet, but he had the key to success. Look at Genesis 15:6, a key verse in the first chapter that shows us Abraham was a prophet:

> **Genesis 15:6**—And he believed the LORD, and he counted it to him as righteousness.

From this we can conclude the Lord is much more concerned about the attitude of the heart than he is about anyone's relative skill at performing the duties they have been called to. Even though Abraham was an imperfect prophet, he was all God needed him to be, for God could work through his faithful heart to accomplish his purposes. In contrast, at a crucial time in Moses' ministry he displayed an unfortunate unbelief (lack of faith):

> **Numbers 20:12**—And the LORD said to Moses and Aaron, "Because you did not believe in me, to uphold me as holy in the eyes of the people of Israel, therefore you shall not bring this assembly into the land that I have given them."

Moses is presented in the Pentateuch as the prophet who didn't believe. In spite of doing many great things, he failed at what counted most. The lesson for us is to place our faith in God and all he has promised to do, not the least of which is to provide a perfect prophet who is all we will ever need.

Moses
Moses received his call to be prophet in Exodus 3–4. Not surprisingly we find some parallels here to the call of Abraham in Genesis 15. In the conversation God had with Abram, he mentioned Abram's descendants would live as slaves in a foreign nation for 400 years before God would deliver them. Immediately following this prediction Abram saw a smoking fire pot and a flaming torch (Genesis 15:13–17), which were probably intended to parallel Moses' burning bush experience just before he began to deliver Abraham's descendants. In Genesis 15:1 God had told Abram he would be his shield, and in Exodus 3:12 he told Moses he would likewise be with him. In Genesis 15:8 Abram asked for a sign, and in Exodus 3:12 God offered one without being asked. Much of Exodus 3 seems to be written with Genesis 15 in mind.

In chapter 4 the purpose of God's call on Moses' life becomes even more clear. Look at verse 12, which describes the prophetic role Moses was to have:

> **Exodus 4:12**—"Now therefore go, and I will be with your mouth and teach you what you shall speak."

That is exactly the biblical picture of a prophet throughout the rest of the Scriptures.

The portrayal of Moses as a prophet continues to grow in Exodus 7. This is where God revealed his plan to Moses and actually even spent some time dealing with Moses' reluctance and unbelief. In 7:1 the Lord made a very shocking statement in light of the strict monotheism of Israel:

> **Exodus 7:1**—And the LORD said to Moses, "See, I have made you like God to Pharaoh, and your brother Aaron shall be your prophet.

It's amazing to me that this could even be in the Hebrew Bible. Even though it's obviously a figure of speech, it seems too controversial to be part of the Israelite Scriptures! In light of that it must have a clear message. I like Robert Alter's analysis: "The reiteration of this bold comparison may have a polemic motivation: Pharaoh imagines himself a god, but I have made you a god to Pharaoh."[5] In other words, whether the audience likes it or not, a prophet always comes with an authoritative message from God. There is no chance of selectively listening to only that which is pleasing. God's messenger has God's message, period.

Since Moses was concerned about his ability to speak, God allowed his brother, Aaron, to speak for him. (This wasn't the first time God had spoken this way; see also Exodus 4:14–16.) In this verse God said Aaron would stand as Moses' prophet—another defining statement regarding the function of a prophet. Moses was like God. Aaron was his prophet. Since Aaron was speaking for Moses, we can understand this to mean that a prophet speaks God's words. So in light of the figure of speech used in this verse, we can affirm that Moses and Aaron were both prophets of the Lord. They both relayed God's message to Pharaoh. Moses was simply on a higher level with regard to their chain of command.

Two very important passages describe the way Moses fulfilled his prophetic role. They are important not for their implications for all future prophets, but because of the connection they give to the greatest prophet of

---

[5] Alter, *The Five Books of Moses*, 345.

all—Jesus Christ. The first of these is in Exodus chapters 19 and 20. Look especially at 19:16–20 to get a feel for the tenor of the passage:

> Exodus 19:16–20—On the morning of the third day there were thunders and lightnings and a thick cloud on the mountain and a very loud trumpet blast, so that all the people in the camp trembled. Then Moses brought the people out of the camp to meet God, and they took their stand at the foot of the mountain. Now Mount Sinai was wrapped in smoke because the LORD had descended on it in fire. The smoke of it went up like the smoke of a kiln, and the whole mountain trembled greatly. And as the sound of the trumpet grew louder and louder, Moses spoke, and God answered him in thunder. The LORD came down on Mount Sinai, to the top of the mountain. And the LORD called Moses to the top of the mountain, and Moses went up.

This was a very scary experience for the people: thunder, lightning, a thick cloud, a very loud trumpet blast, fire, smoke like the smoke of a kiln, and quaking—all causing the people to tremble. All this combines to give the effect that God is unattainable. Even if God permits it, going into his presence is obviously too much for a mere mortal to bear. Moreover, God is so exalted that when he went down in verse 20, he was still at the top of a mountain. The Lord called Moses and met with him at the top of that mountain.

Now look at how the people responded to these factors in the very next chapter:

> Exodus 20:19–21—[The people] said to Moses, "You speak to us, and we will listen; but do not let God speak to us, lest we die." Moses said to the people, "Do not fear, for God has come to test you, that the fear of him may be before you, that you may not sin." The people stood far off, while Moses drew near to the thick darkness where God was.

Just as when God's prophetic word was given to Abraham (Genesis 15:1), here is another command not to fear. Verse 19 is especially key in how it shows the reaction of the people in the face of what they were experiencing. Their request was that Moses mediate between them and God. They were willing to listen to Moses, but they did not want God to speak to them—it was too much for them. John H. Sailhamer has done a great job of explaining why we should understand the people's fear as failure and not as reflective of God's original intention for them.[6] Whether this is true or not, it is clear Moses fulfilled the function of prophet at Sinai, and he did it in the context

---

[6] Sailhamer, *The Meaning of the Pentateuch*, 378-398.

of fear, a mountain, and a belief on the part of the people that God is unap-
proachable. Take special note of these details, for they will become even
more significant in our analysis (below) of Jesus' transfiguration.

The other important passage describes not only the event at Sinai, but
also Moses' customary meetings with God subsequent to it. Exodus 34:29–
35 tells us his face would shine as a result of his conversations with the Lord.

> **Exodus 34:34–35**—Whenever Moses went in before the LORD to speak with
> him, he would remove the veil, until he came out. And when he came out
> and told the people of Israel what he was commanded, the people of Israel
> would see the face of Moses, that the skin of Moses' face was shining. And
> Moses would put the veil over his face again, until he went in to speak with
> him.

Once again the people's reaction was fear. Now not only God was too holy
for them; his mediator was as well! In order to solve this problem, Moses
was forced to wear a veil whenever he was with the people. John picked up
on this in his gospel:

> **John 1:14**—And the Word became flesh and dwelt among us, and we have
> seen his glory, glory as of the only Son from the Father, full of grace and
> truth.

The word John uses for "dwelt" is the Greek verb related to "tabernacle." In
contrast to Moses, who hid his glory with a veil after entering the tent of
meeting, Jesus became our tent of meeting and allows us to see his glory in
all its fullness. This passage will also be an important factor in understanding the transfiguration.

A Prophet Like Me

Our next passage gives us every reason to expect a future prophet who supersedes every other prophet mentioned in the Old Testament. Deuteronomy is a record of what happened just before the Israelites entered the
Promised Land. Moses was about to die, and he gave a series of sermons to
the people to prepare them for what was to come. In chapter 18 he dealt with
the need they would have for a prophetic voice. Look at verse 15:

> **Deuteronomy 18:15**—The LORD your God will raise up for you a prophet
> like me from among you, from your brothers—it is to him you shall listen.

He told them God would give them a prophet in the future. One of the reasons this verse is so important is because of one little phrase pronounced by

Moses: "like me." Many prophets were yet to come in Israel's future, but only one of these would prove to be "like" Moses in the fullest sense of the word. The little phrase "like me" is intended to fill the original hearers, and even us, with high expectations. The fact that the similarities to Moses aren't really defined only serves to heighten the anticipation. Who will he be? What will he really be like? In what sense will he be like Moses? We ought to read the rest of Scripture with an attention to details that help us recognize this promised prophet.

Moses said something else significant about the prophet in verse 15—he will be "from among you, from your brothers." This is important, and I believe Jesus fulfills this promise on two levels. On the surface, of course, this means the prophet had to be an Israelite. When Jesus was born a Jew, it placed him in the right category. But I think there's more, and to understand it we need to hear the phrase the way it was originally heard. When Moses said this, the people must have thought, "Good, he will be one of us; he will be approachable and we can trust him to have our best interest at heart." In this sense also, Jesus fulfills the promise better than anyone else ever could. Many other prophets were human—an unremarkable fact; but it's extraordinary that the Perfect Prophet would be one of us. We now know that Jesus, being God, was made flesh. Therefore, in a special way he is approachable because he is one of us. We can have full confidence that he has the human interest at heart because he is human. In other words, the full significance of this phrase was not completely understood until we realized the promised prophet was God himself. The fact that God became a prophet "from among [our] brothers" makes him the best prophet ever!

In the last part of verse 15, Moses emphasized the importance of listening to the future prophet. As a prophet himself, Moses knew the tendency in people not to listen well. He knew life could be found only by listening to God's words. And Moses certainly knew the future prophet would be even more important than him.

In verses 16–18, Moses refers back to the events of Exodus 20, when the people requested a mediator.

> **Deuteronomy 18:16–18**—Just as you desired of the LORD your God at Horeb on the day of the assembly, when you said, "Let me not hear again the voice of the LORD my God or see this great fire any more, lest I die." And the LORD said to me, "They are right in what they have spoken. I will raise up for them a prophet like you from among their brothers. And I will put my words in his mouth, and he shall speak to them all that I command him."

Moses was establishing that the future prophet would also be a solution to the fear of God's people and our refusal to listen directly to him. Just as Moses was able to give God's words to the people, so the future prophet is the perfect solution for a people who find it impossible to relate with a holy God. In this sense Jesus is exactly what we need: He is a man with flesh and blood just like us. In fact, he is a man who came from the very poorest of roots; he is a simple carpenter with no social advantages to intimidate the very least among us!

The following verses (18b–22) in Deuteronomy 18 further describe the future prophet. Their description is general enough to apply to all future prophets of Israel, but if they are true for *any* prophet, they are especially true for the *perfect* prophet.

> **Deuteronomy 18:18–22** — "I will raise up for them a prophet like you from among their brothers. And I will put my words in his mouth, and he shall speak to them all that I command him. And whoever will not listen to my words that he shall speak in my name, I myself will require it of him. But the prophet who presumes to speak a word in my name that I have not commanded him to speak, or who speaks in the name of other gods, that same prophet shall die." And if you say in your heart, "How may we know the word that the LORD has not spoken?" — when a prophet speaks in the name of the LORD, if the word does not come to pass or come true, that is a word that the LORD has not spoken; the prophet has spoken it presumptuously. You need not be afraid of him.

We are told the prophet will be speaking God's words. The implication of this is that not listening to the prophet will be a rejection of God himself and for this the people will be held responsible by the Lord. There is no room for error on the part of the prophet. If what he says proves not to come true, the people will know with certainty he was not speaking God's words. And in such cases the penalty for the prophet would be death. All these guidelines for prophecy should serve to increase our respect for and value of the one perfect prophet who lacks nothing in his work on our behalf.

Joshua

Moses' prediction of a future prophet like him is a very significant part of the larger message at the end of Deuteronomy. The last chapter of the book records Moses' death. Since Moses was likely responsible for much of the text of the Pentateuch, it is important to note that Deuteronomy 34 could not have been written by him, for it recounts the circumstances of his death. In light of that we must understand this chapter as the viewpoint of an author who was more removed from the situation and able to give a very neutral evaluation of things. Let's see what he wrote.

As soon as the author finished his account of Moses' death and the people's mourning, he mentioned Joshua in verse 9.

> **Deuteronomy 34:9**—Now Joshua the son of Nun was filled with the spirit of wisdom, for Moses had laid his hands on him; and the sons of Israel listened to him and did as the LORD had commanded Moses (NASB).

It's clear Joshua was meant to fill Moses' shoes as his successor. We are told he was "filled with the spirit of wisdom" and "Moses had laid his hands on him." With those details alone, we might suspect him to be a prophet *like Moses.* However, an even more obvious hint leads us to draw this conclusion. Did you notice the phrase "The sons of Israel listened to him"? That's a clear reference back to Deuteronomy 18:15; Moses commanded the people to listen to the prophet who would be like him. It's clear Israel had taken Moses' prophecy to heart; they were full of hope that Joshua would be the perfect prophet.

As readers of the text, we are left with a certain literary tension—we are led to believe Joshua probably was the one. Several other details in the text would support this conclusion. For starters, Joshua's name means "the Lord is salvation" in Hebrew, and I don't believe it is mere coincidence that "Jesus" is the Greek version of the same name. Also, looking ahead to Joshua 5:13–15, we see similarities between him and Moses.

> **Joshua 5:13–15**—When Joshua was by Jericho, he lifted up his eyes and looked, and behold, a man was standing before him with his drawn sword in his hand. And Joshua went to him and said to him, "Are you for us, or for our adversaries?" And he said, "No; but I am the commander of the army of the LORD. Now I have come." And Joshua fell on his face to the earth and worshiped and said to him, "What does my lord say to his servant?" And the commander of the LORD's army said to Joshua, "Take off your sandals from your feet, for the place where you are standing is holy." And Joshua did so.

Joshua encountered a man who was "the commander of the army of the Lord," whom many have interpreted to be the Lord Jesus himself. If this is so, Joshua, like Moses, had a face-to-face encounter with God. Furthermore, he was commanded to remove the sandals from his feet, for the place where he was standing was holy—a clear repetition of Moses' burning bush experience. Any careful reader who observes these details alone will rightly conclude the prophet like Moses had arrived in the person of Joshua.

Nevertheless, the last three verses of Deuteronomy are carefully worded to contradict the hypothesis at which we ought to be arriving. Look especially at verse 10:

> **Deuteronomy 34:10**—Since that time no prophet has risen in Israel like Moses, whom the LORD knew face to face (NASB).

It is as if the author is playing with our minds. He is at one moment showing us Joshua's greatness and potential to be the fulfillment of the perfect prophet we need (verse 9), and at the next moment removing the possibility (verse 10), with the effect that our hope is heightened further still. If Joshua in all his greatness wasn't great enough, the perfect prophet must be great beyond our wildest imagination! In fact, the same holds true for any other Old Testament prophet, however great. This text probably was written much later than Joshua's ministry, potentially even after the exile. John H. Sailhamer shows why we need to understand this verse as written quite late:

> This statement not only reflects an awareness of the existence of an office of prophecy, but also is able, within that chronological frame, to draw the conclusion that such an individual prophet (as envisioned in Deut 18!) had not arisen. Neither Joshua, nor Samuel, nor any of the pre-exilic prophets were in a position to make such a statement. In Joshua's day, the prophetic office had not been established, and in Samuel's day it had only just begun to function. Even during the exile, the office of prophet was still being actively exercised. Deuteronomy 34 says that the prophet promised in Deuteronomy 18 "never came."[7]

Therefore, Deuteronomy 34:10 is likely an addition to the text of Deuteronomy that was added much later to complete the message of the Pentateuch and link it to the rest of Scripture. It was written to disqualify all the prophets of the entire Old Testament and inspire hope in the prophet who was yet to come.

Look at the details of the biblical text. The author states flatly that no prophet has risen like Moses. He couldn't express more clearly that no other prophet measured up. He couldn't say more emphatically that the perfect prophet would have a much greater face-to-face relationship with the Father than anyone else's feeble approximation.

> **Deuteronomy 34:11–12**—none like him for all the signs and the wonders that the LORD sent him to do in the land of Egypt, to Pharaoh and to all his

---

[7] Ibid., 18.

servants and to all his land, and for all the mighty power and all the great deeds of terror that Moses did in the sight of all Israel.

Verses 11 and 12 refer to miracles the perfect prophet would do, miracles that corresponded to those of Moses, but that no other prophet up to that time had done. Those of verse 11 are miracles of judgment like the plagues Moses performed against Egypt. Those of verse 12 are miracles of validation before God's people that the prophet is truly of God. Just as in Moses' case, these miracles of the future prophet are not necessarily pleasant for those who witness them; some even produce "terror" in those who are present. When we read the New Testament we find this to be true in the ministry of Jesus; the terrible miracles of verse 12 are recounted throughout the gospels. On the other hand, the miraculous judgments of verse 11 are mostly described in Revelation.

Other Prophets

A whole bunch of prophets are mentioned in the rest of the Old Testament, but we will take time only to briefly discuss a couple. More attention is given to Elijah and Elisha than all the rest, and they come the closest to being prophets like Moses. God certainly performed many miracles through both of them, and it's interesting to note that both of them emulated Moses very specifically in one way. Look what they did in 2 Kings 2:8.

> **2 Kings 2:8**—Then Elijah took his cloak and rolled it up and struck the water, and the water was parted to the one side and to the other, till the two of them could go over on dry ground.

Later, after Elijah departed for heaven, Elisha repeated the miracle. We probably should see this as a reflection of Moses and Joshua. Moses crossed the Red Sea and Joshua repeated the miracle at the Jordan River. Now Elijah was close to being the prophet like Moses, and Elisha, his successor, walked in the same footsteps as Joshua. When Elisha asked for and received a double portion of Elijah's spirit (2 Kings 2:9–12), it doesn't mean he was twice the prophet Elijah was. His request was in the sense of Deuteronomy 21:17, which established a double inheritance for the firstborn. Thus Elisha received twice as much as what any normal prophet's apprentice would receive. This means Elisha did not supersede Elijah in importance; he simply inherited the same position. Since Elisha followed Elijah in the same way Joshua followed Moses, we might expect Elijah to be more likely to fulfill

Moses' prophecy. Even though that is the correct expectation, the next passage makes clear that the perfect prophet was to supersede even Elijah in greatness.

Elijah is mentioned in another key passage of the Old Testament Scriptures. The traditional Jewish order of the books of the Old Testament (Tanak) does not match what we have in our English Bibles. It was divided into three sections: the law, the prophets, and the writings. The key passage we have analyzed in Deuteronomy 34 comes at the end of the law. At the end of the prophets (which also is the end of our Old Testament) we find Malachi chapter 4. Look at what these final verses say:

> **Malachi 4:5–6** — "Behold, I will send you Elijah the prophet before the great and awesome day of the LORD comes. And he will turn the hearts of fathers to their children and the hearts of children to their fathers, lest I come and strike the land with a decree of utter destruction."

The law ends with a statement in Deuteronomy that a prophet is coming who will be "like Moses." And now we can understand this passage, from the end of the prophets, to say that the coming prophet will be "like Elijah." The Old Testament clearly states in several ways, therefore, that even the best candidates for the perfect prophet within its pages only foreshadowed the only one who can fill those shoes. It wasn't Moses. It wasn't Elijah. In fact, Deuteronomy 34 tells us, viewing all the prophets of Israel, he never came. Those who came closest fell far short. Appropriately, the order of our Old Testament also indicates that we must look beyond those pages for the answer. The last two verses of our Old Testament lead us to turn the page and find the answer in the New Testament. The arrangement of the Tanak results in putting 2 Chronicles 36:22–23 at the end. These two verses are also messianic,[8] not just in a prophetic sense but in a kingly one as well. We'll leave a detailed analysis of this for another time. (Look for it in a future book.)

Jesus

By now it should be no surprise that Jesus is the perfect prophet of whom Moses spoke. Besides making him the focus of our study, I have more than hinted that these particular Old Testament passages point to him. Nevertheless, as we move to look at the New Testament teaching on this topic, I think many of you, like me, will be surprised at just how clearly we are told that Jesus fulfills our hope. What we have seen in the Old Testament will make

---

[8] Ibid., 173-4.

the teaching of the New Testament clearer than it otherwise might be. It's always important to approach the New Testament with a good understanding of the Old. Without full awareness of the prediction, we easily miss the clear statement of fulfillment.

Nowhere is the fulfillment more completely described for us than in Matthew 17 at the transfiguration of Jesus.

> **Matthew 17:1–7**—And after six days Jesus took with him Peter and James, and John his brother, and led them up a high mountain by themselves. And he was transfigured before them, and his face shone like the sun, and his clothes became white as light. And behold, there appeared to them Moses and Elijah, talking with him. And Peter said to Jesus, "Lord, it is good that we are here. If you wish, I will make three tents here, one for you and one for Moses and one for Elijah." He was still speaking when, behold, a bright cloud overshadowed them, and a voice from the cloud said, "This is my beloved Son, with whom I am well pleased; listen to him." When the disciples heard this, they fell on their faces and were terrified. But Jesus came and touched them, saying, "Rise, and have no fear."

Let's look at how many of the details of Jesus' experience correspond with those of Moses. First we are told Jesus went up a high mountain. Although he took his three closest disciples with him, like Moses he left some people behind, for it says they went "by themselves." In verse 2 we are told his face shone like that of Moses in Exodus 34:29, when he came down from the mountain. It's no accident that both Moses and Elijah appeared, talking to Jesus on this mountain. As the two greatest prophets ever, they were there to show that Jesus was in good company.

Peter's response, although meant to honor Jesus, fell far short of the glory Christ deserves. When he offered to build three sacred tents, he was basically recognizing that Jesus was, like the other two, a prophet. In fact, Jesus is presented here as the prophet "like Moses." We are given a hint that he is also like Elijah, but that will become much more explicit when we see the message of Revelation. When the Father claimed Jesus as his son, Peter was supposed to realize Jesus was a prophet whom the Lord knew face-to-face, contrary to all the other prophets since Moses (Deuteronomy 34:10). But he failed to recognize Jesus was in a league by himself. His suggestion was rejected implicitly by a lack of direct response from both the Father and the Son. In fact, the Father's next statement emphasized Jesus to the point of ignoring Moses and Elijah, and when the whole thing was over, the point was made further when Peter saw "no one but Jesus only."

The Father manifested himself in verse five through the overshadowing presence of a cloud, just as he did in Exodus 19:9, 16, when Moses served as a mediating prophet for the people. (I plan to write more about clouds in a future book.) And if it isn't clear by now that Jesus is the prophet like Moses, God quoted Moses' instruction in Deuteronomy 18:15 when he said, "Listen to him!"

The disciples' response in verse 6 was terror. Just as the Israelites needed a mediating prophet because of their fear, the disciples showed that the Father's direct presence was too much for them and they needed Jesus as a buffer. Matthew could not have done a better job of showing that Jesus is the prophet who is like Moses, and yet even greater. If he had come right out and said so, it wouldn't have been more certain, and in the way it's written, it's as if we are there ourselves and able to conclude what the Father is revealing to us!

Although the transfiguration was obviously written to make a clear statement about who Jesus is, it is not the only passage in the gospels to make this claim. Let's look briefly at some other New Testament passages that show us Jesus was a prophet. First, the Sermon on the Mount in Matthew 5 is designed to convey this idea. Matthew tells us of seven mountains on which Jesus performed his ministry. Warren Austin Gage lists them:

> These mountains are 1) the mountain of the temptation (4:8), 2) the mountain of the beatitudes (5:1), 3) the mountain of the separation (14:23), 4) the mountain of the feeding in the wilderness (15:29), 5) the mountain of the transfiguration (17:1), 6) the mountain of the Olivet discourse (24:3), and 7) the mountain of the commissioning (28:16).[9]

Moses was also on mountains during his ministry, four of them—Sinai, Hor, Abarim and Nebo. The fact that Jesus performed his ministry on seven mountains, however, points to the perfection of his ministry (since the number seven represents completion). The second of these mountains is especially clear in its comparison of Jesus and Moses. In Matthew 5 Jesus repeats a phrase several times: "You have heard that it was said…but I say to you." In each case, Jesus is applying the law of Moses in a new, more extreme way that involves not just external obedience but a response of the heart as well (5:22, 27, 32, 34, 39, 44). Thus Jesus is a prophet whose ministry surpasses that of Moses.

---

[9] Warren Austin Gage, *Gospel Typology in Joshua and Revelation: A Whore and Her Scarlet, Seven Trumpets Sound, A Great City Falls* (Fort Lauderdale, FL: St. Andrews House, 2013).

Matthew 11:27 speaks of an important revelatory ministry that Jesus has as prophet:

> **Matthew 11:27** — All things have been handed over to me by my Father, and no one knows the Son except the Father, and no one knows the Father except the Son and anyone to whom the Son chooses to reveal him.

A prophet reveals God. Since Jesus has an intimate relationship with the Father, anyone who has an intimate relationship with Jesus will enjoy the benefits of his revelation.

In Matthew 13:57 Jesus claimed to be a prophet:

> **Matthew 13:57** — And they took offense at him. But Jesus said to them, "A prophet is not without honor except in his hometown and in his own household."

Here Jesus indirectly referred to himself as a prophet by quoting this proverb and applying it to himself.

In Matthew 21:10–11 even the crowds recognized he was a prophet:

> **Matthew 21:10–11** — And when he entered Jerusalem, the whole city was stirred up, saying, "Who is this?" And the crowds said, "This is the prophet Jesus, from Nazareth of Galilee."

We can't always trust what the crowds said as good theology, but this time they got it right; even the common people could recognize a good prophet when they saw him.

In Luke 13:33 Jesus again referred to himself as a prophet:

> **Luke 13:33–34a** — "Nevertheless, I must go on my way today and tomorrow and the day following, for it cannot be that a prophet should perish away from Jerusalem." O Jerusalem, Jerusalem, the city that kills the prophets and stones those who are sent to it!

It isn't always advantageous to be a prophet; Jesus viewed the prophet's ministry as so dangerous that death was automatically assumed as part of the package. It's not flattering to Jerusalem that it was only fitting for his death to happen there, as it had with so many other prophets in the past.

Finally, look at what Jesus claimed as his authority:

> **John 12:49** — For I have not spoken on my own authority, but the Father who sent me has himself given me a commandment — what to say and what to speak.

It's pretty likely Jesus had Deuteronomy 18 in mind. When Moses foretold of a prophet like him, he also warned about prophets who would speak on their own initiative. Jesus, however, claimed everything he spoke was from the Father. There were examples of false prophets in other times during Israel's history. Look at how the following verses contrast with Jesus' claim.

> **Jeremiah 23:16**—Thus says the LORD of hosts: "Do not listen to the words of the prophets who prophesy to you, filling you with vain hopes. They speak visions of their own minds, not from the mouth of the LORD."

> **Ezekiel 13:2–3**—"Son of man, prophesy against the prophets of Israel, who are prophesying, and say to those who prophesy from their own hearts: 'Hear the word of the LORD!' Thus says the Lord GOD, Woe to the foolish prophets who follow their own spirit, and have seen nothing!"

We should never fail to be thankful that we now have a perfect prophet in whom we can place our full confidence, knowing he is speaking God's message to us. For now we experience this as we read his Word. The day will come when we will hear his words directly as we enjoy physically being in his presence!

Peter's Sermon

Jesus was a very effective prophet, so effective that he succeeded in angering many people in Jerusalem who didn't want to hear God's message. Just as foretold, Jesus was killed like many other good prophets. After his death and resurrection his disciples picked up the task of proclaiming his message. In Acts 3:19–26 Peter preached a sermon about the perfect prophet. Peter's point was that Jesus is the prophet spoken about by Moses and his future prophetic ministry will be entirely perfect.

> **Acts 3:19–26**—"Repent therefore, and turn back, that your sins may be blotted out, that times of refreshing may come from the presence of the Lord, and that he may send the Christ appointed for you, Jesus, whom heaven must receive until the time for restoring all the things about which God spoke by the mouth of his holy prophets long ago. Moses said, 'The Lord God will raise up for you a prophet like me from your brothers. You shall listen to him in whatever he tells you. And it shall be that every soul who does not listen to that prophet shall be destroyed from the people.' And all the prophets who have spoken, from Samuel and those who came after him, also proclaimed these days. You are the sons of the prophets and of the covenant that God made with your fathers, saying to Abraham, 'And in your offspring shall all the families of the earth be blessed.' God, having raised

up his servant, sent him to you first, to bless you by turning every one of you from your wickedness."

In the preceding verses (Acts 3:11ff), Peter openly blamed his audience for putting Jesus to death. He declared himself a witness to the fact that God raised him from the dead. And he boldly stated that Jesus was the Christ—the one who was anointed as a prophet for the people. In verse 21 he explained that Jesus is now in heaven waiting for the right time to restore all things as God has promised. He quoted Deuteronomy 18:15 in verse 22 to show Jesus is the prophet like Moses.

Peter's sermon has two more lessons for us related to the office of prophet. The first of these looks backward to all previous prophets. I wonder what each of the prophets thought when God called them to their ministries. It could be that some of them considered whether they would turn out to be the prophet like Moses. We all have a desire to be someone important. Surely most of them were aware of the promise made in Deuteronomy and considered this question seriously. Eventually they all learned who the Scriptures were truly pointing toward. Do you suppose any of them, learning who the prophet was to be, felt a sense of rivalry or even envy toward Jesus? I doubt it; they would have been missing the main purpose for their ministries. Look at what Peter said of them in verse 24:

> **Acts 3:24**—And all the prophets who have spoken, from Samuel and those who came after him, also proclaimed these days.

The prophets looked forward to the great things God would do by sending his Son to be the perfect prophet. Any true prophet would rejoice to see God himself become a prophet! We live in a wonderful age when we can look back at promises that were made, know how they have been fulfilled, and look forward to their ultimate completion in the future work of Jesus Christ!

The second lesson from Peter regards our future hope. In verse 19, he exhorted his hearers to repent; if they would do so, he said God would send the Christ who had been appointed to restore all things. In other words, the Jews at that very moment could have ushered in the kingdom by submitting to the perfect prophet's leadership. Obviously it wasn't meant to be, for it hasn't happened yet, but it will. We have hope because one day all Christ's followers will truly submit to him as our Prophet. We will see him restore his people to God the Father, and we will see him give us hearts of flesh that naturally hear and obey the words the Father gives him (Ezekiel 36:26). In verse 26, Peter tells us the Christ was sent first to Israel to turn them from their wickedness. And the true hope for all of us, no matter who we are, is found in verse 25, for in Abraham's "offspring shall all the families of the earth be blessed." I, for one, am glad Jesus has taken up the task of being our Perfect Prophet!

Our Prophet Accomplished It All

In Romans 10, Paul makes a comparison between Moses and Jesus in their prophetic ministries:

> **Romans 10:5–6**—For Moses writes about the righteousness that is based on the law, that the person who does the commandments shall live by them. But the righteousness based on faith says, "Do not say in your heart, 'Who will ascend into heaven?' " (that is, to bring Christ down)

Moses had to work really hard as a prophet. Many times, just to get God's message, he had to go mountain climbing. When he came back and gave the message to the people, it usually meant they also had to work hard—obeying the law. All through the history of Israel we see that keeping the law was impossibly difficult. In Deuteronomy 30:11–14, at the end of his life, Moses talked about a new way. He talked about a new commandment that was not part of the law. The new way actually is quite old—it is accomplished by exercising the faith of Abraham.

Abraham was presented as the prophet who had faith, and now Moses presented faith as the most important response for every prophet's hearers. Instead of climbing a mountain all the way up to heaven, Moses says obedience by faith is simply a matter of the mouth and the heart. Now here in Romans 10, Paul picks up on Moses' message and makes it even more clearly Christological. He quotes Moses' words when he says no one needed to ascend to heaven. Moses means no one needed to bring down the law; Paul means no one needed to bring down Christ. Jesus Christ has already done everything hard. He is the prophet who came down from the heights of heaven with everything we need to know, and his message is infinitely more effective than the prophetic mountain message of Moses. What a truly great prophet we have! If his message were one of works, we would have no hope. His message of faith is the only means to righteousness we can attain. (In a future book I hope to write more on the message of Romans 10.)

Prophet's Apprentice

Our prophet is so extraordinary, he invites his followers to join him in the prophetic task of sharing God's word. As his people, we all have the incredible privilege of sharing the message, and it was a message of faith from the beginning. Even Deuteronomy 6:4–9 speaks of the message in terms of love as it addresses our responsibility:

> **Deuteronomy 6:4–9**—"Hear, O Israel: The LORD our God, the LORD is one. You shall love the LORD your God with all your heart and with all your soul and with all your might. And these words that I command you today shall be on your heart. You shall teach them diligently to your children, and shall talk of them when you sit in your house, and when you walk by the way, and when you lie down, and when you rise. You shall bind them as a sign on your hand, and they shall be as frontlets between your eyes. You shall write them on the doorposts of your house and on your gates."

While Deuteronomy refers to parents' task of teaching their children, Jeremiah refers to an extended responsibility everyone has. The difference is that Jeremiah looked forward to the completion of the New Covenant, at which time teaching one another to know God will become obsolete:

> **Jeremiah 31:34**—"And no longer shall each one teach his neighbor and each his brother, saying, 'Know the LORD,' for they shall all know me, from the least of them to the greatest, declares the LORD. For I will forgive their iniquity, and I will remember their sin no more."

We still live in an age when teaching others to know God is important. That's what the great commission is all about:

> **Matthew 28:19–20**—Go therefore and make disciples of all nations, baptizing them in the name of the Father and of the Son and of the Holy Spirit, teaching them to observe all that I have commanded you. And behold, I am with you always, to the end of the age."

So for now, we are called to join our Great Prophet and proclaim his message to the world. We, like Elisha, are prophet's apprentices. Just as Elisha received a double portion of Elijah's spirit when he saw the great prophet go up to heaven (2 Kings 2:9–11), so we receive a double portion of the Holy Spirit since the disciples saw our Great Prophet ascend. (Look for a future book to deal more with our position as apprentices.) It's as if Jesus makes us all to be his junior prophets, but at the end of the age this ministry will no longer be needed—just as Jeremiah said, our neighbors will all know God and the prophetic ministry will end.

Validation

During his time on earth, Jesus' prophetic ministry was validated by his miracles, but a future validation is yet to come. Remember what we saw in Deuteronomy 34? We were told that no prophet had arisen like Moses, judging in part based on the lack of miracles.

> **Deuteronomy 34:11–12**—none like him for all the signs and the wonders that the LORD sent him to do in the land of Egypt, to Pharaoh and to all his servants and to all his land, and for all the mighty power and all the great deeds of terror that Moses did in the sight of all Israel.

We observed earlier that the deeds of terror correspond to the miracles Jesus already did while here on earth. Revelation speaks more to the signs and wonders of judgment on the unbelieving world. We don't normally think of a prophet as judging those who reject his message, but for Jesus, the only prophet who is God, it is only fitting that he use his power in that way. When Christ comes in his full strength, he will come with a kind of power that was foreshadowed by Moses and Elijah. Moses displayed it with the plagues on Egypt. Elijah displayed it in a verse in 2 Kings that has always fascinated and puzzled me at the same time. Why did Elijah the prophet seem so stuck on himself that he saw fit to abuse his miraculous power by killing these men?

> **2 Kings 1:9–10**—Then the king sent to him a captain of fifty men with his fifty. He went up to Elijah, who was sitting on the top of a hill, and said to him, "O man of God, the king says, 'Come down.' " But Elijah answered the captain of fifty, "If I am a man of God, let fire come down from heaven and consume you and your fifty." Then fire came down from heaven and consumed him and his fifty.

The context answers pretty well the reason Elijah judged the attitude of the king and his soldiers, but there's a lot more than just the immediate context. Two separate passages in the book of Revelation give us a much better picture of the message behind Elijah's actions. A large purpose behind what Elijah did was to give us a kind of a preliminary reflection of the ministry of the True Prophet to whom he pointed.

The first of these passages in Revelation describes the actions of a couple of men who, like Moses and Elijah, are representatives of the Perfect Prophet. The two witnesses are given power by Christ himself and repeat the actions of Elijah and Moses.

Revelation 11:5–6—And if anyone would harm them, fire pours from their mouth and consumes their foes. If anyone would harm them, this is how he is doomed to be killed. They have the power to shut the sky, that no rain may fall during the days of their prophesying, and they have power over the waters to turn them into blood and to strike the earth with every kind of plague, as often as they desire.

Just as in Elijah's case, these two men are threatened with harm by unbelieving hearers of the message. Just like Elijah they respond by calling down fire on their enemies. In both cases this fire is said to consume those who are judged. They also reflect Elijah with their power to judge the earth through drought (compare 1 Kings 17:1). And like Moses, they are empowered to strike the earth with plagues, apparently very similar to those performed in Egypt. Nevertheless, these men, as powerful as they are, are still not the real deal. They are only precursors to the most powerful prophet.

The Lamb of God is the one truly in charge of all that happens in Revelation, and he gains his ultimate victory in chapter 20. Satan makes one last attempt to foil God's plan; he gathers the rebellious nations to fight the mother of all battles. Unfortunately for him, all they get to do is march.

Revelation 20:7–10—And when the thousand years are ended, Satan will be released from his prison and will come out to deceive the nations that are at the four corners of the earth, Gog and Magog, to gather them for battle; their number is like the sand of the sea. And they marched up over the broad plain of the earth and surrounded the camp of the saints and the beloved city, but fire came down from heaven and consumed them, and the devil who had deceived them was thrown into the lake of fire and sulfur where the beast and the false prophet were, and they will be tormented day and night forever and ever.

Our Perfect Prophet will act from heaven to destroy all the forces which oppose him, and victory will be attained for all of eternity. He does it in a big way after the manner of Elijah, consuming them all with fire. That is one true victory that leaves no shadow of a doubt! At the Mount of Transfiguration Jesus showed he was a prophet like Moses; now in Revelation we see he is also a prophet like Elijah. Nothing is lacking in our Perfect Prophet!

Conclusion

Has your concept of a prophet changed? Jesus is the best prophet who ever was or ever will be. Clearly his job is much more than predicting the future. Jesus, as God himself, brings God's message to the world. Do you think he has the right message? Do you think his message is worth taking seriously?

I sure do. Not everyone cares to listen. Those who reject the message of the prophet are recipients of not only his worst words, but the terrible judgment he has to offer. Those of us who accept the prophet and his message realize how beautiful the message can be. We see the prophet in all his mountaintop glory. We receive the good news regarding how attainable righteousness is through his prophetic word. And we are offered an eternity of hearing his beautiful message in his very presence.

Passages for further study:

Exodus 4:10–12
Exodus 33:11
Numbers 12:6–9
2 Kings 2:19–21
2 Kings 6:1–7
Isaiah 55:4
Jeremiah 1:6–9
Matthew 16:14
John 1:18
John 8:28
John 15:15–16
Hebrews 1:1–3

4
The Perfect Priest

In *The Lion, the Witch and the Wardrobe*, C. S. Lewis wrote a passage that does a great job of illustrating the importance of a priest. In this book, Edmund is a boy who is guilty of being a traitor, and the rules of Deep Magic say he must die. Instead, Aslan the lion willingly chooses to give himself to die in Edmund's place. During the chosen night he walks toward the Witch and all her evil horde. They begin by binding and muzzling him. They seem proud of having accomplished something significant, but everyone knows they were able to overpower the lion only because he has let them do it. After mistreating him in several ways, they drag him to the Stone Table. Then the Witch prepares to do her part with the knife:

> At last she drew near. She stood by Aslan's head. Her face was working and twitching with passion, but he looked up at the sky, still quiet, neither angry nor afraid, but a little sad. Then, just before she gave the blow, she stooped down and said in a quivering voice, "And now, who has won? Fool, did you think that by all this you would save the human traitor? Now I will kill you instead of him as our pact was and so the Deep Magic will be appeased. But when you are dead what will prevent me from killing him as well? And who will take him out of my hand then? Understand that you have given me Narnia forever, you have lost your own life and you have not saved his. In that knowledge, despair and die."[1]

As the story progresses, Aslan returns to life because of the "Deeper Magic from before the dawn of time." The witch was unaware that "when a willing victim who had committed no treachery was killed in a traitor's stead, the Table would crack and Death itself would start working backwards." Therefore, Aslan served as priest in two ways. First, he offered a sacrifice to appease the Deep Magic, allowing Edmund to live. This wasn't just any sacrifice, but astonishingly, he was willing to sacrifice his own life! Additionally, his resurrection gave him the ability to continue to act in favor of all Narnia. The witch had been wrong; death could not keep Aslan from protecting his own. Similarly, our Priest made an infinitely valuable sacrifice for us and now lives to intercede for us before the Father.

---

[1] C. S. Lewis, *The Lion, The Witch, And The Wardrobe* (New York: Collier Books, 1970), 149-152.

The second in the triad of important offices in the Old Testament is that of priest. A priest is someone who provides access to a divine being. God is holy and infinitely perfect. Because he is infinitely superior to us, without some kind of intervention it is impossible for us to communicate directly with him and receive from him what we need for our very lives. Therefore, we need a priest who can bridge the gap between us and God, making him accessible. Adam and Eve were the only two people who ever lived who did not need an intermediary to approach God (at first). They used to walk and talk with the Lord in the Garden of Eden (Genesis 3:8–9). But since sin entered the world, the sin we all share now serves as a barrier in our relationship with our creator. The history of redemption is all about removing the barrier and giving us access to God once again. In the current age we have the incredible privilege of approaching God directly (and it will be even greater in the future), but this would not be true had it not been gained for us by our Perfect Priest. Let's look at what the Bible teaches about how it came about.

Adam

Even though Adam and Eve had no need for an intermediary, that is not to say no priest existed before sin, Genesis 2:15 would have us understand that before sin, even before God formed Eve, Adam served as a priest.[2]

> **Genesis 2:15**—The LORD God took the man and put him in the garden of Eden to work it and keep it.

The two words "work" and "keep" are used here to speak of a priestly responsibility. Both of these words are common words and simple enough when used alone. "Work" is the Hebrew word 'abad, which speaks of "[expending] considerable energy and intensity in a task or function."[3] It is used for serving, cultivating, or encouraging growth, beauty and maturity. "Keep" is the Hebrew word shamar, which means to "limit access and movement of persons or objects in and out of an area, implying protection to or from the

---

[2] For most of the ideas in this paragraph about Adam I am indebted to: Kevin DeYoung and Greg Gilbert, *What is the Mission of the Church? Making Sense of Social Justice, Shalom and the Great Commission,* audiobook (Wheaton, IL: Crossway, 2011). Chapter 8, Seeking Shalom: Understanding the New Heavens and the New Earth.

[3] James Swanson, *Dictionary of Biblical Languages With Semantic Domains: Hebrew (Old Testament),* electronic ed. (Oak Harbor, WA: Logos Research Systems, Inc., 1997), 6268 עָבַד.

object being guarded.[4] One who fulfills this function is making sure that no evil enters an area, or if it does, to judge it and cast it out. The meaning of these two words, when used together, becomes much more specialized. They take on a compound meaning which usually refers to the priestly task of serving and guarding in a temple.[5] In the exceptions the concept of temple is figuratively applied to one's heart, which must also be worked and guarded in order to be devoted to God. Read, for example, this verse which speaks of the Levites' ministry in the tabernacle and includes 'abad and shamar in italics:

> **Numbers 3:8**—They shall *guard* all the furnishings of the tent of meeting, and keep guard over the people of Israel as they *minister* at the tabernacle (emphasis added).

Numbers 18:1–7 is another example that repeats these two words several times as it describes the ministry of the priests. Thus Eden is presented as the perfect temple, the place where God dwelt with man. And Adam is presented as the priest, caring for and protecting the temple in a priestly role. (I will have much more to say on the temple theme in a future book.)

Unfortunately, Adam didn't do very well with his priestly duties. Instead of caring for and guarding God's dwelling with man, he allowed sin to enter and spoil it. Instead of judging the serpent and casting it out of the garden, Adam surrendered to the will of the serpent and joined him in rebellion against God. Because of Adam's failure, God cursed the ground (Genesis 3:17). The rest of biblical history describes the search for a priest who can right his wrongs.

Noah

When Noah shows up, he becomes a partial answer to the search. His name means "relief"; look at why his father named him that:

> **Genesis 5:28–29**—When Lamech had lived 182 years, he fathered a son and called his name Noah, saying, "Out of the ground that the LORD has cursed,

---

[4] Ibid.

[5] See also, Gordon J. Wenham, "Sanctuary Symbolism in the Garden of Eden Story," in *I Studied Inscriptions from before the Flood: Ancient Near Eastern, Literary, and Linguistic Approaches to Genesis 1–11*, ed. R. S. Hess and D. T. Tsumura, Sources for Biblical and Theological Study 4 (Winona Lake, IN: Eisenbrauns, 1994), 399-404; 401. http://www.godawa.com/chronicles_of_the_nephilim/Articles_By_Others/Wenham-Sanctuary_Symbolism_Garden_of_Eden.pdf

this one shall bring us relief from our work and from the painful toil of our hands."

His father's hope was that Noah could give relief from the curse—relief from the difficult labor of making the ground produce. As you think back on what you know about Noah, in what sense do you think he gave relief from work? The flood story is about salvation from judgment—a theme that is certainly related, but not essentially focused on the curse. (I will write a chapter in a future book to discuss one way in which Noah's ark does deal with the curse.) Remarkably, Noah's greatest relief from the curse is found in the verses that immediately follow the account of the flood. God had chosen to destroy life on earth because he "saw that the wickedness of man was great in the earth, and that every intention of the thoughts of his heart was only evil continually" (Genesis 6:5). Look at what happened when Noah came out of the ark:

> **Genesis 8:20–21**—Then Noah built an altar to the LORD and took some of every clean animal and some of every clean bird and offered burnt offerings on the altar. And when the LORD smelled the pleasing aroma, the LORD said in his heart, "I will never again curse the ground because of man, for the intention of man's heart is evil from his youth. Neither will I ever again strike down every living creature as I have done."

This is the very first time an altar is explicitly mentioned in Scripture. Noah built it and gave an offering with a resulting change of God's attitude toward mankind. God committed to never again curse the ground, and it's not because mankind was suddenly better—he knew man's heart was still evil. It's because Noah had become a priest who achieved a certain peace between God and man. God's new commitment about the curse did not mean the curse of Adam had been removed. Rather, the Lord was making a commitment to never again add to that curse. These verses show that Noah was instrumental in achieving it. It turns out Noah's father named him well; he did provide relief from God's anger as a very important priest. In one sense he was a prototype of the coming Levitical priests. In another sense, he was a prototype of Christ himself in that "Noah's sacrifice is effective for all mankind."[6] Thankfully, Jesus' work is effective for removing every vestige of the original curse brought upon us by Adam—a priestly work that goes far beyond that of Noah.

---

6 Gordon J. Wenham, *Genesis 1–15*. Word Biblical Commentary, Vol. 1 (Dallas: Word, Incorporated, 1998), 280.

Abram

Just as Abram was an important prophet, he was also an important priest. Whenever he built an altar he was fulfilling this role: Genesis 12:7–8; 13:4; 18; 22:9. The only place he built an altar, however, was in the land of Canaan—a land that in many texts was represented as a new temple to replace Eden, where God would dwell with his people. Peter J. Gentry and Stephen J. Wellum show this connection:

> We saw above that Canaan is depicted in Edenic language as a mountain sanctuary. Now we see Abram fulfilling an Adamic role: he offers sacrifice as a priest and worships God in this mountain sanctuary.[7]

Genesis chapters 12 and 13 don't actually mention whether he offered any sacrifices on these altars, but Abraham later presented a very significant offering, his son Isaac, and then Isaac's substitute. Genesis 22:9 is especially clear with its priestly allusions.

> **Genesis 22:9**—When they came to the place of which God had told him, Abraham built the altar there and laid the wood in order and bound Isaac his son and laid him on the altar, on top of the wood.

The phrase "the place of which God had told him" is often associated throughout the Old Testament with the temple (Deuteronomy 12:10–11; 16:7). Additionally, arranging the wood and placing a sacrifice on top of it was clearly a priestly duty. Compare Leviticus 1:7–8 which uses some of the same terms.

Melchizedek

One of the key passages to understanding our priest is Genesis 14—the first use of the word "priest" in the entire Bible. In this chapter some of Abram's neighbors got involved in a conflict. Five kings (and their kingdoms) had been subservient to four kings for twelve years. They got tired of the arrangement and rebelled. The four superior kings managed to maintain the status quo by defeating the other five and carrying off many possessions and people. None of this would have concerned Abram if it weren't for the fact that one of the people taken into captivity was his nephew Lot. That ticked off Abram, and he decided to do something about it. The four victorious kings were obviously more powerful than the five weaker kings; nevertheless, they were no match for Abram, who defeated them all with 318

---

[7] Gentry and Wellum, *Kingdom through Covenant*, 5681-5682.

men of his household. Abram's greatness is clearly emphasized in this passage because of a point the author wanted to make in the next verses. Look at what they say:

> **Genesis 14:17–24** — After [Abram's] return from the defeat of Chedorlaomer and the kings who were with him, the king of Sodom went out to meet him at the Valley of Shaveh (that is, the King's Valley). And Melchizedek king of Salem brought out bread and wine. (He was priest of God Most High.) And he blessed him and said, "Blessed be Abram by God Most High, Possessor of heaven and earth; and blessed be God Most High, who has delivered your enemies into your hand!" And Abram gave him a tenth of everything. And the king of Sodom said to Abram, "Give me the persons, but take the goods for yourself." But Abram said to the king of Sodom, "I have lifted my hand to the LORD, God Most High, Possessor of heaven and earth, that I would not take a thread or a sandal strap or anything that is yours, lest you should say, 'I have made Abram rich.' I will take nothing but what the young men have eaten, and the share of the men who went with me. Let Aner, Eshcol, and Mamre take their share."

There are just a handful of verses here, but they are full of significance. Let's analyze what was said. First, we should notice what the author was affirming about greatness in this passage. There seems to be an implicit ranking going on here, based on the details about military power in the context. Five kings were defeated by four, giving honor to those four kings who, even though they were outnumbered, proved to be mightier. Abram, however, is obviously presented as a person deserving of even greater respect for his military prowess, for his disadvantage was higher still. And we must conclude that Melchizedek was the greatest person in this passage, demonstrated by his interaction with Abram. Melchizedek blessed Abram, and according to Hebrews 7:7, this indicates he was superior to Abram. Abram responded by giving him a tenth of everything—another sign, according to Hebrews 7:4, of the greatness of Melchizedek. In spite of Melchizedek's greatness, however, he pointed to someone who is even greater!

Although Melchizedek was clearly very great, I do not think we should understand this as a pre-incarnate appearance of Christ himself. In several other passages I think we do find such appearances of Jesus, but I see no compelling reason to view this one in such a manner. Other authors have written extensively on this subject, so I won't go into detail here. The writer of Hebrews almost makes it seem as if Melchizedek was Jesus, but probably not in a way that's much different from many of the statements in my book about several characters from the Old Testament—people who simply pre-figured our Savior. I believe the author of Hebrews was simply drawing parallels between Jesus and Melchizedek to show that the latter was a type of Christ. In chapter 7 he makes amazing comparisons, but he nevertheless maintains a distinction between the identities of the two men. The points he makes about Melchizedek are exaggerated (although based on fact) in order to more clearly state his foreshadowing of Christ. If it turns out Melchizedek was Jesus himself, everything we learn from these verses will remain the same. I will take the position that he wasn't, but if you disagree, I think you will still find yourself agreeing with my conclusions.

Now let's dig in to the text of Genesis 14 to see what we can learn about priesthood and, more specifically, about the priesthood of Christ. In verse 18, we learn that Melchizedek was king of Salem—apparently an early name for what later became Jerusalem. It's amazing that God would design his Word so this very important person who prefigured Jesus was king of the same city where Jesus eventually carried out his priestly ministry! His name is also significant; *Melchizedek* is a compound word meaning "king of right-eousness." Besides being a king, he was also a priest of God Most High, a profound statement considering how rare it is to find biblical characters who are both priest and king. In fact, in Israel's history this would have been practically impossible; kings came from the tribe of Judah, and priests from the tribe of Levi. I am aware of only seven individuals who in some way reflect both these offices: Adam, Abraham, Melchizedek, Moses, David, Joshua (the son of Jehozadak), and Jesus Christ. We will discuss each of these in turn, seeing that the first six all point forward to Christ in this respect. These indicators of the identity of Melchizedek probably raise more ques-tions than answers. We'd like to know more about who he is, but he is not the point of the Bible—Jesus is. It would be interesting to know more about Melchizedek, but his main purpose in Scripture is to help us know more about Christ.

Did you notice the crazy way in which these verses about Melchizedek show up in the middle of a set of verses about another king—the king of Sodom? This text would flow much more naturally without verses 18–20, which were likely inserted in the middle of the verses about the king of Sodom. This is the very fact the writer of Hebrews references in order to compare him to Jesus in Hebrews 7:3. That is, he shows up without a gene-alogy or an explanation of the beginning (birth) or end (death) of his days.

The writer of Hebrews capitalizes on this fact to make it sound like Melchizedek is eternal because he wants to show how he foreshadows Jesus who truly is eternal.

To the modern reader the interruption of the story of the king of Sodom makes it appear as if the author has made some kind of mistake or somehow an error was made in the transmission of the text, resulting in a confusion of the two kings. We need to give credit, however, to the author of these verses in their final form and realize he purposely made a very significant comparison between the two kings. By placing them so close together in the text, he highlighted the difference in Abram's response to the two men. In verse 20 we are told that Abram gave a tenth of everything to Melchizedek; in verse 21 the king of Sodom asked Abram to give him the people and take everything else. Abram's answer to the king of Sodom was no; he wasn't willing to do with him what we just read that he did with Melchizedek. That is, he wouldn't keep anything for himself; he wouldn't keep 90 percent of the goods; he wouldn't keep even 1 percent. Abram's reason was that he was not willing to accept any material gain from the king of Sodom. All those possessions originally belonged to the king of Sodom and his allies. The reader, who knows what comes in context just a few chapters later, understands why Abram couldn't accept a blessing that originated from Sodom—the representation of everything that was contrary to God. By his answer Abram acknowledged his dependence on God. To him, Melchizedek represented the hand of God; therefore he gave Melchizedek a tithe, recognizing that anything he did not give him—although Melchizedek deserved it all—would be God's provision for him. In this way, the author communicates Melchizedek's position of intermediary between God and Abram.

Melchizedek pointed forward to Jesus Christ by what he did when he met Abraham. In verse 18 he brought out bread and wine. This very significant detail foreshadowed the very thing Jesus did at the Lord's Supper to help us commemorate the pinnacle of his own priestly ministry. It is marvelous to see that God saw fit to include this detail in his Word about the life of a man who lived centuries before Jesus came to earth. This inspires confidence in the fact that God has always been in perfect control of the inspiration of the Bible.

The original readers of the Pentateuch were steeped in tradition and very familiar with the Levitical priesthood. The religion of the day likely exalted the priests who served in a way that was familiar to them. In these verses, however, the author presents Melchizedek as a priest who offered a ministry that predated and (as we shall see later) superseded that of the Levites. This radical message is even more scandalous considering Melchizedek was a gentile through whom God chose to accomplish his will in the lives of his people. Melchizedek was a righteous gentile who had much to offer since he was revolutionary and innovative. In Genesis 14 God was teaching his people they should expect the unexpected when it came to priests. In other words, the best priestly ministry was the one that came from outsiders. This is a recurring message in the theme of priests. We will see other priests who follow the same pattern, the greatest of which is Jesus Christ. Jesus, although not a gentile, was even more of an outsider when it came to the Levitical priesthood. For starters, he was an outsider in the sense that he was not a Levite. What's even more astonishing is that he is God himself—a very unexpected source from which to find a priest who can intermediate between God and man!

Jethro

We will contemplate Melchizedek a little more when we get to Psalm 110 and Hebrews 5–10, but for now let's move ahead to another interesting passage in the Pentateuch. Let's make some comparisons between the passage on Melchizedek we have just seen and Exodus 18. In the latter chapter the main character is Jethro, who displays some amazing parallels to Melchizedek. Take some time right now to read Exodus 18.

Jethro's identity is a significant part of this chapter. Jethro was first introduced in chapters 3 and 4 of Exodus where, as in chapter 18, we are told that Jethro was Moses' father-in-law and a priest of Midian. The biggest question that arises is regarding his identity as priest. What does it mean to be a priest of Midian? Does this mean he was a follower of Jehovah? There is no indication in the Bible that a priest of Midian would be in any way favorable to the religion of the Israelites. In fact, quite to the contrary, Numbers 25 makes it clear the Midianites worshiped Baal of Peor. Exodus 18:11 seems to indicate that Jethro had a conversion during the time he was with Moses: when Moses recounted the exodus experience, Jethro proclaimed that *now* he knew Yahweh is greater than all gods, as if he didn't previously. This leads us to believe Jethro was a priest from another religion, in contrast to Melchizedek, who was a "priest of God Most High."

Jethro's identity is quite surprising in light of the role he plays in Exodus 18. The main point of this chapter is that Jethro taught Moses how to judge the people and apply the law. Moses had been deciding cases of dispute between the people, and it took him all day. In verse 16 he said he made "them know the statutes of God and his laws." Jethro told Moses what he was doing was not good and he was going to wear himself out. In verse 20 he said Moses needed to "warn them about the statutes and the laws," but he had to delegate others who could judge the people. Jethro's counsel is presented as wise; he comes across as the expert on the law and Moses put his counsel into practice. That Moses, through whom the law originated, could submit to the teaching of another person about the law is meant to emphasize just how great Jethro's expertise was. Just like Melchizedek, therefore, Jethro was a righteous gentile priest who had much to offer since he was revolutionary and innovative.

Jethro's similarity to Melchizedek is not coincidental; in fact, they share many more textual details in common. Look at the chart below to see how the author has crafted these similarities:[8]

Melchizedek		Jethro	
Gen. 14:7, 17	Appears after the battle with Chedorlaomer who had defeated the Amalekites	Ex. 17:13	Appears after the battle with Amalek
Gen. 14:18	Priest of God Most High	Ex. 18:1	Priest of Midian
Gen. 14:18	King of Salem (*shalom*) (*Jerusalem* means "city of peace")	Ex. 18:17	Jethro and Moses greet each other (The word for "greet," *shalom*, means peace).
		Ex. 18:23	Gives solution for peace (*shalom*)
Gen. 14:18	Brings bread and wine	Ex. 18:12	Brings burnt offering and sacrifices
Gen. 14:20	Abram tithes to him.	Ex. 18:12	Aaron eats bread with him.
Gen. 15:13	The Lord shows Abram in a vision that his seed will be a "sojourner (*ger*) in another's land."	Ex. 18:3	Moses' son is named Gershom because, he says, "I have become a sojourner (*ger*) in a foreign land."

---

[8] This chart is a representation of material in: John H. Sailhamer, *The Pentateuch as Narrative: A Biblical-Theological Commentary* (Grand Rapids, MI: Zondervan Publishing House, 1992), 280-281.

Gen. 15:2	The "son of Abram's house" is Eliezar. Eliezar epitomizes God's help for Abram.	Ex. 18:4	The "son of Moses" is Eliezar. Eliezar's name means "God is my help."

The message presented through the lives of Melchizedek and Jethro is meant to come as a challenge to the reader of the text. The account of these two men teaches us that the best priests aren't always those we would expect. Abraham and Moses, the two greatest men in the Pentateuch, learned from two priests who were clearly superior to the prevailing priests in these books. It's no wonder the author of Hebrews believed Melchizedek pointed to a better priest; no Israelite who paid attention to the details of these texts should have been content with the status quo.

You Speak to Us

Moreover, the status quo as presented in Exodus 19 was only a second-best alternative. The details of Exodus 19 show us that God's original design for the priesthood was later adjusted to fit the weakness of the people. These are details we often overlook, but the text is clear. In the first part of the chapter, the language is tender and loving. God speaks of making a kingdom of priests in verse 6.

> **Exodus 19:6**—And you shall be to me a kingdom of priests and a holy nation. These are the words that you shall speak to the people of Israel.

Remember, a priest has direct access to God; the Lord wanted the *entire nation* to be able to approach him and maintain a relationship with him. We have here an early description of the priesthood of all believers. Furthermore, in verses 11 through 13, God's desire was to meet with all the people on the mountain. They were to stay away from it until the third day, but on the third day they were *all* to go up on the mountain.

> **Exodus 19:11–13**—And be ready for the third day, for on the third day the LORD will come down on Mount Sinai in the sight of all the people...When the ram's horn sounds a long blast *they may go up on the mountain* (emphasis added) (NET).

Most Bible versions attempt to harmonize verse 13 with the fact that later in this chapter the people were not allowed to climb the mountain with Moses (see verse 24 for example). There seems to be confusion in the text about whether the people were supposed to meet with God, or if only Moses was to do so. Therefore, to avoid this confusion many versions say the people are to go up *to* the mountain. In spite of the apparent contradiction in the context, verse 13 is clear in the original when it speaks of the people being *"on* the mountain." In fact, the very same Hebrew preposition is used in other places like Exodus 24:18, to speak of Moses' own experience in the presence of the Lord:

> **Exodus 24:18**—Moses entered the cloud and went up *on* the mountain. And Moses was *on* the mountain forty days and forty nights (emphasis added).

The reason for the confusion in these verses has been analyzed well by John H. Sailhamer.[9] He explains that at first God's desire was that all the nation meet with him. But later, because of the people's sin, they were not allowed to accompany Moses. Not all of these verses are arranged in chronological order. Although chapter 19 shows the change in God's posture toward the people, we don't find a clear explanation of the reason until we arrive at Exodus 20:

> **Exodus 20:18–21**—Now when all the people saw the thunder and the flashes of lightning and the sound of the trumpet and the mountain smoking, the people were afraid and trembled, and they stood far off and said to Moses, "You speak to us, and we will listen; but do not let God speak to us, lest we die." Moses said to the people, "Do not fear, for God has come to test you, that the fear of him may be before you, that you may not sin." The people stood far off, while Moses drew near to the thick darkness where God was.

In these verses we see that by the people's own choice they ultimately were not allowed on the mountain. The people felt so intimidated by God's holiness and transcendence that they were overcome with fear. This interpretation agrees with a later analysis of the story by Moses:

> **Deuteronomy 5:5**—I stood between the Lord and you at that time, to declare to you the word of the Lord. For you were afraid because of the fire, and you did not go up into the mountain.

Since their fear was sinful, it was the very thing that required their separation from the presence of a holy God. In other words, their desire for separation from God required separation from God. But humanly speaking, how can we blame them? For even though their fear was sinful, their undeniable need for a priest was correctly demonstrated. Deep down inside, they know

---

[9] Sailhamer, *The* Meaning *of the Pentateuch,* 378-92.

they needed an intermediary to bridge the gap between them and God—a gap that was much too wide to pretend it didn't exist. In view of this need, Moses stands, fulfilling the role of a priest. John Sailhamer shows how this fits with the overall theological movement within the Pentateuch:

> Viewed within the larger context of Exodus 19–Numbers 10, when the people ask Moses to go before God, they appear to be asking for a priesthood to represent them, to teach them, and to stand before God in their place. They want priests, like Moses, to go in their place, to receive God's words and to come back, like Moses, to teach them the law. Curiously, this is the same interest that we saw in the advice given Moses by Jethro in the narrative leading up to Sinai (Ex 18). It is here again confronting us in this additional narrative that has been attached to the Sinai pericope. Clearly, the purpose of this small segment of narrative is to alert the reader to the coming discussion of the importance and place of the priesthood in the Sinai covenant, and with it, the tabernacle-sanctuary. The laws regulating the priesthood and tabernacle worship, which are immediately enumerated in the following section (Ex 25:1–30:17), are given an appropriate historical context by this narrative.[10]

Thus, Moses is presented as the first priest of the Israelites in the wilderness. Since he was a leader of God's people, the task naturally fell to him. They were simply incapable of operating without a priest, and Moses became the man. In a sense, we can say he informally became a priest before the formal priesthood was ever established. Remember this, for it will soon become significant.

Levitical Priests

In the following chapters the priesthood is formally established. Exodus 28:1 states God's command that Aaron and his four sons (Nadab, Abihu, Eleazar, and Ithamar) serve as priests. The first two, Nadab and Abihu, ended up dying for exercising their ministry incorrectly (Leviticus 10). Eleazar and Ithamar took over, and of these two Eleazar appears to have gained prominence. He was Moses' nephew, and he could potentially be considered as the high priest. We are not told the reason for his prominence, but many times over we find the phrase "Moses and Eleazar the priest." They seem to have worked closely together on all priestly matters. This gives us reason to question whether Moses was or was not considered a priest himself. Regardless of the historical reality, the text itself seems to cast Moses in that light—

---

[10] Ibid., 390.

making him out to be informally the truest priest the people had at this time. Whether this can be inferred from Numbers or not is actually superfluous, for by the time we get to Deuteronomy the message is very clear.

Moses

Without actually coming right out and saying it, Deuteronomy 33:29 comes as close as possible to declaring Moses was a priest, not according to the order of his brother, Aaron, but according to the order of Melchizedek. The careful reader who is familiar with Hebrews (5:6) will recognize the equivalence of this statement to one quoted there about Jesus—coming from Psalm 110:4. Neither Hebrews nor the book of Psalms is presenting this as an original idea; this declaration has its roots in the Pentateuch itself. Let me show you why.

The entire chapter of Deuteronomy 33 is a poetic account of Moses' blessing pronounced on the nation of Israel before he died. Moses named each of the tribes in turn and gave his blessing—much as Israel did to his sons in chapter 49 at the end of Genesis. These verses also share some very important characteristics with Genesis 14, the account of Melchizedek's blessing of Abraham:

Melchizedek		Moses	
Gen. 14:19	He blessed him and said "blessed…"	Deut. 33:1	"The blessing with which Moses the man of God blessed the people…"
Gen. 14:18	King of Salem	Deut. 33:5	He[11] became king in Jeshurun.
Gen. 14:20	This text uses the Hebrew word *mawgan* (מָגֵן), which means "delivered." (This is its only use in the Pentateuch; it is used three times in the OT.)	Deut. 33:29	This text uses the Hebrew word *mawgane* (מָגֵן), which means "shield." (It is used only two times in the Pentateuch—here and Genesis 15:1; it is used 60 times in the OT.)

---

[11] Some English versions say that *God* became king, but the original Hebrew text has "he."

Gen. 14:20	God Most High "has delivered your enemies into your hand."	Deut. 33:29	"Your enemies shall come fawning to you, and you shall tread upon their backs."
Gen. 14:21	Melchizedek abruptly disappears from the text.	Deut. 34:1	Moses goes up to Mount Nebo to die.

Just as Melchizedek blessed the father of the Israelites in Genesis 14, so Moses blessed the entire nation in Deuteronomy 33. Melchizedek was one of the few people in the entire Bible who was said to be both priest and king. Here we see that Moses also shares that distinction. We have already seen how Moses was presented as a priest earlier in the Pentateuch. In Deuteronomy 33:5 the other half of his connection to Melchizedek is presented by mentioning his kingship. Some people interpret this verse to say that God became king, but the text simply uses the pronoun "he." We must look at the context to see who the pronoun refers to. The most natural antecedent is Moses who is mentioned in verse 4.[12] Jeshurun is "a poetic reference to Israel,"[13] so since he was leader of the nation, this poem recognizes him as king. Both Melchizedek and Moses used a rare but important term in their blessings (*mawgan* and *mawgane*). These terms are etymologically related, the only difference being the final vowel. Considering Hebrew spelling originally ignored the vowels altogether, the similarity of the two words is even more significant. Both men made a statement about God's defeat of the enemy and then exited the biblical stage, so to speak. These parallels are intended to help us see that Moses was a priest after the order of Melchizedek. To be a priest in this order implies the normal expectations of the Levitical priesthood wouldn't apply. Moses was a priest, but not just any old priest like Aaron his brother—Moses had more to offer since he was revolutionary and innovative. And since he shared in all three of the Old Testament offices—prophet, priest, and king—he points in a special way to the other priest we know who is a priest after the order of Melchizedek.

If any doubt remains as to whether the Pentateuch truly affirms Moses was a priest, we have a clear indication of it in Psalm 99:6. This verse tells us, "Moses and Aaron were among his priests." The purpose of this psalm is to give us reason to praise the Lord; even though he is exalted high above his people, he is accessible and answers the prayers of the leaders of his people.

---

[12] Sailhamer, *The Pentateuch as Narrative*, 477.

[13] Sharon Pace Jeansonne, "Jeshurun." Ed. David Noel Freedman. *The Anchor Yale Bible Dictionary* 1992: Volume 3 (London, UK: Yale University Press, 1992), 771.

The sense of the word "priest" is that this person serves as a mediator between the exalted Lord and his people. That is clearly the job Moses fulfilled.

David

David was not a priest, but a couple of passages come really close to placing him in that role. Because David so closely foreshadowed Christ, it is important to mention here the verses that almost present him as a priest-king. In the first of these passages (1 Samuel 21:1–6) he was running from Saul and arrived at the tabernacle in Nob. David and his men were hungry, so they asked for bread from the priest who was there. The only bread he had to offer was the holy bread from the tabernacle. Leviticus 24:9 makes clear that only priests were allowed to eat this bread; nevertheless, the priest gave it to David. In Matthew 12:3–4 (and parallel passages) Jesus uses David's actions as an argument to show he had authority to allow his disciples to pluck heads of grain on the Sabbath. The implication is that even though David was not a priest, he likewise had authority to eat the priests' bread. From where was that authority derived? From the fact that he was king? From his necessity? Maybe it's a combination of both. The answer is not crucial to the point I am making here; it's enough to note that the text describes him doing something only priests did. Jesus claimed the same authority, and in doing so he claimed to walk in the steps of David.

The other passage describes two more priestly actions of David. Look at what he did when he brought the ark up to Jerusalem:

> **2 Samuel 6:13–14**—And when those who bore the ark of the LORD had gone six steps, he sacrificed an ox and a fattened animal. And David danced before the LORD with all his might. And David was wearing a linen ephod.

He made a sacrifice and wore an ephod—these were not kingly actions, but priestly ones. In Hebrew, the description of David's clothing is the same as that given of Samuel serving as a priest's apprentice in 1 Samuel 2:18. We could study this passage in more depth, but again the point is simply that the text allows David to appear as a priest. He was a king who acted like a priest on two occasions; his descendant has since proven to be the Perfect King who, to an even greater extent than David, fulfills his role as Perfect Priest.

David's Descendant

Psalm 110 is another very significant passage to consider in this context. In this psalm, King David wrote about his son who would be a priest after the order of Melchizedek. Because of what we have seen in the Pentateuch, we should expect David's message to be about a priesthood that would be revolutionary and innovative. To confirm this, let's especially analyze the first four verses. All seven of these verses are strongly messianic, but since verses 5–7 focus on our Savior's kingly characteristics, we will not discuss them in this context.

In verse 1 we learn about to whom David was writing. He said, "The LORD says to my Lord...." He used two different Hebrew words for "Lord." The first is *Jehovah*, a name for God. The second is a word that refers to one's master or ruler. This term is also often, but not always, used to refer to God. So we need to understand that in this verse God is addressing someone David deeply respects—his master or ruler. The most important ruler in all the Old Testament was the promised Messiah. In fact, David was given a promise in 2 Samuel 7 that his descendant would be the great messianic king in whom rested all the hope of the Old Testament. Jesus mentioned this verse in Matthew 22:44–45, making clear that David was referring to his son. It would be unusual for anyone to refer to their son as their Lord, but because of David's awareness of the surpassing greatness of the Messiah, he chose a term of the deepest respect.

One of the points David made about this future king emphasized his victorious defeat of the enemy. Verses 1 and 2 especially focus on this truth:

> **Psalm 110:1–2**
> The LORD says to my Lord:
>   "Sit at my right hand,
> until I make your enemies your footstool."
> The LORD sends forth from Zion
>   your mighty scepter.
>   Rule in the midst of your enemies!

Notice that victory over the enemy was also a major part of Genesis 14:20, in the case of Melchizedek, and Deuteronomy 33:29, in the case of Moses. In fact, the end of verse 1 is strikingly similar to the blessing Moses gave in Deuteronomy when he said Israel would tread upon the back of the enemy. In both phrases, contact of the foot with the enemy shows dominance. It's even likely we are intended to connect this thought with the prophecy of Genesis 3:15, saying the seed of the woman would crush the head of the serpent.

If verses 1 and 2 present the Messiah as king, verse 4 presents him as priest.

Psalm 110:4

The LORD has sworn
   and will not change his mind,
"You are a priest forever
   after the order of Melchizedek."

In the context of this psalm the Messiah's similarity to Melchizedek is probably mostly in the fact that he is both priest and king. The sheer significance
of this can be seen in the way verse 4 is stated as a solemn declaration.

Having seen the roles of king and of priest, we can now look at the in-
tervening verse, verse 3. This verse is loaded with meaning for both a king
and a priest. The first half describes the Messiah and his followers with three
important terms.

Psalm 110:3a

Your people will offer themselves freely
   on the day of your power,
   in holy garments.

The first important word here is translated into the English phrase "offer
themselves freely." In Hebrew this word is a noun (*nadabah*), quite full of
priestly connotations; in almost all its occurrences in the Bible it is translated
with the phrase "freewill offering." Strong's defines it as an "offering or sacrifice that is voluntary and not compulsory, and thus prompted only by the
impulse of the donor."[14] Only four out of a total of twenty-six occurrences
are translated differently in the ESV. Besides the passage at hand, the other
three exceptions are found in Hosea 14:4; Psalm 68:9; and 2 Chronicles 35:8.
The first two of these are verses that describe an action *God* performs "freely"
or in full measure. The verse in 2 Chronicles describes something that is basically the same as a freewill offering, and it even could be translated that
way. So we can see that this word is a technical term for a freewill sacrificial
offering when applied to humans. It seems to me it is used in Psalm 110 in
the same sense as Romans 12:1.

Romans 12:1—I appeal to you therefore, brothers, by the mercies of God, to
present your bodies as a living sacrifice, holy and acceptable to God, which
is your spiritual worship.

---

[14] Swanson, *Dictionary of Biblical Languages with Semantic Domains*, 5607 נְדָבָה.

In Psalm 110, David already had the concept of a living sacrifice in mind, and Paul developed it further in Romans. Under the Levitical sacrificial system, God's people needed a priest to offer regular sacrifices for them. David, however, was looking forward to the day of the Perfect Priest who would come in the order of Melchizedek. Although Psalm 110:3 does not explain how, it holds out hope that the future priest will somehow enable all God's people to enjoy a direct relationship with God, being priests who offer themselves.

The verb that corresponds to this word for "freewill offering" is also helpful for our study. It is *nadab* and is used seventeen times in the Old Testament. An especially important passage where it is found is Judges chapters 4 and 5. In this pericope Deborah was a judge of Israel who had to defend the nation from the evil King Sisera. She commissioned Barak to lead an army of Israelites in battle against the enemy. Because Barak had a weak level of commitment, Deborah prophesied that Sisera would be defeated by a woman. After Barak's military successes, Sisera fled on foot and arrived at Jael's tent, seeking refuge. Jael was a Kenite woman. Although Kenites were not Israelites, they generally got along well with them.[15] Jael murdered Sisera by driving a tent pet through his head while he slept peacefully, thinking he had found safety. The striking part about this passage is that in many ways the person who ultimately gained victory over the oppressing king was the weakest and least expected of all options. In spite of the unlikelihood, God used Jael to crush the head of the enemy, a foreshadowing of his future work through the serpent crusher. Judges 5:2 describes Jael's willingness to offer herself to help defeat Sisera with the word *nadab*, to freely offer. She made her own life a living sacrifice to the God of Israel, foreshadowing people from every nation—the weakest and least expected—who would also be invited to sacrificially serve the perfect priest-king. Her life became a spiritual offering in the midst of a military setting—the joining of two very opposing roles (priest and king). Now our perfect priest-king leads us in giving ourselves like Jael in a freewill offering for God's kingdom, by which we defeat our spiritual enemy and unite ourselves to the cause of Christ our King.

The second important word in Psalm 110:3 is the word translated "power." We are told the freewill offering of the Messiah's people will be "on the day of [his] power." This word is much more common, found 243

---

[15] Baruch Halpern, "Kenites," *The Anchor Yale Bible Dictionary*, ed. David Noel Freedman (New York, NY: Doubleday, 1992), Volume 4, 17.

times in the Old Testament. Although it most often refers to military might, looking back to some of the other passages we have already seen, we can find it has been used already in a priestly context. It is used in Exodus 18:21, 25 to describe the "able men" Jethro recommended as helpers for Moses. In Deuteronomy 33:11, where Moses was presented as a priest, he asked the Lord to bless the Levites with *strength* (God's Word Translation)—one priest requesting power from God in the ministry of other priests. Even though the word is not used in Genesis 14 when Melchizedek blessed Abram, the concept is included in Abram's military victory before he encountered the priest-king. Other very significant verses with this word include Psalm 33:16; Habakkuk 3:19; and Zechariah 4:6; each of which help us develop the idea further. It seems the biblical message for us is that the followers of the priest-king have all the power they need to defeat the enemy, not coming from their own ability, but from their leader himself.

The third important word in Psalm 110:3 is most often translated "holy garments" or some equivalent in the English versions. Behind this phrase there is actually a textual variant, and we are not completely sure which is the correct reading. The two possible options are represented by only the substitution of one letter for another letter very similar in appearance in the Hebrew. The word "garment" is supported by the Masoretic Text, but another very reliable reading has instead, "on the holy mountains." So it affirms the Messiah's people will be either in holy garments or on the holy mountains. Either way, this phrase carries significant impact on the priestly ministry of God's people. If it refers to garments, there is a connection with the priestly garments of Exodus 28:2:

> **Exodus 28:2**—And you shall make holy garments for Aaron your brother, for glory and for beauty.

The challenge to understanding it in this sense is that the two passages use different Hebrew words for "garment." Nevertheless, Psalm 110 could be affirming that in the future God's people will have clothing corresponding to the new role of priest every follower of the Messiah will share. Revelation 19:14 is a very clear parallel, describing the armies of heaven dressed in white linen and following Christ on white horses. 1 Chronicles 16:29 is even more amazingly close to this reading of Psalm 110:

> **1 Chronicles 16:29**
> Ascribe to the LORD the glory due his name;
>   bring an *offering* and come before him!

> Worship the LORD in the *splendor of holiness* [literally, in holy garments] (emphasis added).

Therefore, the first possible reading of this verse is full of hope for the future capacity of God's people to directly approach Jehovah in worship because of a work he does to make them worthy of being in his presence.

The second possible reading of the verse is likewise rich in priestly significance for God's people. If we are to read "Your people will give a freewill offering in your day of power on the holy mountains," this verse points both backward and forward to significant details in the lives of the two most prominent priests of the Bible. Remember how Exodus 24:18 and other verses in context tell how Moses met with God on Mount Sinai as an intermediary for the people of Israel. They had told him in Exodus 20:18–19 that they were too afraid to meet with God and wanted only him to do so. Psalm 110:3 may be affirming that God's future work will make it possible for *all* his people to meet directly with him as priests who have had the barrier of fear removed.

The term "mountain" also looks forward to the future ministry of Jesus, a priest who infinitely surpasses Moses in greatness. Like Moses, Jesus met with God on a mountain; the difference was that he often took his followers along with him to be in his Father's presence. Remember how we noted in Chapter 3 that Matthew arranged his gospel around seven mountains. Warren Gage noticed chiasm in this arrangement, and he observes that two of the mountains make special use of typology from Joshua:

> The seven Matthean mountains are arranged chiastically, with corresponding pairs arrayed around the central mountain of the wilderness feeding. The mountains relevant to the Joshua typology are the second mountain and the sixth, which frame Matthew's five discourses.[16]

Chiasm is a writing structure in which the author repeats himself in reverse order. The result is often intended to emphasize the central part of the structure. The chiastic pairs in Matthew can be mapped out like this:

---

[16] Gage, *Gospel Typology in Joshua and Revelation.*

A The mountain of the temptation (4:8)
  B The mountain of the beatitudes (5:1)
    C The mountain of the separation (14:23)
      D The mountain of the feeding in the wilderness (15:29)
    C' The mountain of the transfiguration (17:1)
  B' The mountain of the Olivet discourse (24:3)
A' The mountain of the commissioning (28:16)

I believe Gage is right to say that B and B' connect the life of Joshua with that of Jesus. Furthermore, it seems to me that C and C'—the third and fifth mountains—connect typological details from the life of Moses to that of Jesus. In the case of the third mountain, Jesus went up the mountain alone to pray—much as Moses communicated with God alone on the mountain. In chapter 17, that of the fifth mountain, he took three disciples with him up the mountain of transfiguration. They saw Jesus in his glory as he was validated by Moses, Elijah, and God himself. (See chapter 3, "The Perfect Prophet," for more about this passage.) On that day Peter, James, and John partially fulfilled what seems to be predicted in Psalm 110:3. Now *all* God's people are able to accompany him on the mountain and see his glory because of Christ's work, removing the barrier between us and the Father. John tells us of a future encounter on a mountain that will be even more glorious than what we experience in the present:

> **Revelation 14:1**—Then I looked, and behold, on Mount Zion stood the Lamb, and with him 144,000 who had his name and his Father's name written on their foreheads.

In Psalm 110, we have seen how David spoke of his coming son in terms of a priest-king who shared some important characteristics with Melchizedek. He asserted that the Son of David would do a work of hugely significant proportions that would benefit the people of God. Like Moses, this priest is only mildly associated with the Levitical priesthood, and is instead part of an order that is much more transcendental. Like Melchizedek and Jethro, the Son of David is a righteous man from the outside who has much to offer since he is revolutionary and innovative.

Uzziah
Up to this point in redemption history we have noticed a handful of men who were presented as both king and priest. Our next focus will be on a man who made a failing attempt to take on both roles. For one man to fill both

offices was not normal; his failure was inevitable if his actions were not authorized by God. But this man's failure serves a positive purpose as a foil of the true priest-king. Look at what happened when King Uzziah tried to fulfill the office of priest:

> **2 Chronicles 26:16–19** — But when [King Uzziah] was strong, he grew proud, to his destruction. For he was unfaithful to the LORD his God and entered the temple of the LORD to burn incense on the altar of incense. But Azariah the priest went in after him, with eighty priests of the LORD who were men of valor, and they withstood King Uzziah and said to him, "It is not for you, Uzziah, to burn incense to the LORD, but for the priests, the sons of Aaron, who are consecrated to burn incense. Go out of the sanctuary, for you have done wrong, and it will bring you no honor from the LORD God." Then Uzziah was angry. Now he had a censer in his hand to burn incense, and when he became angry with the priests, leprosy broke out on his forehead in the presence of the priests in the house of the LORD, by the altar of incense.

King Uzziah's problem was pride. Verse 16 tells us his pride was a result of growing strong. Apparently he was a man who had become used to getting his way. We don't know why he felt like he needed to burn incense in the temple, but when he did, eighty-one priests followed him in to confront him about his error. They probably were hoping their large number would make a difference in convincing him or at least protecting them from his anger. It is interesting that Uzziah was not punished until he became angry. Maybe the Lord was demonstrating his patience so no one could claim the king was not aware of how serious his error was. In any case, when Uzziah failed to submit and listen to the priests' rebuke, God saw fit to punish him with leprosy.

The passage about Uzziah in 2 Chronicles is a lot less familiar than another one we have all heard from Isaiah 6. Nevertheless, the chronicler sheds some very important light on the meaning behind Isaiah 6:1–4:

> **Isaiah 6:1–4** — In the year that King Uzziah died I saw the Lord sitting upon a throne, high and lifted up; and the train of his robe filled the temple. Above him stood the seraphim. Each had six wings: with two he covered his face, and with two he covered his feet, and with two he flew. And one called to another and said:
> "Holy, holy, holy is the LORD of hosts;
>   the whole earth is full of his glory!"
> And the foundations of the thresholds shook at the voice of him who called, and the house was filled with smoke.

The time stamp Isaiah gave to this chapter is not insignificant—he included it for a reason. Uzziah had leprosy until the day he died as punishment for his sin. Now Isaiah records a vision he had that contrasts with Uzziah's experience. Many have noted that the person in his vision is a pre-incarnate appearance of God the Son, and rightly so. Jonathan McLatchie states it especially well:

> Fascinatingly, Isaiah begins his sixth chapter by writing, "In the year that King Uzziah died, I saw the Lord, high and exalted, seated on a throne; and the train of his robe filled the temple." Several textual indicators suggest that it is Christ whom Isaiah beheld in this chapter, and we are told as much explicitly in John 12:39–41. Isaiah thus seems to draw a contrast between the man who wanted to be a high priestly king and the one who would ultimately be the true high priestly king.[17]

Christ successfully fills the roles of king and priest that Uzziah was punished for attempting to fill. We are told he is sitting on a throne (as a king) and the train of his robe fills the temple (as a priest). This is another way of saying he is actually worthy of occupying both offices. Uzziah died for claiming what didn't belong to him, but Isaiah's vision confirms that someone would come who had every right to take it.[18]

Isaiah further develops his message about the true priest-king later in his book. Look at just one of his amazing statements in chapter 53:

Isaiah 53:10
Yet it pleased the LORD to bruise Him;
He has put *Him* to grief.
When You make His soul an offering for sin,
He shall see *His* seed, He shall prolong *His* days,
And the pleasure of the LORD shall prosper in His hand (NKJV).

Isaiah recognizes that the suffering servant will fulfill a priestly task in regard to a guilt offering. The unusual part of this statement, however, is that in the case of this priest, instead of offering an animal as the sacrifice, the priest himself becomes the sacrifice! The most literal translations of this verse help us see that the Father makes the soul of the son an offering for sin. That doesn't mean the Father has become the priest; it simply means the

---

[17] Jonathan McLatchie, *'Jesus Foreshadowed by Joshua the High Priest.'* CrossExamined.org. 25 November 2011. Web. http://crossexamined.org/jesus-foreshadowed-by-joshua-the-high-priest/ Accessed 5 June 2015.
[18] Ibid.

sacerdotal ministry of this priest is extreme—beyond any other mediating act the world has known or ever will. This priest is committed enough that his sacrifice goes to the ultimate level.

Joshua the High Priest

Before we see what the New Testament teaches us about this ministry of Jesus, let's look at one more book in the Old Testament. Zechariah shows us another man who was priest-king and thus foreshadowed Jesus. In contrast to Uzziah he actually had authorization to fill both rolls. This man's name was Joshua, and he was the high priest in Jerusalem after the people came back from exile. Two passages refer to him—Zechariah 3:1–10 and 6:11–13. He is not very well known, but he points forward to Jesus in several ways.

First, he has the same name as Jesus. His name in Hebrew sounds like *Yehoshua*, but the English pronunciation has evolved into Joshua. Jesus' name is *Yeshua* in Hebrew, which is just a shortened form of *Yehoshua*. The difference between these two names is heightened by the fact that *Yeshua* was first translated into Greek for the writing of the New Testament, and from there to English. In Greek his name is *Iesous*, which is rendered "Jesus" in English.

Now look at what the prophet Zechariah records about this man, Joshua. In chapter 6 God gave instructions to Zechariah concerning Joshua:

> **Zechariah 6:11–13**—Take from them silver and gold, and make a crown, and set it on the head of Joshua, the son of Jehozadak, the high priest. And say to him, 'Thus says the LORD of hosts, "Behold, the man whose name is the Branch: for he shall branch out from his place, and he shall build the temple of the LORD. It is he who shall build the temple of the LORD and shall bear royal honor, and shall sit and rule on his throne. And there shall be a priest on his throne, and the counsel of peace shall be between them both."

In verse 11 he makes the effort to mention the name of Joshua's father, Jehozadak. Jehozadak means "Jehovah is Righteousness," which should remind us of Melchizedek (King of Righteousness). He wants us to catch his clue that what we have in these verses is another Melchizedek who becomes priest-king. God gives him the nickname Branch in verse 12. This is a clear title for the promised Messiah from Isaiah 11 and other passages. In verses 12 and 13 we are told he is the one who shall build a temple of the Lord. This should remind us of the promises God gave to David about his son who would build a temple. For a moment Joshua looks like he could be the Son of David who will be both priest and king and the fulfillment of every messianic promise. Look, however, at Zechariah 3:8, where he also mentions the messianic term "servant" along with "Branch."

> **Zechariah 3:8**—Hear now, O Joshua the high priest, you and your friends who sit before you, for they are men who are a sign: behold, I will bring my servant the Branch.

Although Joshua the high priest was in a small way the branch Israel needed, God was not affirming that he was the Messiah; rather, he was simply indicating that Joshua was the man for the hour. Because of the exile, the temple and the sacrificial system were in ruins. God's people needed someone who could restore the religious structure as they returned to the land. An article on GotQuestions.org expresses clearly the role of Joshua:

> Joshua was already the high priest, and the prophet was to symbolically crown him king. The coronation was to serve as an encouragement to Joshua in his work of rebuilding the temple. Also, it was a visual prophecy of the future Messiah—who would be both high priest (Hebrews 6:20) and king (Matthew 27:11).[19]

The rest of Zechariah is very full of messianic images and promises. See, for example, Zechariah 9:9:

Zechariah 9:9
Rejoice greatly, O daughter of Zion!
　　Shout aloud, O daughter of Jerusalem!
Behold, your king is coming to you;
　　righteous and having salvation is he,
humble and mounted on a donkey,
　　on a colt, the foal of a donkey.

At this time, only a relatively little time was left before Jesus' coming, and he ultimately proved to be the real fulfillment of these promises. Zechariah, close to the end of the Old Testament, was building up to his soon coming. Even though Jesus came just as predicted, he still hasn't fulfilled all of Zechariah's promises. In many ways the book of Revelation shows us how Jesus will, in the future, fulfill the rest of the prophecies in the book of Zechariah.

---

[19] GotQuestions.org. '*Who Was the Joshua In Zechariah 3:1-10?*' N.p., 2015. Web. Accessed 6 June 2015. http://www.gotquestions.org/Joshua-in-Zechariah.html

New Testament

When we turn to the New Testament, we see that its writers focus very heavily on Jesus' priestly ministry. Look, for example, at this verse in 1 Timothy, where Paul describes the mediatorial role of Christ as our priest:

> **1 Timothy 2:5** — For there is one God, and there is one mediator between God and men, the man Christ Jesus.

The New Testament writers also echo the idea which Isaiah first proclaimed — shockingly, this priest actually becomes the sacrifice! Jesus was so committed to making an effective sacrifice that he would stop at nothing but the best — a sacrifice of his own life, the only sacrifice that permanently heals the relationship between his people and their God. Look at some of the verses:

> **Matthew 20:28** — The Son of Man came not to be served but to serve, and to give his life as a ransom for many.

> **Hebrews 1:3** — He is the radiance of the glory of God and the exact imprint of his nature, and he upholds the universe by the word of his power. After making purification for sins, he sat down at the right hand of the Majesty on high.

> **John 10:15** — The Father knows me and I know the Father; and I lay down my life for the sheep.

In all previous experiences the sheep were the sacrifice offered by the priest. In Jesus' case however, the priest is the sacrifice offered for the sheep!

Caiaphas

Caiaphas was the high priest of the Jews when Jesus was on earth. As we might expect, he and his ministry serve as a contrast to the only true High Priest who was worthy to have his position. Look at this amazing passage in John:

> **John 11:47–53** — So the chief priests and the Pharisees gathered the council and said, "What are we to do? For this man performs many signs. If we let him go on like this, everyone will believe in him, and the Romans will come and take away both our place and our nation." But one of them, Caiaphas, who was high priest that year, said to them, "You know nothing at all. Nor do you understand that it is better for you that one man should die for the people, not that the whole nation should perish." He did not say this of his own accord, but being high priest that year he prophesied that Jesus would

die for the nation, and not for the nation only, but also to gather into one the children of God who are scattered abroad. So from that day on they made plans to put him to death.

Caiaphas made an amazing statement that was even more true than he realized. He believed it was better to kill Jesus than to be at risk of upsetting the Romans and causing the entire nation to suffer at their hands. John captures the irony of what he said when he states that Jesus "should die for the people." Thus, even Caiaphas viewed Jesus' death as a sacrifice of sorts. In verse 51, John tells us Caiaphas' statement was a prophecy; that is, it was truth that came directly from God in spite of Caiaphas' lack of intentionality to serve God in this way. And John goes on to tell us Jesus really was a substitute, not only for the nation of Israel, but for the entire world. Eventually Caiaphas had his way:

> **Matthew 26:3–5**—Then the chief priests and the elders of the people gathered in the palace of the high priest, whose name was Caiaphas, and plotted together in order to arrest Jesus by stealth and kill him. But they said, "Not during the feast, lest there be an uproar among the people."

Caiaphas was an unworthy priest who ironically offered the greatest sacrifice ever made. The only reason it was successful was that Jesus, superseding him in priestly status, in reality had his hand in the same sacrifice—offering himself!

Hebrews
Hebrews picks up much of what we have seen in the Old Testament and presents it in the same way.

> **Hebrews 5:1–10**—For every high priest chosen from among men is appointed to act on behalf of men in relation to God, to offer gifts and sacrifices for sins. He can deal gently with the ignorant and wayward, since he himself is beset with weakness. Because of this he is obligated to offer sacrifice for his own sins just as he does for those of the people. And no one takes this honor for himself, but only when called by God, just as Aaron was. So also Christ did not exalt himself to be made a high priest, but was appointed by him who said to him, "You are my Son, today I have begotten you"; as he says also in another place, "You are a priest forever, after the order of Melchizedek." In the days of his flesh, Jesus offered up prayers and supplications, with loud cries and tears, to him who was able to save him from death, and he was heard because of his reverence. Although he was a son, he learned obedience through what he suffered. And being made perfect,

he became the source of eternal salvation to all who obey him, being designated by God a high priest after the order of Melchizedek.

Hebrews does a lot of comparison and contrast between Jesus and all the other priests who came before him:

> **Hebrews 7:26–27**—For it was indeed fitting that we should have such a high priest, holy, innocent, unstained, separated from sinners, and exalted above the heavens. He has no need, like those high priests, to offer sacrifices daily, first for his own sins and then for those of the people, since he did this once for all when he offered up himself.

Hebrews also makes a close connection between Jesus and Melchizedek, showing that Jesus, the ultimate priest and ultimate king, serves in an infinitely greater way than all the other priest-kings before him. Allen P. Ross synthesizes this message of Hebrews regarding the priest in the Bible Knowledge Commentary:

> That ancient unity of priest and king in one person [is] reunited in the Messiah, a fact which necessitates the end of the line of Aaron's priesthood. This is precisely the point of the writer to the Hebrews, who four times said Melchizedek is a type of Christ (Heb. 5:6; 6:20; 7:17, 21). As a Priest Jesus sacrificed Himself by His death on the cross (Heb. 7:27–28; 10:10). Not in Aaron's line (cf. Heb. 7:11–18), He is the eternal High Priest (cf. Heb. 7:21–26, 28) of the New Covenant (cf. Heb. 8:13; 9:15). Because He is also the promised Davidic King, both offices are united in one Person.[20]

A Living Priest

Remember the story of Aslan? The witch told him his sacrifice was futile; when he was dead, he would have no power to continue to protect Edmund and the rest of Narnia from her schemes. Unfortunately for her, she was unaware of the Deeper Magic from before the dawn of time. Aslan defeated death with his sacrifice and returned to life, completely destroying the witch's curse on the land. That's the way some verses speak of Jesus' priestly death and resurrection:

> **Romans 5:9–10**—Since, therefore, we have now been justified by his blood, much more shall we be saved by him from the wrath of God. For if while

---

[20] Allen P. Ross, "Psalms," *The Bible Knowledge Commentary: An Exposition of the Scriptures*, ed. J. F. Walvoord and R. B. Zuck (Wheaton, IL: Victor Books, 1985), Ps 110:4, Volume 1, 874.

we were enemies we were reconciled to God by the death of his Son, much more, now that we are reconciled, shall we be saved by his life.

That is, we are reconciled to God by Christ's death, but we are actually saved by his life!

> **Romans 8:34–39**—Who is to condemn? Christ Jesus is the one who died— more than that, who was raised—who is at the right hand of God, who indeed is interceding for us. Who shall separate us from the love of Christ? Shall tribulation, or distress, or persecution, or famine, or nakedness, or danger, or sword? As it is written,
> "For your sake we are being killed all the day long;
> we are regarded as sheep to be slaughtered."
> No, in all these things we are more than conquerors through him who loved us. For I am sure that neither death nor life, nor angels nor rulers, nor things present nor things to come, nor powers, nor height nor depth, nor anything else in all creation, will be able to separate us from the love of God in Christ Jesus our Lord.

Praise our Lord that he not only died for us, but lives to protect us from all evil and will one day defeat it completely! His most defining act as priest was at the moment of his death; today, however, he continues to serve as priest in life. Because he already propitiated our sins, he is now able to serve as our advocate. That is, he comes between us and God as a reminder to the Father that our sins have been paid:

> **1 John 2:1–2**—My little children, I am writing these things to you so that you may not sin. But if anyone does sin, we have an advocate with the Father, Jesus Christ the righteous. He is the propitiation for our sins, and not for ours only but also for the sins of the whole world.

A Kingdom of Priests
Remember what we saw in Exodus 19:6? God intended for his people to be a kingdom *of* priests, but because of their fear, he made them a kingdom *with* priests. Jesus' ministry, as perfect as it is, finally accomplishes the original goal:

> **1 Peter 2:5, 9**—You yourselves like living stones are being built up as a spiritual house, to be a *holy priesthood*, to offer spiritual sacrifices acceptable to God through Jesus Christ...But you are a chosen race, a *royal priesthood*, a holy nation, a people for his own possession, that you may proclaim the excellencies of him who called you out of darkness into his marvelous light (emphasis added).

In other words, Jesus is not the only legitimate priest today. It is true that he completely replaced the Levitical priesthood. Now, however, Jesus is more than just a priest; he is our high priest, and all his followers are priests who serve under his authority. The mediation he offered between us and the Father was so effective that nothing is lacking in our relationship with God. We have *direct* access to the Father because of Jesus' once-for-all sacrifice which purchased our right to carry out the role of priest! That is, we now join him in offering sacrifices—not bloody physical sacrifices, but spiritual ones. Part of our priestly task is to proclaim his excellencies, thus bridging the gap between people who are still in darkness and the marvelous light into which we call them.

> **Revelation 5:9–10**—And they sang a new song, saying,
> "Worthy are you to take the scroll
>   and to open its seals,
> for you were slain, and by your blood you ransomed people for God
>   from every tribe and language and people and nation,
> and you have made them a *kingdom* and *priests* to our God,
>   and they shall reign on the earth" (emphasis added).

Jesus' priestly act makes us not only priests, but an important part of his kingdom as well. It seems John has purposely changed the phrase used in Exodus 19:6 from "a kingdom of priests" to "a kingdom and priests," giving emphasis to both messianic roles. Since Jesus is a priest-king, his followers adopt the same identity. That is, we not only serve as priests under the authority of our High Priest, we also rule under the authority of the King of kings. Verse 10 tells us we will "reign on the earth" as priests to our God! (For more, see Chapter 5, "The Perfect King.")

A Living Sacrifice

You might be asking how we can serve as priests if Jesus already made the perfect sacrifice. What is left to do? If so, you're asking the right question, and Paul answers it for us in Romans 12:1:

> **Romans 12:1**—I appeal to you therefore, brothers, by the mercies of God, to present your bodies as a living sacrifice, holy and acceptable to God, which is your spiritual worship.

Even though this verse is commonly quoted, I had failed to understand the significance of it until I read it in terms of a priestly ministry. Jesus offered his body in death to serve as our priest. Now that he has made us priests we are called to follow him by doing the same. We also offer our bodies as sacrifices. The only difference is that our sacrifices do not result in death; to the contrary, our bodies are *living* sacrifices! That is, we give all we have to God—our very selves—and we get to keep doing it continually. Our very lives belong to God, and we offer them up to him for his glory! The only reason this has any value at all is because our High Priest, out of his mercies, offered his own body first in the ultimate sacrifice of the Perfect Priest!

Conclusion

Ever since sin entered humanity's reality, God was too distant for us. There was no way for us to find, on our own, the access to him we desperately needed. To make matters worse, left to ourselves we don't even want that access—we aren't even willing to admit its importance. Jesus is the perfect priest-king who not only provides our access to the Father, but also makes us priests who can and do offer sacrifices directly to God. He has solved in infinite measure the worst problem we ever had! Aren't you glad he is your priest? Aren't you glad he died to remove your barrier to the Father? But it doesn't stop there. Now he lives to continually connect you to your God! The witch was wrong because Aslan had the solution. Jesus' solution is also the final and complete removal of everything that keeps us from our God!

Passages for further study:

Numbers 25:6–13

Deuteronomy 33:11

Deuteronomy 33:19

Psalm 4:5

Psalm 51

Psalm 116:17

Isaiah 56:1–8—Imperfect gentiles
    will become priests.

Isaiah 61:6

Isaiah 66:20–21

Jeremiah 17:24–26

Jeremiah 33:11

Jonah 2:9

Malachi 3:1–3

Philippians 4:18

Hebrews 2:17

Hebrews 3:1

Hebrews 4:14–15

Hebrews 5:5

Hebrews 6:20

Hebrews 8:1

Hebrews 9:11

Hebrews 10:21

Hebrews 13:10–16

Revelation 1:6

Revelation 20:6

5
The Perfect King

King Louis XIV of France was the epitome of an absolute monarch. He reigned 72 years—the longest-lasting kingdom of all the European kings. He constructed Versailles—a palace of exaggerated luxury—and he was always most concerned about his own glory. He is known for developing the ultimate model of absolutism. In his memoirs he wrote some pretty bold statements illustrating the doctrine of the Divine Right of kings:

> As he [the king] is of a rank superior to all other men, he sees things more perfectly than they do, and he ought to trust rather to the inner light than to information which reaches him from outside…occupying, so to speak, the place of God, we seem to be sharers of His knowledge as well as of His authority.[1]

Louis XIV liked to be called "Louis the Great" and is often attributed with the statement "I am the state."[2]

Shortly after the death of Louis XIV a large crowd was gathered at Sainte-Chapelle to honor their revered former king. At the prescribed moment, the preacher, Jean Massillon, approached the pulpit. David Lee Rubin writes "dazzling light was everywhere."[3] Surely the congregants expected a great eulogy. Unexpectedly, however, Jean Massillon defiantly began his sermon proclaiming, "God alone is great, my brothers."[4] I'm sure Massillon's bold statement was not part of expected protocol. In fact, he might have feared what the outcome of his words might be. In spite of the risk, he did not shy away from declaring truth about the greatest king of the universe.

In many cultures throughout history, the overriding assumption has been that a king always deserves the utmost loyalty of his subjects. In ex-

---

[1] W. H. Lewis, *The Splendid Century: Life in the France of Louis XIV* (Garden City, N.Y.: Doubleday, 1957), 28.

[2] Laurence Bradford Packard, *The Age of Louis XIV* (New York: Hold, Rinehart and Winston, 1957), 16.

[3] David Lee Rubin, *The Sun King: the ascendancy of French culture during the reign of Louis XIV* (Washington: Folger Shakespeare Library; London: Associated University Presses, 1992), 61.

[4] Ibid., 47, 62. On page 47 Rubin incorrectly translates "brother" in the singular. On page 62 he insinuates that a plural translation is better.

change for protecting the kingdom from all threats both external and internal, the subjects owe the king their very lives. He protects them from enemies through his military power. This justifies him in expecting their submission to his rule over them. He governs them and expects them to obey the laws he sets in place. If he is a good king, the laws will reflect the goodness of his character and, instead of being a burden, they will be a cause for the joy of his people. In even the worst of cases, the king's subjects often submit to him because it is better than the alternative of being dominated by evil enemies.

Our divine King infinitely supersedes all other kings in the measure of his goodness. Our King is infinitely worthy of our submission and obedience. Only when we follow him will we be truly happy and safe from our enemies. For this reason he is worthy of the greatest amount of glory we can give him—much more worthy than Louis XIV or any other king. Jesus will one day display the full extent of his glory, which far surpasses that of even Louis XIV, and he will deserve every bit of it, for he is God. Not only is Jesus the perfect prophet and the perfect priest, he is also the perfect king, thus fulfilling all three offices established by God in the Old Testament.

Let's look at what the Bible teaches us regarding Jesus' kingdom and his right to the throne. Of the three offices, that of king is probably most prominently declared about our Lord; the Bible is replete with declarations to this effect. In these pages we'll simply summarize its teaching and trace the overall development of the theme of king. When we understand the big picture, individual pieces of Scripture can be interpreted and appreciated on a whole new level.

Adam

Just as in the case of the prophet and the priest, our study of the king must start with Adam. Adam gives us a picture of Christ by carrying all three biblical offices. Both Adam and Eve served roles as royalty, as seen in Genesis 1:

> **Genesis 1:26–28**—Then God said, "Let us make man in our image, after our likeness. And let them have dominion over the fish of the sea and over the birds of the heavens and over the livestock and over all the earth and over every creeping thing that creeps on the earth."
> So God created man in his own image,
>   in the image of God he created him;
>   male and female he created them.

And God blessed them. And God said to them, "Be fruitful and multiply and fill the earth and subdue it, and have dominion over the fish of the sea and over the birds of the heavens and over every living thing that moves on the earth."

Twice in these verses God mentioned Adam and Eve's dominion over creation—in his purpose and in his command. The unstated assumption in this text is that the Lord himself is the high king of the universe, and he is establishing humans in a position of vicegerents. They are to rule in his stead with the power and authority he has delegated to them. Even the term "image of God" is loaded with royal significance. Being in the "image of God" was a prestige that was commonly claimed by kings in the ancient Near East. It was the justification for their position and their authorization to represent divinity and carry out his will.[5] The delegated position that Adam and Eve were given makes their eventual rebellion even more heinous. T. Desmond Alexander describes well the irony of their choice:

> In the light of their royal status and their divine commission to rule over the animals, it is especially noteworthy that Adam and Eve obey the serpent's instructions rather than those of God. By submitting to the serpent, Adam and Eve fail to exercise their God-given dominion over this crafty animal...The ones through whom God's sovereignty was to be extended throughout the earth side with his enemy. By heeding the serpent they not only give it control over the earth, but they themselves become its subjects.[6]

Patriarchal Promises

Likewise, Abram rounded out his resume when God gave him the privilege of also being a king. Without explicitly stating it, Genesis 12:1–3 puts him in that light:

> **Genesis 12:1–3** — Now the LORD said to Abram, "Go from your country and your kindred and your father's house to the land that I will show you. And I will make of you a great nation, and I will bless you and make your name great, so that you will be a blessing. I will bless those who bless you, and him who dishonors you I will curse, and in you all the families of the earth shall be blessed."

---

[5] T. Desmond Alexander, *From Eden to the New Jerusalem: An Introduction to Biblical Theology* (Grand Rapids, MI: Kregel, 2008). pp. 76-77.

[6] Ibid., 78-79.

Bill T. Arnold observed that "to have a great name given to one by God in the Hebrew Scriptures is to be viewed as a royal figure."[7] Thus Abram is being viewed as having a royal future. This same term is repeated to King David in 2 Samuel 7:9, confirming that Abram is in good royal company. Other terms in these verses, like "land" and "nation," support our understanding that God was giving Abram a political domain.

Genesis 14 also hints that Abram was a king when it recounts an event in his life in the context of other kings. This chapter describes a battle in which four greater kings defeated five lesser ones. It concludes with Abram handily defeating the four victors in order to rescue his nephew Lot. The implication is that Abram was an even more powerful king than the four in all their combined strength.

Among all the kings mentioned in Genesis 14, a tension exists with regard to who was truly the greatest. As it's the first passage in the Bible to use the word "king," it is surprising to find eleven royal figures. Of the others I have mentioned, Abram is the most prominent, but superseding him is Melchizedek. We should understand him as greater due to the fact that he blessed Abram and Abram gave him a tithe. Nevertheless, seen in the context of Genesis 17 and the rest of the Bible, Abram maintains a certain level of God-given greatness. In Genesis 17:6 we learn for the first time that God has a plan for blessing his people that includes kings. In verse 6 he gives a promise to Abram that he will be the father of a plurality of kings, one of whom will turn out to be the King of kings:

> **Genesis 17:5–6**—No longer shall your name be called Abram, but your name shall be Abraham, for I have made you the father of a multitude of nations. I will make you exceedingly fruitful, and I will make you into nations, and kings shall come from you.

And in verse 16, he repeats the promise in a similar way, only this time it applies to Sarai:

> **Genesis 17:15–16**—And God said to Abraham, "As for Sarai your wife, you shall not call her name Sarai, but Sarah shall be her name. I will bless her, and moreover, I will give you a son by her. I will bless her, and she shall become nations; kings of peoples shall come from her."

---

[7] Bill T. Arnold, *Genesis* (Cambridge, UK: Cambridge University Press, 2009), 132.

It is significant that the Abrahamic covenant mentions kings; it shows how important this theme is to the development of God's perfect plan throughout history. Ultimately it will be through a king that God provides his solution to all that has gone wrong with the world. A truly great king will be required to fix the rebellion started by the Lord's first vicegerents.

Kings are mentioned again in Genesis 35:10–11, when God reaffirms his covenant with Abraham's grandson Jacob:

> **Genesis 35:10–11**—And God said to him, "Your name is Jacob; no longer shall your name be called Jacob, but Israel shall be your name." So he called his name Israel. And God said to him, "I am God Almighty: be fruitful and multiply. A nation and a company of nations shall come from you, and kings shall come from your own body."

It's interesting that in all three cases where God gave this promise, he changed the name of the beneficiary—Abraham, Sarah, and now Israel—once again emphasizing the importance of this theme to salvation history. Jacob obviously took God's promise to heart, as we shall see in the next passage.

The Lion of Judah

At the end of Genesis, in chapter 49, Israel gave his blessing to each of his sons in turn. The importance of this passage is illustrated by the extra effort that was made to craft it into poetry.[8] The poems of the Pentateuch carry the weightiest theological meaning of the books and usually communicate something about the hope of a future king.[9] The most significant blessing in this chapter is the one he gave to Judah:

> **Genesis 49:8–11**
> "Judah, your brothers shall praise you;
> > Your hand shall be on the neck of your enemies;
> > Your father's sons shall bow down to you.
> "Judah is a lion's whelp;
> > From the prey, my son, you have gone up.
> > He couches, he lies down as a lion,
> > And as a lion, who dares rouse him up?
> "The scepter shall not depart from Judah,
> > Nor the ruler's staff from between his feet,
> > Until Shiloh comes,

---

[8] Sailhamer, *The Meaning of the Pentateuch*, 277-78.
[9] Ibid., 572.

And to him *shall be* the obedience of the peoples.
"He ties *his* foal to the vine,
   And his donkey's colt to the choice vine;
   He washes his garments in wine,
   And his robes in the blood of grapes" (NASB).

Look with me at several aspects of these verses that are kingly in meaning. In verse 8 we see Judah's brothers would bow down to him someday. This is intended to contrast with the immediate context, the story of Joseph serving as prime minister of Egypt. Joseph dreamed his brothers and parents would bow before him, and just a few chapters later his dream was fulfilled. In these last few chapters of Genesis there is a literary tension between Joseph and Judah as we wait to see who will surface as the favored son of Israel. In the immediate context it proves to be Joseph, who became king and saved the entire world from famine. In 49:8, however, in the words of Israel the reader is told there would be a future work of Judah who, through his descendant, would accomplish something far greater than Joseph.

The message is expanded further through the imagery of verse 9. The reference to a lion—the king of the beasts—is obviously meant to confirm that the tribe of Judah would prove to be royal.

Verse 10 is the clearest yet. It refers to a scepter and a ruler's staff, special implements used by a king. And Jacob asserted that the tribe of Judah would always be the source of these kings until Shiloh would come. The term *Shiloh* is an untranslated Hebrew word that means "the one to whom it belongs" (cf. NIV). The reference here is so clearly directed at the Messiah that many writings, even very early translations of the Old Testament, understood it to be a messianic title,[10] and for that reason it remains untranslated in many English versions. Significantly, then, this prophecy about the tribe of Judah was intended to be eternal. Judah was to be the source of kings until the Perfect King arrived, the king from the tribe of Judah who would never need to be replaced because of his perfect and eternal rule.

Balaam's Prophecy

Another long passage of poetry is found in Numbers 23 and 24, and it too conveys the royal message of the Pentateuch. This passage is a record of the

---

[10] Allen P. Ross, "Genesis", *The Bible Knowledge Commentary: An Exposition of the Scriptures*, ed. J. F. Walvoord and R. B. Zuck (Wheaton, IL: Victor Books, 1985), Ge 49:8-12. Volume 1, 98.

blessings of Balaam on God's people. Their enemy, Balak the Moabite king, requested that Balaam place a curse on the Israelites (22:1–5). Balak had full confidence that Balaam was a true prophet and everything he said would be fulfilled. Balaam started off somewhat carelessly to do the work of his "contract" with Balak. God responded with drastic measures to get his attention and ensure that he proclaimed only the divinely authorized message about God's people. He used both a talking donkey and the appearance of an angel to deliver his warning to Balaam. Instead of the curse Balak wanted, Balaam proclaimed God's blessing. Chapters 23 and 24 are the resulting message from God, delivered through his prophet. The first of these chapters focuses on the entire nation of Israel as the reader expects, but the second narrows the scope of the blessing to someone more specific. Observe, for example, the national aspect of the blessing in 23:24:

Numbers 23:24
"Behold, a people! As a lioness it rises up
    and as a lion it lifts itself;
it does not lie down until it has devoured the prey
    and drunk the blood of the slain."

These verses echo the theme of the lion as it was presented to Judah in Genesis 49. In both chapters there is a corporate sense in which these words apply to the nation of Israel. In Numbers 24, however, the message focuses on the future King who would eventually emerge as a more complete fulfillment of the royal prophecy in Genesis. Observe how the pronouns are converted to singulars and the extent of the promise becomes more extreme:

Numbers 24:7–9
"Water shall flow from his buckets,
    and his seed shall be in many waters;
his king shall be higher than Agag,
    and his kingdom shall be exalted.
God brings him out of Egypt
    and is for him like the horns of the wild ox;
he shall eat up the nations, his adversaries,
    and shall break their bones in pieces
    and pierce them through with his arrows.
He crouched, he lay down like a lion
    and like a lioness; who will rouse him up?
Blessed are those who bless you,
    and cursed are those who curse you."

Important messianic words here include *water, seed, king, Egypt, lion, bless,* and *curse,* among others. All of them in important ways point to Christ. Verse 8 also describes him defeating his enemies, a promise given first in Genesis 3:15 and picked up over and over afterward in other messianic passages. Balaam's prophecy reaches a high point in verse 17:

> **Numbers 24:17**
> "I see him, but not now;
>   I behold him, but not near:
> a star shall come out of Jacob,
>   and a scepter shall rise out of Israel;
> it shall crush the forehead of Moab
>   and break down all the sons of Sheth."

The star of Bethlehem was doing a lot more than just attracting the attention of some curious magi; it declared the arrival of the king Balaam beheld so long ago. This star would be like a scepter that identifies the authority of the king who wields it. The star would point to the king who is the star prophesied long before his birth. In spite of Jesus' weakness as a baby in the manger, he was identified from the beginning as the greatest king of all time. He is the king who crushes the head of his enemies—not just Moab, but even the ancient serpent from Eden!

Moses
Because Moses typifies Christ, it's important to note that he is also presented in the Pentateuch as a king. We have already seen that Moses filled the roles of prophet and priest. That of prophet was the most clearly stated of the three, but the roles of priest and king are also both mentioned in Deuteronomy 33. Some textual clues in this chapter connect Moses with Melchizedek, the priest-king of Genesis 14. (See chapter 4, "The Perfect Priest.") For right now, let's just focus on verses 4 and 5:

> **Deuteronomy 33:4–5**
> "Moses charged us with a law,
>   A possession for the assembly of Jacob.
> "And He was king in Jeshurun,
>   When the heads of the people were gathered,
>   The tribes of Israel together" (NASB).

Many translations render verse 5 as "And the Lord was king in Jeshurun," or something similar. The subject of the verb in this clause is not stated in

Hebrew. "He" is the most literal translation, and because Moses is the subject in verse 4, it is most natural to understand him as the referent of verse 5. Apparently, many prefer to understand the referent to be the Lord based on the fact that he is mentioned in verses 2 and 3. Duane L. Christensen is among them:

> In giving the Torah, Moses functions as a prophet; but he also takes on much of the functions of "a king" in his capacity as leader in ancient Israel. At the same time, it is important to note that Moses never takes upon himself the name or the position of royalty. Like Gideon in another day, Moses would have declared: "I will not rule over you, and my son will not rule over you; the LORD will rule over you" (Judg 8:23). It is YHWH himself who is declared king in Jeshurun, "when the chiefs of the people [including Moses] assembled in conclave the tribes of Israel" (v 5).[11]

It certainly is true that Moses was humble enough not to seek the title of king, but the most natural reading of verse 5 is that he did act in that role. John H. Sailhamer does a better job of interpreting the meaning of the pronoun here.[12] He shows how the immediate context leads us to conclude that it was Moses who acted in the role of king. Moreover, since Deuteronomy 33 and 34 mention the offices of prophet, priest and king, the end of the Pentateuch shows how God was able to unite the three offices in one person. Therefore, Moses, being compared directly with Melchizedek, prefigures a time when the Lord himself fills the kingly role as our ruler in the person of Christ. Thus Moses as prophet, priest, and king is an image, weak though it be, of Jesus—our perfect Prophet, Priest, and King.

Royal Requirements
Earlier in the book of Deuteronomy, Moses laid down specific guidelines for the nation regarding the required character of a king. As in the case of many other messianic themes, these guidelines should be read with both kings (plural) and the One King (singular) in mind. That is, these verses expound the expectations God had for *all* the kings of Israel, and they all failed in some sense or another. Additionally, they are the expectations given for the Messiah himself, and he fulfills them to the "T." Read Deuteronomy 17, starting with verses 14–17.

---

[11] Duane L. Christensen, *Deuteronomy 21:10–34:12*, Word Biblical Commentary (Dallas: Word, Incorporated, 2002), 838.

[12] Sailhamer, *The Pentateuch as Narrative*, 477.

> **Deuteronomy 17:14–17**—"When you come to the land that the LORD your
> God is giving you, and you possess it and dwell in it and then say, 'I will
> set a king over me, like all the nations that are around me,' you may indeed
> set a king over you whom the LORD your God will choose. One from among
> your brothers you shall set as king over you. You may not put a foreigner
> over you, who is not your brother. Only he must not acquire many horses
> for himself or cause the people to return to Egypt in order to acquire many
> horses, since the LORD has said to you, 'You shall never return that way
> again.' And he shall not acquire many wives for himself, lest his heart turn
> away, nor shall he acquire for himself excessive silver and gold.

Let's observe the principle components of these requirements. First of all,
according to verse 15, it should be God who chose the king. From the outset,
the people had to recognize their dependency on God's leadership for the
governance of the nation. For the nation of Israel that was demonstrated
even in the choice of the king.

Verse 16 speaks of horses. To say that the king should not acquire many
horses was really the contemporary way of saying he should not have a
powerful army. The equivalent today would be a command against acquiring many tanks, night vision goggles, fighter airplanes, and nuclear war-
heads. When he said they should not return to Egypt, he meant they should-
n't depend on human means of defense; there was no need even to keep the
business card for the arms dealer of the day. Why was God so determined
that Israel's king not be a great military leader? Deuteronomy 31:3 helps put
it in perspective:

> **Deuteronomy 31:3**—The LORD your God himself will go over before you.
> He will destroy these nations before you, so that you shall dispossess them,
> and Joshua will go over at your head, as the LORD has spoken.

The prohibition against building a great army was intended to force God's
people to place their faith in him. He was going to fight for them; they didn't
need to worry about it. With a God like Yahweh they didn't even need to
develop any contingency plans! We see this over and over in the history of
Israel. They won victories against great odds, not because of their skill or
power, but because God was simply giving the victory into their hands. The
king, as the governing leader of the nation, more than anyone else, needed
to be aware of this principle. That is the reason for the prohibition of his
acquisition of many horses.

Verse 17 states a prohibition against acquiring many wives. Moses based
this on the likelihood that they would turn the king's heart away from the

Lord. It seems clear enough that a king who was principally focused on his own pleasure was likely to abandon his love for God and all that mattered most to him.

Likewise there was a prohibition against acquiring many riches. This was probably for protection both against an unbalanced focus on selfish pleasure and against self-sufficiency. Just as in the case of military strength, God did not want the king to think he could accomplish great things because of his quantity of silver and gold; God wanted the king to depend on divine intervention.

Interestingly, the three prohibitions given in this passage concern the common downfalls of all men throughout history: money, sex, and power. Many people have pointed out the capacity of one or more of these three vices to corrupt anyone who allows himself to be dominated by them. And kings of every culture have shown themselves to be among the most susceptible of anyone to corruption. Israel's king was to avoid this possibility completely. The king who could successfully relinquish his privilege to these three attractions would prove to be the Perfect King; that is, he would be the Messiah himself.

Until now, the passage has focused on prohibitions for the king. We know what he wouldn't be like, but how would he be characterized positively? Verses 18–20 answer this question for us. They tell us that Yahweh's king would be a man of God's law. Look at how this is described:

> **Deuteronomy 17:18–20**—"And when he sits on the throne of his kingdom, he shall write for himself in a book a copy of this law, approved by the Levitical priests. And it shall be with him, and he shall read in it all the days of his life, that he may learn to fear the LORD his God by keeping all the words of this law and these statutes, and doing them, that his heart may not be lifted up above his brothers, and that he may not turn aside from the commandment, either to the right hand or to the left, so that he may continue long in his kingdom, he and his children, in Israel."

He would write for himself a copy of God's law. We shouldn't understand the term "law" here to refer to what we normally think of as laws that govern our behavior. Of course it includes that, but that is only a modest part of the whole that is referred to. This "law" refers to the Pentateuch and, by extension, to all of Scripture. It should be taken in the sense of Psalm 1:2: "But his delight is in the law of the LORD, and on his law he meditates day and night," a verse which also speaks in its ultimate sense of the Messiah. That is, we are told that Scripture would be so important to the Messiah that he would run, as it were, to the nearest copy machine to make a copy he would never lose. He would be more like a scribe than what is normally thought of when one thinks of a king. Not only would he have a copy of the law, but he would be required to read it every day.

The expectations don't stop there; the emphasis of verse 19 is given by repetition. He must keep the law, he must do it. That is, righteousness is expected of him. The more righteous our king, the more perfect he is. He is not better than his brothers in the sense that he is not above the law. The second half of verse 20 repeats themes that are common in Deuteronomy: walking the straight path will result in the blessing of God. Just as Israel could stay in the land by obedience, her king could remain in his position through the same strategy. As you can see, these verses describe a king who is radically different than the norm. Instead of a powerful military leader, Israel was to have a humble spiritual leader.

The expectations have been laid out. Deuteronomy 17 is the key to understanding almost every other passage in the Bible on kingship. Now we need to move forward and see how successfully the nation of Israel and her kings lived up to these requirements.

Request for a King

The next passage we need to analyze comes as somewhat of a surprise in light of what we have seen in Deuteronomy. In 1 Samuel the people had become tired of being ruled by judges, especially those who had proven to be corrupt. Look at what they proposed to Samuel:

> **1 Samuel 8:4–9**—Then all the elders of Israel gathered together and came to Samuel at Ramah and said to him, "Behold, you are old and your sons do not walk in your ways. Now appoint for us a king to judge us like all the nations." But the thing displeased Samuel when they said, "Give us a king to judge us." And Samuel prayed to the LORD. And the LORD said to Samuel, "Obey the voice of the people in all that they say to you, for they have not rejected you, but they have rejected me from being king over them. According to all the deeds that they have done, from the day I brought them up out of Egypt even to this day, forsaking me and serving other gods, so they are also doing to you. Now then, obey their voice; only you shall solemnly warn them and show them the ways of the king who shall reign over them."

The surprising part is in verse 6, where we see that Samuel was displeased by their request for a king. Our first reaction might be to argue with Samuel, "Don't you know, Samuel, that even Moses mentioned this day would come way back in Deuteronomy 17?" We might think Samuel was too close to the situation. Maybe he was taking it personally that the people weren't accepting the rule of his sons. But then we notice that even God seems to have been upset in verse 7; he claimed the people had rejected him as their king. So both Samuel and the Lord were taking this personally—for different reasons.

The key to understanding the message of this chapter is in one phrase from the mouths of the people: "like all the nations." This is the very part of the request that is not repeated in verse 6 when Samuel expresses his displeasure. It's as if he was unable to utter the part that most offended him. Ironically, though, this phrase is also found in Deuteronomy 17:14, where God looked positively on the idea. He had said through Moses that when they wanted a king *like all the nations*, they could indeed establish one. Therefore, there is nothing wrong with the phrase itself, depending on what is meant. The problem is that this phrase can be interpreted in a couple of different ways. If Israel had meant they wanted to be like the other nations in the sense that they didn't want to be without a king, that was fine. I think, however, that what they meant in this verse is that they wanted a king who was like the kings of the other nations. Whether or not they were fully aware of their exact desires might be in doubt, but God knew their hearts, and he knew they were rejecting him in the kind of king they were seeking.

God decided to give them what they asked for, knowing they would eventually realize how undesirable it was. A king like the other nations was exactly the wrong kind of king. Therefore, God told Samuel to warn the people about what the king would be like. Samuel did just that in the following verses. In spite of the warnings, the people were firm in their desire:

> **1 Samuel 8:19–20**—But the people refused to obey the voice of Samuel. And they said, "No! But there shall be a king over us, that we also may be like all the nations, and that our king may judge us and go out before us and fight our battles."

Here in verse 20 we finally get to the bottom of the issue. The author has delayed defining the real issue to heighten its seriousness. In fact, it doesn't show up until the end of a string of motives in verse 20. The real root of the problem is their desire that the king fight their battles. Remember the guidelines in Deuteronomy 17? Israel's king was not supposed to be a military leader; he was supposed to be a spiritual leader. Now the people wanted to put their confidence in a human king's ability to protect them from their enemies. They were rejecting the Lord as their king in light of God's promise to go before them in battle (Deuteronomy 31:3). Even more significantly, they were already rejecting God's plan to give them a Perfect Future King, the Messiah who would completely fulfill Deuteronomy 17.

God Gave Them Saul

The next few chapters detail the process of choosing and establishing the king. God chose Saul as the person for the job. He was a man from the tribe of Benjamin who wasn't necessarily seeking the position, but was confirmed by the Lord as the man for the job. Look at Samuel's speech to the people in chapter 12:

> **1 Samuel 12:13–15**—And now behold the king whom you have chosen, for whom you have asked; behold, the LORD has set a king over you. If you will fear the LORD and serve him and obey his voice and not rebel against the commandment of the LORD, and if both you and the king who reigns over you will follow the LORD your God, it will be well. But if you will not obey the voice of the LORD, but rebel against the commandment of the LORD, then the hand of the LORD will be against you and your king.

Samuel made it clear that God was giving his people and their king a chance to prove they could handle this whole matter correctly. It may have been a hypothetical chance, but it was a chance nonetheless. Everything depended on how the people and the king responded in the face of this opportunity. If they acted in obedience, we are told that all would be well. I think God fully intended for them to consider every possibility at this point; they even must have wondered whether Saul would prove to be the Promised One.

The answer regarding Saul's identity comes very quickly in the following text of 1 Samuel. We find it in the very next chapter, a sad description of Saul's sin. His error in these verses is connected to 10:8, where we find instructions Samuel gave to Saul even before he had been crowned king.

> **1 Samuel 10:8**—"Then go down before me to Gilgal. And behold, I am coming down to you to offer burnt offerings and to sacrifice peace offerings. Seven days you shall wait, until I come to you and show you what you shall do."

Look at what happened when it came time for Saul to follow these instructions:

> **1 Samuel 13:8–14**—He waited seven days, the time appointed by Samuel. But Samuel did not come to Gilgal, and the people were scattering from him. So Saul said, "Bring the burnt offering here to me, and the peace offerings." And he offered the burnt offering. As soon as he had finished offering the burnt offering, behold, Samuel came. And Saul went out to meet him and

greet him. Samuel said, "What have you done?" And Saul said, "When I saw that the people were scattering from me, and that you did not come within the days appointed, and that the Philistines had mustered at Michmash, I said, 'Now the Philistines will come down against me at Gilgal, and I have not sought the favor of the LORD.' So I forced myself, and offered the burnt offering." And Samuel said to Saul, "You have done foolishly. You have not kept the command of the LORD your God, with which he commanded you. For then the LORD would have established your kingdom over Israel forever. But now your kingdom shall not continue. The LORD has sought out a man after his own heart, and the LORD has commanded him to be prince over his people, because you have not kept what the LORD commanded you."

Now to be fair to Saul, I must say it seems like it would have been easy for me to make the same decision he did. I can understand the pressure he was under and how easy it would have been to rationalize his choice. Saul did wait seven days as Samuel had said. The people were losing confidence in Saul and beginning to leave him. It felt like the only wise thing to do was to offer the sacrifices himself. Nevertheless, the Lord was not pleased with Saul. Sin is never justified or excused simply because it feels like the right thing to do at the moment. In addition, the seriousness of Saul's offense apparently was magnified by the position he was in. That is, Saul showed a lack of dependence on God in the face of battles—again a rejection of the Lord as the military leader. If Saul were to be the kind of king God desired, he needed to show obedience to the law (Deuteronomy 17:19) and leave the outcome of the battle to God himself (Deuteronomy 31:3). Instead, he wanted to be a strong military leader, and he showed a lack of wisdom in regard to spiritual things.

Notice the textual clues about what happened here. Verses 9 and 10 give a subtle hint about the timing of the whole thing. In verse 9, Saul asked someone to bring the burnt offering and the peace offerings. Then verse 10 tells us Saul offered only the burnt offering. He didn't even have time to complete his plans concerning the peace offerings before Samuel showed up! It sounds like Saul was so impatient, he barely waited seven days and jumped to action. A few more moments of patience would have proven enough for Samuel's arrival. In other words, Saul was probably looking for every excuse to move ahead, and when he found one he took advantage of it.

Not only that, but Saul was also trying to avoid responsibility for his actions. In verse 11 he blamed Samuel in an underhanded way when he said, "You did not come within the days appointed." Then in verse 12 he said he "forced himself" to do the offering. It's like he was saying he didn't really want to do it but he had no other option, a statement which in God's eyes simply was not true.

Verse 13, by mentioning God's command, emphasizes the fact that Saul did not fulfill the requirement of the king to "keep all the words of the law" (Deuteronomy 17:19). Samuel told him he had been given a chance at having an eternal kingdom, but he blew it. In this statement we can see that the Lord already had his mind on the Messiah and Saul definitely was not the one. Instead, the Lord had a plan to establish a king after his own heart. In the context here and in Acts 13:22, the meaning of this phrase is given as someone who would do God's will. Someone who pursued the heart of God, someone who sought to do what God loves. That is, the king after God's own heart would definitely (among other things) keep all the words of his law.

A Man After God's Own Heart

In 1 Samuel 17:12 the new man shows up. Here we are told, "David was the son of an Ephrathite of Bethlehem in Judah." Already, anyone reading this verse who knows the Bible well can conclude that there might be more hope for David than there was for Saul. David was from the tribe of Judah, and we are meant to recall the blessing on Judah way back in Genesis 49. Saul, on the other hand, was from the tribe of Benjamin (9:1–2). So it seems David actually has a chance, but would he prove to be the promised king? The answer is "yes" and "no." Yes, he did become an eternal king in one sense because his dynasty is eternal. God told him his sons would always be on the throne. And yet the answer is also "no" because David was told he would also have a much greater son who would truly fulfill God's promise in every way. So even though David was a really great king, God had in mind a plan that was even more amazing.

What kept David from being the King God had in mind? First Samuel 13:13–14 leads us to believe David had a hypothetical possibility of being the Messiah. That is, when the Lord took the possibility from Saul, he mentioned he would give it to his successor, the man after God's own heart. And yet we know David was not the Messiah. It's probably helpful to state what *didn't* keep him from being the perfect king. It wasn't David's sin that disqualified him from the position. By that I mean there was not one individual sin that was a deal-breaker. Of course we know that the real Messiah is sinless, and that David, just like the rest of us, could not be Christ and offer an effective atonement for the sins of the rest of humanity. But what I mean to say is that scripturally speaking, David's *big* sin—committing adultery with Bathsheba and murdering her husband (2 Samuel 11)—was not what kept him from being the perfect king. And when you think about it, that is actually quite incredible! The hypothetical possibility of an eternal kingdom was removed from Saul because of his errant sacrifice, but in spite of David's sin (which to us seems much bigger), he was given an eternal dynasty. What made the difference? In light of God's severe response to Saul's sin, wouldn't we expect his response to David to be even heavier? Even though I don't completely understand why God chose to respond as he did, I'm really glad for it. This shows God's grace. The Lord's election of David is a lot like our salvation; it doesn't depend so much on what we do or even on whether or not we can prove our worthiness. Rather, it depends on God doing a work in our hearts. That is, he is the one who makes us people after his own heart!

Let's look at 2 Samuel 7 to see what it has to say about David's connection to the Messiah. The closest the Bible comes to stating why David himself did not completely step into the role of Messiah is what it says about the temple. David wanted to build a temple for Jehovah, but he was not allowed. Second Samuel 7 doesn't tell us why, but three other verses make it clear. First Kings 5:3; 1 Chronicles 22:8; and 1 Chronicles 28:3 all say it was because David was a man of war. These texts don't clarify how this disqualifies him, but they seem to indicate that in some way David fell short of full messianic greatness. Maybe the point is less about what he was and more about what he wasn't. As a king of war, David prefigured Christ's attack against evil, but his focus on war distracted him from prefiguring Christ in other ways. Irving L. Jensen considers how Solomon completed what David was unable to do:[13]

> David wanted to build a temple for God, but Solomon was given the privilege. Undoubtedly the character of David's life work for God was fighting, not building. But even by this fighting he was clearing the way for another to lay the foundation of that house of worship which his heart had so fondly desired to build. After the warring was over, Solomon erected the temple from materials which David had prepared. David represents Christ in His suffering and victory over the great enemy. Solomon represents Christ in His glory after the suffering and the conflicts are finished. The church, which is the true temple of God, having Christ for its chief cornerstone, will

---

[13] Irving L. Jensen, *I & II Samuel*, p. 92. as quoted in William MacDonald, *Believer's Bible Commentary: Old and New Testaments*, ed. Arthur Farstad (Nashville, TN: Thomas Nelson, 1995), 330-31.

be manifested in the last day. Now in the church's days of suffering and conflict the materials are being prepared for this glorious building for God.

So David, as a man of war, couldn't fully fill the shoes that were intended for Solomon—a king of peace and glory. Jesus is such a great king that the two greatest kings of Israel's history combined aren't equal to him. It takes both of them to show us what is only a pale image of Jesus' greatness!

When God told David he would not be the one to build a temple, he gave him some amazing promises. There is a play on words here in the original language. "Temple" and "dynasty" could both be spoken of as a house. After David expressed his desire to build a house (temple) for God, God promised to build a house (dynasty) for David. The house he would receive was the kingly line which ultimately produced the Messiah. Look at the most significant verses:

> **2 Samuel 7:12–16**—When your days are fulfilled and you lie down with your fathers, I will raise up your offspring after you, who shall come from your body, and I will establish his kingdom. He shall build a house for my name, and I will establish the throne of his kingdom forever. I will be to him a father, and he shall be to me a son. When he commits iniquity, I will discipline him with the rod of men, with the stripes of the sons of men, but my steadfast love will not depart from him, as I took it from Saul, whom I put away from before you. And your house and your kingdom shall be made sure forever before me. Your throne shall be established forever.

These verses apply both to the entire line of Davidic kings and also in a special way to Jesus as the greatest son of David. Let's see how.

One of the key words here is *offspring* in verse 12, also potentially translated as "seed." This word is important because it takes us back to Genesis 3:15, where God promised that the seed of Eve would crush the head of the serpent, solving once and for all the problem of sin in this world. So the Lord's promise to David is meant as a further clarification as to who that seed would be and the character of his royal position.

Verse 14 mentions his father/son relationship with God. This is a beautiful description of intimacy that all the kings of Israel could share with the Lord. Yet it applies most fully to Christ, who has always existed as son to God the Father. Scripture hints at the existence of God the Son long before it clearly teaches who he is.

In the same verse we also see a reference to the sins of the future kings:

> When he commits iniquity, I will discipline him with the rod of men, with the stripes of the sons of men.

It's most natural to apply this to the entire line of Davidic kings; God promises he will discipline them when they need it. But this statement also speaks of Jesus. It is true that Jesus never committed and never will commit iniquity. Nevertheless, as he was on the cross he was carrying all our sins, having received our sin by imputation. In fact, he was just as guilty for all my sin as if he had committed it himself. No other person, king or otherwise, has ever been nearly as guilty as Jesus was for committing iniquity. That's why he needed to be disciplined by God.

God says his discipline will be carried out by men. The first of the two words used for the imagery in this passage is *rod*, a messianic term. A rod is an implement used to strike people in punishment. It is also the scepter in Genesis 49:10 and Numbers 24:17 and "rod" in 2 Samuel 7:14; 18:14; and Micah 7:14. It's a messianic term for a tool Christ uses to dominate his enemies and comfort his sheep. (I plan to write a chapter on Rod in a future book.) The messianic rod is applied to Israel's kings and even to the Messiah himself, before he is allowed to use it for punishing his enemies.

Isaiah apparently notices the use of "stripes" in 2 Samuel 7:14; he picks up the same term in chapter 53 of his prophecies, where it is translated with the English word "stricken":

Isaiah 53:8
By oppression and judgment he was taken away;
    and as for his generation, who considered
that he was cut off out of the land of the living,
      stricken for the transgression of my people? (emphasis added)

Thus Jesus' suffering was a very prominent part of God's promise to David concerning his son, the Messiah.

Even though David was disqualified from being the Messiah, the Lord was pleased with him and consequently gave him the honor of engendering the Messiah. David's son would indeed prove to have an eternal reign according to verse 16. Jesus is the king who will rule forever. The temple he builds for his Father is the New Jerusalem, the final and complete meeting place for his people with God. You and I know that Jesus is the One, but David and his contemporaries didn't. In faithful expectation that God would fulfill his word, they no doubt kept a very close eye on each of David's sons. Even Scripture deals with them with a certain literary tension. Who will prove to be the promised son of David? The storyline eventually leads us to Solomon.

A Glorious King

Just like Saul and David, Solomon had a hypothetical chance to be the promised king. Look at the following condition given by the Lord to Solomon:

> **1 Kings 9:4–7**—And as for you, if you will walk before me, as David your father walked, with integrity of heart and uprightness, doing according to all that I have commanded you, and keeping my statutes and my rules, then I will establish your royal throne over Israel forever, as I promised David your father, saying, 'You shall not lack a man on the throne of Israel.' But if you turn aside from following me, you or your children, and do not keep my commandments and my statutes that I have set before you, but go and serve other gods and worship them, then I will cut off Israel from the land that I have given them, and the house that I have consecrated for my name I will cast out of my sight, and Israel will become a proverb and a byword among all peoples.

Verse 5 makes it clear that Solomon could have been the promised king, if only he would have walked in righteousness—a condition that is truthfully impossible for any of us to meet. Since we are human, we have an unavoidable bent toward sin. Thankfully, there was one human who was able to conquer sin—the only king who truly is the Messiah! The author of Kings plays with the reader for a couple of chapters. He leads us toward the conclusion that Solomon was doing everything right and eventually would prove to be the Messiah. If you read chapters 9 and 10, you will see the extreme measure of glory the Lord gave to him, contributing to his messianic appearance.

In spite of the reader's expectation, however, the author shatters our positive opinion of King Solomon in 1 Kings 10:26 to 11:6. His analysis is based on Deuteronomy 17. It follows it so closely, in fact, that it's as if he's using Moses' law as a rubric to grade Solomon's performance. Let's compare the two passages:

Deuteronomy 17		1 Kings 10–11	
Verse 16	Must not acquire many horses for himself. Must not go to Egypt to get them.	10:26, 28	Acquired 1,400 chariots and 12,000 horsemen. Imported horses and chariots from Egypt.

Verse 17	Shall not acquire many wives for himself, lest his heart turn away.	11:1–4	Loved many foreign women, including the daughter of Pharaoh. Had 700 wives and 300 concubines. They turned his heart away after other gods.
Verse 17	Nor shall he acquire for himself excessive silver and gold.	10:27	Silver was as common as stone.

Solomon's failures are not listed as random weaknesses in his character; the author of Kings is purposely showing us that Solomon was not the promised king of Deuteronomy, and likewise not the promised son of David of 2 Samuel 7. Solomon had a very glorious reign, but the clear message is that someone much greater was yet to come! And in case we miss the point, he makes it even clearer in 11:4–6 by comparing him with David. Twice (for emphasis) he tells us King Solomon's heart was not devoted to the Lord "as was the heart of David his father."

Another One Bites the Dust
A long list of kings followed Solomon in the history of Israel. The writer of Kings is mostly interested in sharing with us their successes and failures so he can help us evaluate whether each one might possibly be the true and perfect king. Let's look at just some of these evaluations. They are written in formulaic style at the end of the account of each king's life.

> **1 Kings 15:1–3**—Now in the eighteenth year of King Jeroboam the son of Nebat, Abijam began to reign over Judah. He reigned for three years in Jerusalem. His mother's name was Maacah the daughter of Abishalom. And he walked in all the sins that his father did before him, and his heart was not wholly true to the LORD his God, as the heart of David his father.

> **1 Kings 15:25–26**—Nadab the son of Jeroboam began to reign over Israel in the second year of Asa king of Judah, and he reigned over Israel two years. He did what was evil in the sight of the LORD and walked in the way of his father, and in his sin which he made Israel to sin.

> **1 Kings 15:33–34**—In the third year of Asa king of Judah, Baasha the son of Ahijah began to reign over all Israel at Tirzah, and he reigned twenty-four years. He did what was evil in the sight of the LORD and walked in the way of Jeroboam and in his sin which he made Israel to sin.

> **1 Kings 16:18–19**—And when Zimri saw that the city was taken, he went into the citadel of the king's house and burned the king's house over him with fire and died, because of his sins that he committed, doing evil in the sight of the LORD, walking in the way of Jeroboam, and for his sin which he committed, making Israel to sin.

> **1 Kings 16:25**—Omri did what was evil in the sight of the LORD, and did more evil than all who were before him.

> **1 Kings 16:30**—And Ahab the son of Omri did evil in the sight of the LORD, more than all who were before him.

As my dad would say, it sounds like a broken record—repeating the same thing over and over. This formula to evaluate kings is found all through 1 and 2 Kings. The main theme of these books could be titled "Another One Bites the Dust." They were written to help us in our search for the perfect king. Most of the kings of Judah failed miserably; the kings of Israel were even worse. The list of failures goes on and on and on. It seemed like there was no hope. God needed to act.

Dim Rays of Hope

Not everything was entirely negative; dim lights were shining here and there. Consider the account of Josiah, who didn't have a copy of the law, but when it was found, recognized its value, almost qualifying as Messiah in terms of Deuteronomy 17:18–20. He was a high point in the middle of many low ones.

> **2 Kings 22:1–2**—Josiah was eight years old when he began to reign, and he reigned thirty-one years in Jerusalem. His mother's name was Jedidah the daughter of Adaiah of Bozkath. And he did what was right in the eyes of the LORD and walked in all the way of David his father, and he did not turn aside to the right or to the left.

Read 2 Kings 22 and 23 to see the encouraging things recorded about Josiah. Yet moments like this were only the exception to a generally very steep decline in the history of God's people.

> **2 Kings 23:25–26**—Before [Josiah] there was no king like him, who turned to the LORD with all his heart and with all his soul and with all his might, according to all the Law of Moses, nor did any like him arise after him. Still the LORD did not turn from the burning of his great wrath, by which his anger was kindled against Judah, because of all the provocations with which Manasseh had provoked him.

Josiah was a great king, but even he was unable to reverse God's judgment for the accumulated sins of his people and her kings.

After Josiah, three of his sons and one of his grandsons each took their turn at ruling Judah, and they did a poor job of it. God responded with the exile; the kingdom was gradually dismantled during the reign of each of these kings. Eventually, Jehoiachin was deported to Babylon. The last two chapters describe the extremely sad conclusion of Israel's sovereign existence—punishment from God for generations of sin. Yet the book doesn't end on the lowest note. Look at the last four verses:

> **2 Kings 25:27-30**—And in the thirty-seventh year of the exile of Jehoiachin king of Judah, in the twelfth month, on the twenty-seventh day of the month, Evil-merodach king of Babylon, in the year that he began to reign, graciously freed Jehoiachin king of Judah from prison. And he spoke kindly to him and gave him a seat above the seats of the kings who were with him in Babylon. So Jehoiachin put off his prison garments. And every day of his life he dined regularly at the king's table, and for his allowance, a regular allowance was given him by the king, according to his daily needs, as long as he lived.

The king of Babylon graciously freed Jehoiachin from prison. Although he continued to live in exile, he was treated with respect. This ending to Kings is meant as a sign that God still desired to have mercy on his people. Moreover, he was not willing to completely wipe out the dynasty of Davidic kings in light of the promise he had given in 2 Samuel 7:16.

A Messianic Gentile

The biblical usage of the term "messiah" teaches us more about our perfect king. In the Old Testament, prophets, priests and kings were all anointed with oil to demonstrate that they were set aside for a special purpose, to serve God through their office. The word for "anointed one" in Hebrew is *mashiyach*, from which we get the term "messiah" in English. Translating this word to Greek produced the term "christ." The word "messiah" isn't commonly used in the Old Testament to refer directly to our Lord in the full sense of what that means to us. Nevertheless, it is used to refer to people who typify Jesus Christ. One of the most striking examples of this is found in Isaiah. Look at the only time this book uses the word "messiah:"

> **Isaiah 45:1**
> Thus says the LORD to his *anointed*, to Cyrus,
>   whose right hand I have grasped,
> to subdue nations before him

> and to loose the belts of kings,
> to open doors before him
>   that gates may not be closed: (emphasis added)

When Isaiah calls Cyrus "anointed" he is literally calling him the Lord's messiah. Cyrus had a special anointing from God to deliver his people from Babylonian captivity. What makes this most astonishing is that Cyrus was king of Persia, a gentile and not even a follower of the true God. Just like Melchizedek the priest-king, Cyrus was a gentile who showed that the perfect king could come from unexpected sources. Although the Ultimate Messiah needs to be from the tribe of Judah, the message regarding Cyrus is that our true king might have some unexpected characteristics about him. Our savior fits this pattern in that he is from a humble family in Nazareth (John 1:45–46). No one would have expected a king to come from his roots. (I plan to write more about Cyrus in a future book.)

Hope Against All Odds

Cyrus' significance was exceptional, but he certainly wasn't the promised king from the tribe of Judah. The prophet Jeremiah maintained his message of hope in the middle of some of Israel's darkest times. In chapter 33 he proclaims that God's promise to bring the King is still good:

> **Jeremiah 33:14–17**—"Behold, the days are coming, declares the LORD, when I will fulfill the promise I made to the house of Israel and the house of Judah. In those days and at that time I will cause a righteous Branch to spring up for David, and he shall execute justice and righteousness in the land. In those days Judah will be saved, and Jerusalem will dwell securely. And this is the name by which it will be called: 'The LORD is our righteousness.' For thus says the LORD: David shall never lack a man to sit on the throne of the house of Israel."

Although the days of the glory of Solomon's reign were long over, the message was clear: another son of David would come whose reign would outshine Solomon's! Jeremiah's words seemingly hung in the air for a few hundred years. Not a lot was happening in regard to kings, but the faithful maintained their hope in God's Word. That is the hope with which a young woman named Mary was waiting for the coming king. One day, out of the blue, she received a visit from the angel Gabriel, and Luke recorded what he said about the baby she was to have:

> **Luke 1:32–33**—"He will be great and will be called the Son of the Most High. And the Lord God will give to him the throne of his father David, and he

will reign over the house of Jacob forever, and of his kingdom there will be no end."

Gabriel's announcement is powerful enough, but when we understand it in the light of all the Old Testament background it is an almost incredible declaration! After waiting for so long, God's people would finally have their true and perfect king! Mary surely had a hard time comprehending the favor of God on her to allow her to be his mother. Mothering any king would be an honor, but no other king has ever been the subject of a declaration this lofty.

The Surpassing Glory of Christ
Jesus proved himself to be the kind of king his Father had in mind in all the prophecies. He relinquished his claim on money, wives, and power during his life on earth. This shows his complete obedience to Deuteronomy 17: in each area of Solomon's failure, Jesus passed with flying colors. He proved he could live the life of the Perfect King without acquiring that which all other kings need in order to artificially sustain their reign. In his future, consummated kingdom he will add each of these prohibited kingdom components to the point of perfection. For example, his kingdom will contain so many riches that gold will be used as pavement. Nothing will be held back in regard to his power; we will see his omnipotence without any reserve. In fact, Armageddon will be such a decisive victory that it's the last battle he'll need to fight. And although Christ never married during his first coming, we, the church, are the true bride of Christ. The marriage will be consummated after his second coming. Jesus will not acquire many wives, but his one bride certainly will include many individuals.

Before immersing ourselves fully in the teaching of the New Testament on the kingship of Jesus, let's look at one more Old Testament passage.

> **Zechariah 9:9–10**
> Rejoice greatly, O daughter of Zion!
>   Shout aloud, O daughter of Jerusalem!
> Behold, your king is coming to you;
>   righteous and having salvation is he,
> humble and mounted on a donkey,
>   on a colt, the foal of a donkey.
> I will cut off the chariot from Ephraim
>   and the war horse from Jerusalem;
> and the battle bow shall be cut off,
>   and he shall speak peace to the nations;

> his rule shall be from sea to sea,
>> and from the River to the ends of the earth.

Zechariah tells us the king would come riding on a donkey. In other words, he would not need horses; he would not need military power in order to establish himself as king. The true king is so unquestionably worthy of his position, he would take his throne in deep humility and without any need for force. That's the kind of king Deuteronomy 17 envisioned, and that's the kind of king Jesus is capable of being! His kingdom will extend across the whole earth! Zechariah is quoting from Psalm 72, a psalm written by King Solomon himself. His psalm concerns his own reign but also alludes to the glory of the future messianic reign.

Inaugural Displays of Kingship

When Jesus came to earth, he came as the rightful king of the universe, but this wasn't obvious to everybody. That's because although Jesus' kingdom has already been made a reality, we still don't see its consummation. During his presence here on earth he left sufficient clues as to his identity as king, and he demonstrated his rule over all. Yet Scripture teaches us that the future holds hope for a dominion that fulfills our deepest longings for a perfect king. Matthew 21 shows an example of one of the few times his real identity as king shone through more clearly:

> **Matthew 21:4–11**—This took place to fulfill what was spoken by the prophet, saying,
>> "Say to the daughter of Zion,
>> 'Behold, your king is coming to you,
>>> humble, and mounted on a donkey,
>>> on a colt, the foal of a beast of burden.'"
>
> The disciples went and did as Jesus had directed them. They brought the donkey and the colt and put on them their cloaks, and he sat on them. Most of the crowd spread their cloaks on the road, and others cut branches from the trees and spread them on the road. And the crowds that went before him and that followed him were shouting, "Hosanna to the Son of David! Blessed is he who comes in the name of the Lord! Hosanna in the highest!" And when he entered Jerusalem, the whole city was stirred up, saying, "Who is this?" And the crowds said, "This is the prophet Jesus, from Nazareth of Galilee."

Jesus' entrance into Jerusalem fulfilled Zechariah's prophecy of a king on a donkey. The people recognized he was the worthy king, the long-awaited Son of David. They even quoted from Psalm 118, another messianic psalm.

And Jesus, by his actions, was making a statement: "I am your king, the one Zechariah told you about." He did nothing to gain acceptance by force; the people recognized and proclaimed his identity by their own choice. In fact, he came in peace; unlike a king of war prepared for battle, he came on a donkey—humble and vulnerable. For now, Jesus is not building a military. Like Moses in Deuteronomy 17:16, he wants our focus elsewhere—that is, on God's provision for our protection, especially spiritual protection. In his second coming, he will indeed come with military force. Then we will see how God wins *all* our battles for us—both spiritual and physical. In verse 11, the people took things a step further. They said Jesus was not only king, but also prophet. I don't believe it's a stretch to say they meant he is *the* prophet, the one Moses had predicted. The crowd seems to have had a full understanding of who Jesus is, so complete that it is amazing to think that the religious leaders were even able to have him crucified just a few days later! The only reason they could was because of the fact that Jesus came with humility and vulnerability.

Understanding the Bible's presentation of Jesus as the Perfect King is key to capturing the full sense of many of its verses. See, for example, Matthew 28:18, a familiar text that jumps out in a different light when seen through a royal lens:

> **Matthew 28:18–20**—And Jesus came and said to them, "All authority in heaven and on earth has been given to me. Go therefore and make disciples of all nations, baptizing them in the name of the Father and of the Son and of the Holy Spirit, teaching them to observe all that I have commanded you. And behold, I am with you always, to the end of the age."

Jesus is here claiming to have all authority; he is claiming nothing short of being king of the universe! On that basis he sends his followers to extend the reality of his eternal reign. When we disciple others, we are teaching them to submit to their king. Through baptism Jesus' subjects make a statement to the world that they willingly choose to belong to the kingdom of the only true king who exists!

World leaders have been accused of not being very "presidential" at times. Jesus, however, is always fully expressing his royal character as it is most appropriate for each moment. Even at his lowest point, during his rejection and crucifixion as a criminal, the Bible is careful to show us that he was acting as a king.

> **John 19:2–5**—And the soldiers twisted together a crown of thorns and put it on his head and arrayed him in a purple robe. They came up to him, saying, "Hail, King of the Jews!" and struck him with their hands. Pilate went out again and said to them, "See, I am bringing him out to you that you may know that I find no guilt in him." So Jesus came out, wearing the crown of thorns and the purple robe. Pilate said to them, "Behold the man!"

The details John chose to record in this passage are what give us an indication of his theological message. By mentioning the crown, the robe, and the mocking praise of the soldiers, John revealed his desire that we see Jesus' royal character. The irony here is in the fact that not one of these three kingly indicators was intended seriously. The mocking sarcasm of the soldiers in words and actions were meant to emphasize his failure to measure up to the throne. Nonetheless, John was not afraid to record it for the world; in fact, he used it to teach us his theological lesson: what Satan intends as evil, God uses for good. Both God and Satan orchestrated the details of Jesus' passion, each with a different purpose. Satan was looking to not only mock Jesus' kingship, but also find a way to terminate it. In the same details, God's purpose was to show that Jesus was the true king and any effort to put an end to his rule was futile. In spite of the mockery and his ultimate death, the Lord turned Satan's purpose on its head and made Jesus' kingship even more obvious.

Jesus himself made patently clear his claim to preeminent kingship.

> **Luke 11:31**—The queen of the South will rise up at the judgment with the men of this generation and condemn them, for she came from the ends of the earth to hear the wisdom of Solomon, and behold, something greater than Solomon is here.

He recognized Solomon as the most glorious son of David to this point. At the apex of the glory of the kings of Israel, 1 Kings recounts for us the visit of the Queen of Sheba. She came to see if the reports she had heard were true. Because of Solomon's wisdom and prosperity, news of God's glory had begun to spread to the nations. In contrast, Jesus expressed his disappointment in his contemporaries from Israel who couldn't even recognize that the Christ was among them when it was obvious. The resulting condemnation is made even stronger by the fact that Jesus is an infinitely greater king than Solomon.

The context of Luke 11:31 is also noteworthy. This verse is sandwiched between two verses about Jonah. Similarly to his statement about Solomon, Jesus stated that "something greater than Jonah is here." This time, instead of focusing on the office of king, Jesus compared himself to one of the greatest prophets. Just like Solomon, Jonah was instrumental in reaching a foreign nation with the truth of the greatness of the God of Israel. And now Jesus as the greatest prophet-king was offering himself to Israel and to the world. Unfortunately for Israel, even Nineveh was more perceptive; while they repented, many of Jesus' contemporaries did not.

Proclaiming the Kingdom

I want us to notice two psalms that proclaim Christ's kingdom in the face of opposition. Look first at this beautiful messianic psalm:

Psalm 2:1–6
Why do the nations rage
    and the peoples plot in vain?
The kings of the earth set themselves,
    and the rulers take counsel together,
        against the LORD and against his Anointed, saying, .
"Let us burst their bonds apart
    and cast away their cords from us."
He who sits in the heavens laughs;
    the Lord holds them in derision.
Then he will speak to them in his wrath,
    and terrify them in his fury, saying,
"As for me, I have set my King
    on Zion, my holy hill."

Psalm 2 glorifies Jesus for his kingly office. All the powerful kings of the earth scoff at God's anointed. Even though he seems at first to be the lowliest of all leaders, in the end he gains full preeminence. The Father establishes his Christ as king in spite of the contempt of humanity. Only those who join his kingdom will find themselves on the winning side.

One of the biggest themes in the book of Psalms is kingship. It's not by accident that the largest chunk of Psalms were written by King David. Let's look at just one more and see how it is picked up by Peter in the book of Acts. Psalm 16 is a psalm of David in which he speaks of God's protection for him in a special way as the king.

Psalm 16:8–11
I have set the LORD always before me;
    because he is at my right hand, I shall not be shaken.
Therefore my heart is glad, and my whole being rejoices;
    my flesh also dwells secure.

> For you will not abandon my soul to Sheol,
> > or let your holy one see corruption.
> You make known to me the path of life;
> > in your presence there is fullness of joy;
> > at your right hand are pleasures forevermore.

These words of David, although he wrote them about himself, can also be applied to all of us in some sense. Like David, we can have confidence that God is looking out for our best interest because he loves us. Verse 10 is especially significant in its promise for the future. David had confidence that his Lord had secured eternal life for him. That's what God does for his children: even after one's body turns to dust, the spirit continues to live in God's presence without abandonment or corruption. The path of life on which God has set us results in eternal pleasures at his right hand.

Now let's look at what Peter said about this psalm in Acts 2. On the day of Pentecost, Peter gave a great sermon about Jesus which marked the beginning of the church. He quoted and expounded Psalm 16. Read his sermon in Acts 2:22–41. Peter did not deny that Psalm 16 had an application for David, but he showed that it is more fully applicable to Jesus. Regarding Psalm 16:10 and the corruption of the body, David's body is currently in the grave, but Jesus' is not. David was given a promise that his son would rule as king—and would be a much greater king than David himself. One of the characteristics of Jesus' rule is that it is eternal, a promise that is possible only if the Son of David somehow defeats death. Jesus' resurrection, therefore, is part of his royal ascension to the throne. It enables him to rule forever and is also the basis of all spiritual blessings for the rest of God's children. In verse 23 Peter makes it clear that his listeners are guilty of rejecting and killing the king, but that is not the end of the story. Verse 36 glorifies God for his ultimate victory:

> **Acts 2:36**—Let all the house of Israel therefore know for certain that God has made him both Lord and Christ, this Jesus whom you crucified."

You and I are also guilty of rejecting the king. Praise the Lord that he is great enough to overcome our evil stupidity! Our response needs to be the same as what Peter enjoined from his listeners:

> **Acts 2:38**—And Peter said to them, "Repent and be baptized every one of you in the name of Jesus Christ for the forgiveness of your sins, and you will receive the gift of the Holy Spirit.

We need to make ourselves increasingly subject to the rule of this king. My submission needs to grow at the same rate that my understanding of his worthiness increases. Not only is he worthy, but his reign is also good for me. The greater my level of submission, the better equipped I will be to face whatever he allows in my life.

Consummated Reign

Jesus Christ is our king and we do well if we realize the implications of that fact for the here and now, but even more significant is our hope for the future because of who our king is. Revelation 17 shows us how he will defeat all the forces of evil.

> **Revelation 17:14**—"They will make war on the Lamb, and the Lamb will conquer them, for he is Lord of lords and King of kings, and those with him are called and chosen and faithful."

Even the most powerful and malevolent of all of God's enemies will not stand a chance against the Lamb. Christ is presented here as a Lamb because it was his sacrificial death that earned him the right to claim his position as king over everything. A lamb is a picture of weakness, but the power of God's weakness far exceeds the strength of the strongest second best. If we are on the right side, we can have every confidence that we will triumph in the end. It's not because of what we do, but because our king is so strong, that he can come as a lamb and still defeat the enemy easily. It's as if God wants to show us he is capable of winning the victory with just his little pinkie finger.

Although our king often likes to display his power in the context of weakness, a day is coming when he will fully defeat his enemies with nothing held back. There will then be no doubt left in anyone's mind as to his surpassing and overwhelming dominance over his enemies. Loyal subject and enemy alike will see his kingly strength.

> **Revelation 19:11–16**—Then I saw heaven opened, and behold, a white horse! The one sitting on it is called Faithful and True, and in righteousness he judges and makes war. His eyes are like a flame of fire, and on his head are many diadems, and he has a name written that no one knows but himself. He is clothed in a robe dipped in blood, and the name by which he is called is The Word of God. And the armies of heaven, arrayed in fine linen, white and pure, were following him on white horses. From his mouth comes a sharp sword with which to strike down the nations, and he will rule them with a rod of iron. He will tread the winepress of the fury of the

> wrath of God the Almighty. On his robe and on his thigh he has a name
> written, King of kings and Lord of lords.

In this chapter our king is introduced with a horse. Do you realize how significant that is? Deuteronomy prohibited the king from having much to do
with horses because the victory in war was to be left up to God himself. But
Jesus actually *is* God; and at his second coming he will make that fact plain
to all. At Jesus' first coming he took his throne in humility and quietness, but
when he comes again, we will finally see him on a horse! That's another way
of saying he will arrive with all his guns blazing—nothing held back. He
won't be violating the spirit of Deuteronomy because as God he has every
right to gain the victory with full military strength at the time when he
deems it appropriate (Deuteronomy 31:3).

Notice the implements he will use, according to verse 15. From his
mouth comes a sharp sword. As the Word of God incarnate, he is most qualified to use God's written Word to defeat evil. (I'll write a chapter on the
Word in a future book.) We also find he will rule with a rod of iron. The
word *rod* points us way back to Genesis 49:10; 2 Samuel 7:14; and other passages promising that the Messiah would work to dominate his enemies and
comfort his people. (Look for a chapter on Rod in a future book too.)

Look at one of the best verses of Revelation, indeed of the whole Bible:

> **Revelation 11:15**—Then the seventh angel blew his trumpet, and there were
> loud voices in heaven, saying, "The kingdom of the world has become the
> kingdom of our Lord and of his Christ, and he shall reign forever and ever."

Is there something that frustrates you about this world? Everything we dis-
like, every imperfection, every sin, and the consequences of sin are all produced by the fact that this world is in rebellion against its king. The kingdom
of this world is currently in the hands of a foreign power, a ruler and an
ideology that are contrary to those for which it was designed. Our frustration with these conditions can lead us to despair if we aren't aware of our
hope. In the future the kingdom of the world will change its loyalty. This
kingdom already belongs to the Messiah; he bought it with his blood. A day
is coming when he will come to claim that for which he has already paid. I
look forward with tremendous hope to the day when we can see it done.
Nothing will ever make my heart more glad than to say, "Christ has become
king!" Once that happens we will never again face frustration, for "he shall
reign forever and ever!"

Our Response

We can already praise our king for his perfect reign, but in the future we will have a very concrete way to demonstrate our attitude toward him. God will make us rulers (compare to Joseph in chapter 7, "Discerning Good and Evil") by giving us crowns (see also a chapter in a future book on Crown).

> **Revelation 4:4**—Around the throne were twenty-four thrones, and seated on the thrones were twenty-four elders, clothed in white garments, with golden crowns on their heads.

The twenty-four elders in John's vision represent God's people from all of history. Amazingly, Jesus sees fit to makes us rulers alongside him. What we do with those crowns will display real decorum:

> **Revelation 4:10–11**—The twenty-four elders fall down before him who is seated on the throne and worship him who lives forever and ever. They cast their crowns before the throne, saying,
> "Worthy are you, our Lord and God,
>   to receive glory and honor and power,
> for you created all things,
>   and by your will they existed and were created."

We will have no other recourse but to recognize that the only real true king is Jesus Christ. As God he deserves nothing less than complete dominion over all creation. He makes us rulers by his side, but our focus will remain on the only one worthy of ruling; thus we will yield our crowns to him.

Many themes run through the storyline of the Bible, and one of the biggest is the message of our Perfect King. It's hard to read God's Word without noticing its passion for the King. Nonetheless, it seems altogether too easy to miss the royal message in some spots that are less than obvious or maybe too familiar to us. Let's make a renewed, concerted effort to notice throughout Scripture that Jesus Christ is presented as The True King. During our reading we need to be more aware of key words and concepts that convey a kingly message: *Christ, Messiah, anointed, Son of David, throne, scepter, kingdom,* and others. As we grow in our understanding of this message, we should also let the response of our hearts grow. Let's worship Jesus for being our King! Let your heart feel joy with the confidence that redemption history is moving forward to a completely realized reign of our king! In the meantime, these biblical truths should have an effect on our current allegiance. We need to realize that Christ legitimately deserves to reign as king in our lives right now. It's true that we can't make him the king of this world by

our own will; what we can do is make him our own personal king. We each
have individual control over how pervasive his sovereign rule becomes in
our lives. Also, we can show our allegiance to the king by maintaining our
hope in the reality of his promised future kingdom. Our hopeful, confident
hearts are a testimony to the level of our submission to our king. Like those
in the Old Testament who maintained hope in spite of long generations of
waiting for Jesus' first advent, we can wait tirelessly for his second coming
to establish his victorious kingdom.

In the history of humanity, some really magnificent kings have ruled on
this earth. I think it would be exciting to be in the kingdom of some of the
greatest. That's one of the reasons I enjoyed reading *The Lord of the Rings*—
imagining helping to establish one of the greatest kingdoms ever. Aragorn
is the man in this story who is the rightful heir to the kingdom of Middle
Earth, but Sauron is a wicked being who has blocked him from taking the
throne and is seeking to dominate Middle Earth with his evil. Sauron's entire
plan hinges on a ring and the power it gives him. The only hope to save
Middle Earth lies in the small, unlikely characters of Frodo and his fellow
hobbits. Despite seemingly insurmountable challenges, Frodo successfully
destroys the ring and even Sauron himself. My favorite part of the whole
story is close to the end, when Aragorn is crowned king in a glorious cere-
mony. Aragorn is a worthy king, and in the face of impossible circumstances
he is able to take what rightfully belongs to him. Reading it, I find my heart
rejoicing as if he were my king! As much as that story captures my imagination, another will prove to be even greater. Aragorn is only a feeble image
of the King of the universe. And the very best part of Jesus Christ and his
reign is that they are real, and I will experience his coronation firsthand.
Instead of just reading about it, I will live it!

Passages for further study:

Isaiah 9:7   Luke 22:30
Jeremiah 23:5   Luke 23:42
Jeremiah 30:21–22   John 1:49
Jeremiah 36:30–31   John 18:36–37
Daniel 7:14   1 Corinthians 15:25
Daniel 9:25–26   Philippians 2:10
Matthew 2:2   Hebrews 1:8
Matthew 16:28
Matthew 25:34

6
Dueling Serpents

In *Little House on the Prairie*, Laura Ingalls Wilder describes how her Pa and Ma saved their house from the threat of an approaching prairie fire. First they dug a furrow between the fire and the house. Then they set a small fire between the furrow and danger. This small, controlled backfire burned all the fuel on a strip of land, so when the prairie fire arrived there was nothing left to lead it toward the house. The wind blew the fire past, flanking the house on all sides.

> "I couldn't plow but one furrow; there isn't time," Pa said. "Hurry, Caroline. That fire's coming faster than a horse can run...."
>
> Pa was going along the furrow, setting fire to the grass on the other side of it. Ma followed with a wet sack, beating at the flames that tried to cross the furrow. The whole prairie was hopping with rabbits....
>
> Pa's little fire had made a burned black strip. The little fire went backing slowly away against the wind, it went slowly crawling to meet the racing furious big fire. And suddenly the big fire swallowed the little one.
>
> The wind rose to a high, crackling, rushing shriek, flames climbed into the crackling air. Fire was all around the house.
>
> Then it was over. The fire went roaring past and away.
>
> Pa and Ma were beating out little fires here and there in the yard. When they were all out, Ma came to the house to wash her hands and face. She was all streaked with smoke and sweat, and she was trembling.
>
> She said there was nothing to worry about. "The back-fire saved us," she said, "and all's well that ends well."[1]

Maybe you've heard of fighting fire with fire. Maybe you've even used the expression. In the early history of the United States, when settlers began to build homes in the prairie states, it wasn't long before they realized the potential of a grass fire to destroy everything they owned. If lightning struck the dry grass, it would sometimes start a fire that could wipe out everything in its path for miles. Somewhere someone (probably well before the history of the United States) conceived a brilliant idea—to burn an area of grass with a purposeful fire before a senseless, uncontrolled fire could do any damage.

---

[1] Laura Ingalls Wilder and Garth Williams. *Little House On The Prairie* (New York, NY: Harper & Bros., 1971), 277-282.

Although fighting fire with fire sounds like a foolish—potentially even ineffective—method of protection, it is surprisingly powerful against the destructive forces of flames that otherwise leave no hope of escape. The Bible also describes an ironically effective method that God uses to protect us from the destructive forces of sin. An analysis of salvation history shows us that God sometimes chooses to fight serpents with a serpent. As in the case of a prairie fire, the very nature of the tool used for protection is apparently just as evil as that which is being fought.

Another Serpent

For any serious student of the Bible, it's no news that Satan is described as a serpent; his very first appearance is as a snake in the Garden of Eden. What likely comes as a shock is the fact that Jesus Christ is also described in a few places as a serpent. God's Son comes to earth as a figurative snake, ready to meet the devil "on his own terms" and defeat him at his own game. The reason this is difficult to accept is that Jesus is the only sinless man who ever lived and because the serpent is a symbol for evil, we don't readily see Jesus in that sense. Perhaps it will help, however, if we remember that at the moment of the cross Jesus carried the sins of the world:

> **1 Peter 2:24**—He himself bore our sins in his body on the tree, that we might die to sin and live to righteousness. By his wounds you have been healed.

In that moment, Jesus was guilty for all my sins, all your sins, and all sins ever committed throughout human history—judicially, he was more evil than any single human ever. (See also 2 Corinthians 5:12.) So just as the flame of preservation is almost as scary as the destructive fire, God's serpent of preservation was, in one sense, just about as evil as the serpent he came to defeat.

The image that comes to my mind is that of a duel in the Old West. Western movies are often complicated; it's sometimes hard to say who the good guy is and who the bad guy is. We often see a character with mixed qualities who comes to save the day. More often than not, he faces off against the troublemaker in a gun battle. The movie camera focuses on the men's eyes and focuses on their hands, and tension builds while we wait to see who will draw his gun first. In the end, the victor is not necessarily the first to draw; rather, it depends most on wit and lightning reflexes.

Jesus is presented in the Bible as the character who comes to save the day. Although there are moments when we are left with a certain tension as

to whether or not he is really a good guy, by the end there is no doubt what-
soever that he is perfectly good and perfectly capable of beating the bad guy
at his own game.

If you're like me, you're surprised that I could write some of what you
just read: that Jesus is represented by a symbol for evil; that judicially, Jesus
is as evil as Satan himself; and that the Bible has verses which leave literary
tension over his moral goodness. Actually, I would expect you to react that
way. So before delaying further, let's look at the text and see if it indeed
teaches that Jesus is like a serpent who came to defeat Satan at his own game.

The Original Serpent

First we need to observe the account of the appearance of the original serpent. Let's look briefly at Genesis 3, where Adam and Eve fell in the Garden
of Eden. The text of verse 1 introduces the story by telling us the serpent was
the craftiest of all the creatures God had made. Before getting much farther
in the story, this analysis is proven by the words of the serpent. He shows
his character by twisting God's words in order to accomplish his own evil
purposes. Through clues in this passage and the context of all Scripture, we
know he is really Lucifer, a fallen angel who is appearing in the garden as a
serpent. (See Chapter 1, "A Seed of Hope.") The text is not clear as to
whether he only has the appearance of a serpent or is actually embodying a
material snake. Nevertheless, the symbolic significance of his appearance is
established from the beginning.

The punishment meted out to the serpent in verse 14 of this chapter
finds its basis in his physical form:

Genesis 3:14
The LORD God said to the serpent,
"Because you have done this,
cursed are you above all livestock
and above all beasts of the field;
on your belly you shall go,
and dust you shall eat
all the days of your life."

The first question that naturally comes to mind is regarding the method of
travel the serpent had used up to this point. Many have said it might have
had legs on which to walk until God cursed the serpent. Of course, it is possible that the serpent had always crawled on its belly, but for the first time
its mode of travel had theological significance in connection to the curse.
The only remaining option is that it had previously flown—a suggestion

that is on the one hand less likely, but not impossible, considering the fact that the snake is a representation of Lucifer, an angel who potentially had wings. The possibility is slightly augmented by two passages we will examine below (Isaiah 14:29 and Revelation 12:3, 14). Nevertheless, statements about his previous state are only conjecture; what we can say for sure is that his curse included the fact that he would now be crawling on his belly and eating dust. That is an important fact to which we will return later.

Did you notice that the Lord told the serpent he was cursed above all other animals? This leads us to believe that, of all animals in the Bible, snakes are most representative of evil. In our own lives, I fully believe snakes are morally neutral. I have a friend who collects and studies snakes, and I don't have any problem with him pursuing that activity. Although I'm not very excited about joining him, it's only because I have a lack of interest and a kind of disgust for snakes. It's not because I think there is anything generally evil about the snakes that exist in our world today. Nevertheless, as we read God's Word, we ought to understand that anytime a serpent is mentioned, there are pretty likely some symbolic evil undertones. Each of the authors after Moses knew the way he had introduced the history of the world with the story of a snake, and if they mention one themselves, the original serpent and his evil characteristics have to be at the back of their minds.

A Serpentine Staff

This assumption of snakes' evil symbolism leads me to interpret two passages later in the Pentateuch in a slightly different way than I might otherwise. First let's look at the first few verses in Exodus chapter 4. These verses are part of the passage in which God appeared to Moses at the burning bush. Moses was concerned that he would be unable to fulfill God's call to lead his people out of Egypt; he was worried that the people would not believe. In response, God gave him two miraculous signs to help the people exercise faith. Let's look at the first of these—turning his staff into a serpent.

The very nature of the animal God chose for this miracle is what best conveys the lesson he wanted to teach through it. Have you ever wondered why God chose for Moses' staff to turn into a *snake*? There's got to be more to it than the fact that the staff was already similar in shape to that of a snake. God just as easily could have had the staff turn into a cute little kitty-cat which then purred and rubbed against Moses' feet. That certainly would have been enough to inspire faith in the miracles God could do. But inspiring faith in the miraculous was not the full extent of God's purpose here. He

wanted Israel to believe that Moses, through God's help, was able to dominate their enemies. The serpent, as a symbol of the worst evil imaginable,
was the perfect animal for Moses to conquer in the sight of any who might
doubt him.

Look at how the miracle unfolded. Moses threw his staff on the ground,
and after it turned into a snake, he ran from it. Moses had no confidence in
his own ability to prevail over the power of the serpent. Nevertheless, God
next told him to grab it by the tail! There are a lot of different opinions about
the safest methods for grabbing a snake; sometimes they vary based on the
kind of snake one is dealing with. Some people prefer the head and some
people prefer the tail, but no one will ever say that grabbing the tail guaran-
tees safety. God wanted to show Moses that he intended to dominate the
snake through Moses; he wanted to show that he was able and willing to
defeat evil for his people. His plan was to defeat Pharaoh and the Egyptians,
and ultimately he intended for this experience to show his power to defini-
tively defeat Satan himself for us.

The Bronze Serpent

These ideas are developed further as we move on to the next important passage regarding serpents.

> **Numbers 21:4–9**—From Mount Hor they set out by the way to the Red Sea,
> to go around the land of Edom. And the people became impatient on the
> way. And the people spoke against God and against Moses, "Why have you
> brought us up out of Egypt to die in the wilderness? For there is no food
> and no water, and we loathe this worthless food." Then the LORD sent fiery
> serpents among the people, and they bit the people, so that many people of
> Israel died. And the people came to Moses and said, "We have sinned, for
> we have spoken against the LORD and against you. Pray to the LORD, that
> he take away the serpents from us." So Moses prayed for the people. And
> the LORD said to Moses, "Make a fiery serpent and set it on a pole, and eve-
> ryone who is bitten, when he sees it, shall live." So Moses made a bronze
> serpent and set it on a pole. And if a serpent bit anyone, he would look at
> the bronze serpent and live.

Here we see that serpents can carry both a negative and a positive connotation. First we see the terrible snakes that came as a result of the people's sin.
Because they complained against God and against Moses, God punished his
people by sending awful snakes whose bite resulted in death.

Now, there is some controversy here about exactly what the Hebrew
text means when it describes these snakes. The ESV translates this phrase as

"fiery serpents," but the word used for "fiery" is the Hebrew word *seraphim*. The New American Bible opted for a more literal translation:

> **Numbers 21:6**—In punishment the LORD sent among the people saraph serpents, which bit the people so that many of them died (NAB).

"Seraph" is used very little in the Bible—only in the Pentateuch and the book of Isaiah. Most of its four uses in Isaiah clearly refer to angels (a special kind called seraphim, as opposed to cherubim; we'll analyze the one exception below); the three occurrences in the Pentateuch all relate to the snakes of Numbers 21 (two occurrences in this passage and one in Deuteronomy 8:15). The Hebrew word is derived from the word for "burn," thus the ESV's translation as "fiery." As we consider the meaning of this word, we must conclude one of the three following options. Either the seraphim have an appearance similar in some way to snakes,[2] the snakes described in Numbers 21 are in some way like angels,[3] or both the snakes and the angels are in some way like fire.[4] The latter is the most common assumption and usually

---

[2] This is the conclusion offered by BDB, one of the most used Hebrew lexicons (BDB is the abbreviation of its authors' last names): "...beings orig. mythically conceived with serpents' bodies." Brown, *Enhanced Brown-Driver-Briggs Hebrew and English Lexicon*, 977.

[3] "When most people think of Seraphim, they think of angels, but earliest usages of the term refer to serpent demons. The concept of the serpent as a demon was well known to the Egyptians, Babylonians and Assyrians." Deliriumsrealm.com, 'Seraphim: Fiery Serpent Demons.' N.p., 2015. Web. Accessed 7 December 2014. http://www.deliriumsrealm.com/seraphim/

[4] Word Biblical Commentary takes this position with the following statement: "It is often supposed that there is a reference here to the venomous bite of the snakes, and the burning inflammation produced (cf. e.g. G. B. Gray, 277-78; A. H. McNeile, 112; L. E. Binns, 138; N. H. Snaith, 280-81; J. Sturdy, 148). It is arguable that שרפים "fiery" is strictly a description of the creatures themselves, rather than of their bite (G. W. Coats, Rebellion, 117 n.51)." Phillip J. Budd. *Numbers*, Word Biblical Commentary (Dallas, TX: Word, Incorporated, 1998), 234.

Similarly, HALOT (The Hebrew and Aramaic Lexicon of the Old Testament), one of the most renowned lexicons for Biblical Hebrew, states that this word "signifies the colour or burning pain of a bite: glowing, burning, or the glowing one, the burning one....", Ludwig Koehler, Walter Baumgartner, et al. *The Hebrew and Aramaic Lexicon of the Old Testament* (Leiden, Netherlands: Brill, 1994–2000), 1360.

the only debate is about whether fire describes the appearance of the serpents or their bite.[5]

Regardless of the meaning of the word "seraph," the fact that the author chose it for this passage leads us to make a connection to an earlier passage in the Pentateuch. I think it's likely that the snakes were described as "fiery" in order to reflect either their appearance or their bite. Nevertheless, it's probably not an accident that this word can also be used for angels. After all, Genesis 3 describes a fallen angel who appears as a serpent. Whether the Israelites were being attacked by demons or literal snakes, we are intended to conclude that there is a connection between the original serpent in Eden and the fiery serpents of Numbers 21. Therefore, the outcome of the conflict in Numbers 21 will reflect in some way the curse which was given to the original serpent.

A careful look at the text shows us that God did not solve the issue of the serpents in the way the people would have chosen. In verse 7 the people requested that the Lord take the serpents away. Their request sounds like the logical thing to do, but God had different plans. Instead of removing the source of their trouble, he took away the power of the snakes' bite by providing an antidote. This is God's pattern of work throughout the ages. In our case, he operates in a similar way. Instead of removing Satan from this world, he gives us victory over him through Jesus Christ. God could have done away with Satan in the Garden of Eden immediately after the first sin. Instead, he promises to provide a means to defeat him over time. And ultimately he will completely remove Satan from the picture.

The antidote the Lord gave against the fiery serpents was a bronze serpent set upon a pole. Again the New American Bible gives a literal translation of verse 8. It's interesting to note that God's command doesn't even mention the phrase "bronze serpent":

---

[5] It's also interesting to consider the possibility of this passage giving a description of dragons, of which BDB also hints. Dragons are usually taken as mythical beings, but it's possible that they were a type of dinosaur that somehow actually breathed fire. Isaiah 14:29 and 30:6 mention the "flying fiery serpents." Thus we potentially have a description of reptiles who fly and breathe fire. These verses also connect with the concept found in Revelation of the ancient serpent who appears once again as a dragon (12:9). The woman of Revelation 12:14 escapes from this dragon by flying away with borrowed wings.

Numbers 21:8—And the LORD said to Moses, "Make a saraph and mount it on a pole, and if anyone who has been bitten looks at it, he will recover" (NAB).

The author cites the Lord as simply commanding Moses to make a seraph. Other translations have added the word "serpent," making it "fiery serpent," an interpretation that is likely correct though not explicit in the text of this verse. The context (especially verse 9) makes it clear that making a bronze serpent was God's intention for Moses, because after Moses did so, God honored Moses' actions by healing the wounded. I believe God probably told Moses to make a bronze serpent but the command was so shocking that Moses couldn't bring himself to write it exactly that way. He "censored" God's command, so to speak, because he wanted to avoid recording any statement from God that appeared to contradict the commandment in Exodus regarding graven images. Therefore, as it is written God technically did not command Moses to make a graven image. Rather, Moses writes it in a way that lays the responsibility on himself.[6] It's as if he is willing to take the fall for God's command. In 2 Kings 18:4 we learn that the bronze serpent was later given the name Nehushtan and became an object of worship. If Moses was the author of the text in Numbers, he was willing to take the flak for his actions in order to avoid any semblance of evil on the part of God. Although he knew God could not have commanded something that was wrong, he wanted to avoid the controversy. The shocking nature of God's command was augmented by the fact that he wanted a snake. Not only did God require a graven image, but it was an image of the worst creature imaginable.

This text is where we first recognize that when it comes to serpents, God is fighting fire with fire. In light of the symbolism behind serpents, it's really surprising to the reader of Numbers that God would choose to defeat the serpents with an image of a serpent. He just as easily could have asked Moses to make an image of a flower, the Ark of the Covenant, or anything else that displays beauty and goodness. Clearly, however, the idea in this text is that the people had to exercise faith by looking upon something very evil in order to be saved from that which was even more evil.

---

[6] Sailhamer, *The Pentateuch as Narrative*, 403.

A Type of Christ

The New Testament tells us Jesus is like the bronze serpent. We are all very familiar with John 3:16, but many people aren't aware of the context provided by the verses that immediately precede it. Read John 3:14–16 and see if you are at all surprised by what you find.

> **John 3:14–16**—And as Moses lifted up the serpent in the wilderness, so must the Son of Man be lifted up, that whoever believes in him may have eternal life. "For God so loved the world, that he gave his only Son, that whoever believes in him should not perish but have eternal life."

John tells us that "as Moses lifted up the serpent in the wilderness, so must the Son of Man be lifted up." Both the serpent and Jesus were hung on wood. Both the serpent and Jesus are objects of faith for those who are dying. In one case, the faith results in physical life; in the other it results in spiritual and eternal life as well. In both cases, exercising faith is required. I wonder if in Moses' day there were people who refused to look. I can imagine someone getting bitten by a snake. His friend tells him not to worry. He says, "If you just look behind you at that bronze snake, you are guaranteed to be healed; God has promised it." But maybe he scorns the idea and refuses to make the small effort required to look at the serpent. Before long he wastes away and dies, just a small distance away from the object that could have saved his life if only he would have believed. That would be a really sad and even incomprehensible conclusion for such a person. But the same is true for those who reject Jesus and fail to exercise the small faith it takes to be saved by him from their sin.

There is one more similarity between the bronze serpent and Jesus Christ. Both were made surprisingly similar to the evil they were intended to destroy. We have already discussed how ironic it is that the life-giving serpent was an image of the serpents who were killing the Israelites. Could it be that Jesus also shares a surprising degree of evil in his character? Yes, he does. I would never want to characterize Jesus as evil, but in two ways he does come really close. First, he was made flesh, that is, he became a human like us. Although it is true that he was the only sinless human, it's really quite shocking to consider that God could and would choose to share our human nature—one that is in all other cases characterized by sin. It should never cease to amaze us that God became one of us! And in this sense Jesus shares a similarity with the bronze serpent. Fred Hartley Wight noticed the irony behind this:

The serpent on the pole that brought deliverance was made in the likeness of those serpents that bit the Israelites. Even so: "God sending his own Son in the likeness of sinful flesh, and for sin, condemned sin in the flesh" (Rom. 8:3).[7]

The second way Jesus was made surprisingly similar to evil is even more clear. According to 2 Corinthians 5:21, something really significant happened while he was on the cross:

> **2 Corinthians 5:21**—For our sake he made him to be sin who knew no sin, so that in him we might become the righteousness of God.

Don't pass lightly over this verse and its amazing statement. Jesus did not even know sin; he previously had nothing to do with it. But the Father not only introduced Jesus to what sin was, he made him to *be* sin. There is no more emphatic way to say that Jesus became evil, all so we could become righteousness. Of course, it was only in a judicial sense that Jesus was made evil. While he was dying on the cross he was guilty of my sins and guilty of your sins. He was guilty of the combined sins of the whole world. So he was, in fact, at that moment more evil than any single person who has ever lived. It was for that reason that he died; he was punished by God with the punishment he did not actually deserve, but did deserve judicially. This is why Jesus is compared to a serpent, the most cursed of all animals. Jesus "became a serpent" so he could meet the serpent on his own terms and gain the ultimate victory for his people, who were formerly under the serpent's power!

Remember Who Defeats the Serpent

Our perspective changes when we are conscious of who has defeated the serpent. If we start to think we do it in our own power, we are sure to lose focus. Moses challenged the Israelites with this very truth. When they arrived at the edge of the Promised Land and looked back at their experiences in the wilderness, one of their key memories was the experience of Numbers 21. Their reflection, in Deuteronomy 8, on the incident of the snakes has some lessons for us as we look back on Jesus' saving work in our lives.

> **Deuteronomy 8:11–17**—"Take care lest you forget the LORD your God by not keeping his commandments and his rules and his statutes, which I command you today, lest, when you have eaten and are full and have built good houses and live in them, and when your herds and flocks multiply and your

---

[7] Fred Hartley Wight, *Devotional Studies of Old Testament Types* (Chicago, IL: Moody Press, 1956), 128.

silver and gold is multiplied and all that you have is multiplied, then your heart be lifted up, and you forget the LORD your God, who brought you out of the land of Egypt, out of the house of slavery, who led you through the great and terrifying wilderness, with its fiery serpents and scorpions and thirsty ground where there was no water, who brought you water out of the flinty rock, who fed you in the wilderness with manna that your fathers did not know, that he might humble you and test you, to do you good in the end. Beware lest you say in your heart, 'My power and the might of my hand have gotten me this wealth.'"

In verse 11 Moses warned the people about the possibility of forgetting the Lord their God. He recounted the great things God had done for them, which included, in verse 15, leading them through a place occupied with "fiery serpents"—a clear reference to Numbers 21. Moses warned them about the danger of beginning to feel complacent and self-congratulatory. The most threatening error the people could make was to forget that their blessings had come from God. In a similar way, the biggest mistake you and I can now make is to think we have saved ourselves from the obstacles that were keeping us from enjoying him and the salvation he offers. If they forgot, the Israelites were likely to fail to keep the law, according to verse 11.

On the other hand, forgetting Jehovah's work in our favor to save us from the ancient serpent can result in two extremes. We might be tempted to think our ongoing salvation depends on our current performance. In that case, we are likely to try to gain our salvation through good works and thus, ironically, never truly receive it. The other extreme is that we too might forget that we owe our very lives to our Savior. Because of gratitude for our new lives, we ought to be living ever-increasingly righteous lives. So as Moses warned so long ago, we need to beware of forgetting that God deserves wholehearted obedience to him in exchange for having redeemed us from the serpent's claim on our lives.

We can see similar reasoning from Paul in 2 Corinthians 11:1–4. He teaches us that it is important to keep our focus on Christ, who has won the victory for us.

2 Corinthians 11:1–4—I wish you would bear with me in a little foolishness. Do bear with me! For I feel a divine jealousy for you, since I betrothed you to one husband, to present you as a pure virgin to Christ. But I am afraid that as the serpent deceived Eve by his cunning, your thoughts will be led astray from a sincere and pure devotion to Christ. For if someone comes and proclaims another Jesus than the one we proclaimed, or if you receive

a different spirit from the one you received, or if you accept a different gospel from the one you accepted, you put up with it readily enough.

In these verses we are taught that we owe our loyalty to Christ as a result of what he has done for us. Just as Eve was led away from loyalty to God, we have the potential to be led away from a sincere and pure devotion to our Lord Jesus Christ. The assumption in these verses is that the very same serpent could lead us away if we allow him to. Paul's biggest concern here is that we might accept a different gospel; if we adopt false teaching, we are going the way of Eve in the presence of the serpent.

Victory in the Christian life is pictured very graphically in terms of serpents.

> **Luke 10:17–20** — The seventy-two returned with joy, saying, "Lord, even the demons are subject to us in your name!" And he said to them, "I saw Satan fall like lightning from heaven. Behold, I have given you authority to tread on serpents and scorpions, and over all the power of the enemy, and nothing shall hurt you. Nevertheless, do not rejoice in this, that the spirits are subject to you, but rejoice that your names are written in heaven."

The seventy-two disciples returned to Jesus with joy, for they realized they had power over even the demons. Jesus put their joy into perspective on a couple of levels. First, he reminded them he saw Satan fall like lightning from heaven. With that kind of power over the ancient serpent, he had authority to give the same power to his disciples. In verse 19, he even said they were able to "tread on serpents." This phrase should remind us of the curse in Genesis 3 and the promise that someone would crush the head of the serpent. Only Jesus is fully capable of this kind of victory, but his followers are able, in little ways, to do the same with Jesus' help. Amazingly, you and I can share daily in little victories that ultimately build toward the final victory our redeemer will have over Satan! Nevertheless, the other piece of perspective he gives in verse 20 is that our daily victories over Satan are small compared to the victory of salvation that Christ already won for us. We need to be sure to value that which is of most lasting value; if we get distracted by external manifestations over the powers of evil, we will be missing the point of the whole thing—which was removing the eternal suffering the bite of the serpent can inflict.

The Ultimate Defeat of the Serpent

Until now we have studied what the Bible teaches about how God takes away the power of Satan to kill us with his bite. Instead of removing the serpent, he chose to give us an antidote. Because of Jesus' first coming, the serpent's bite no longer has power over us. But God's victory doesn't end there. His Word also teaches us that he will ultimately defeat the serpent himself! When that happens the victory will be even more complete than the victory achieved through the antidote.

An interesting verse in Job refers to the defeat of Satan. Job 26:5–14 is full of terms that look back to creation. Look especially at verse 13:

Job 26:13
By his wind the heavens were made fair;
      his hand pierced the fleeing serpent.

The word that is here translated "wind" has a broad meaning; it can mean "wind," "breath," or "spirit." Think back to Genesis 1:2; this is the very same word used to say that the "the Spirit of God was hovering over the face of the waters." Just a few verses later in Genesis, God created an expanse which he called heaven. The New Living Translation makes the connection clearer when it translates Job 26:13a, "His Spirit made the heavens beautiful." Thus, the first part of this verse is clearly referring to creation.

The amazing part of verse 13 is found in the second half. He says here that "his hand pierced the fleeing serpent." In a series of verses referring to creation, the author has included a clause about something else that occurred at approximately the same time. He is apparently referring to the appearance of the serpent in Genesis 3 soon after creation is recounted. The glorious part of this clause is that its perspective on Genesis 3 focuses on Yahweh's victory! In spite of the apparent victory of the serpent in introducing sin and defiling God's perfect creation, the focus is on the Lord's punishment of the serpent. The proclamation of his curse in Genesis 3:14–15 is presented here in Job as a completed fact, through the use of two words: "pierced" and "fleeing." The serpent knew from the beginning that he had been defeated, and the only option he had was to flee. The Hebrew word for "pierced" is not all that common in Scripture, but it's interesting to note that one of the other occurrences is in Isaiah 53:5, where we are told that our Savior would be pierced for our transgressions. Just as Genesis 3:15 refers to reciprocal wounds for the serpent and the seed of the woman, Job and Isaiah describe their corresponding wounds with the same word. The two serpents, Jesus and Satan, ultimately pierce each other, but the effect on each of them is drastically different because Jesus' power is infinitely greater! Furthermore, even though we have been waiting for all of human history for Satan's defeat, Job describes it as a done deal from the beginning!

A Latent Victory

Besides Numbers 21 and John 3:14, at least one more verse uses the term *serpent* in a positive sense; that is, in reference to Christ. In Isaiah 14:29 the serpent is clearly a representation of Jesus Christ.

Isaiah 14:29
Rejoice not, O Philistia, all of you,
    that the rod that struck you is broken,
for from the serpent's root will come forth an adder,
    and its fruit will be a flying fiery serpent.

This verse is a warning to Philistia that it has no reason to rejoice. Philistia was an enemy of God's people and by extension, in this poetic verse represents all enemies of God's people, including Satan himself. Although the enemy might be tempted to rest easy due to the apparent downfall of God's servant, the final outcome is yet to be seen. This verse uses two very clearly messianic terms: *rod* and *root*. The rod is the object the anointed one uses to dominate his enemies. *Root* is a term which implies that the Messiah and his line survive against overwhelming odds, including death and extinction. (See especially Isaiah 11:1, and look for my chapters in a future book on both Rod and Root). So even though the rod is broken and the line is extinct, the root will produce a serpent—bad news for the original serpent. The word used for "fiery serpent" is *seraph*, taking us back to the snake of Numbers 21. But this heroic serpent won't be any ordinary snake—he can fly! There aren't many reptiles which have this ability. The one which most easily comes to our mind is a dragon. Whether Isaiah knew it to be an actual creature which has since fallen into extinction, or simply a mythical beast whose imagery he uses, his point is that no one, not even Satan himself, can survive its power. Jesus Christ will defeat Satan with all the power of a dragon. We will soon see that Satan seeks to emulate the strength of this creature, according to the text of Revelation.

Impending Doom

Let's look at more verses that focus on the future reality of Satan's judgment. The messianic rod shows up in the context of a serpent once again in Micah 7:14–17. This time the serpent is clearly a representation of God's enemies.

Micah 7:14–17
Shepherd your people with your shepherd's rod,
the flock that belongs to you,
the one that lives alone in a thicket,

in the midst of a pastureland.
Allow them to graze in Bashan and Gilead,
as they did in the old days.
"As in the days when you departed from the land of Egypt,
I will show you miraculous deeds."
Nations will see this and be disappointed by all their strength,
they will put their hands over their mouths,
and act as if they were deaf.
They will lick the dust like a snake,
like serpents crawling on the ground.
They will come trembling from their strongholds
to the LORD our God;
they will be terrified of you (NET).

The rod is mentioned in verse 14 as a tool of the shepherd for the good of his flock. Many translations have substituted "scepter" or "staff" because "rod" is not usually used with a positive connotation. Shepherds had two sticks: a staff which directly cared for the sheep and a rod which indirectly benefited them by striking the sheep's enemies.[8] *The New Manners and Customs of Bible Times* describes the two sticks this way:

> For weapons the shepherd used a heavy club and a sling. The club is referred to as a "rod" in Psalm 23:4, but it was a heavy weapon, and flints (later nails) were often embedded into its heavy "working end" to make it more effective.... The shepherd was also equipped with a staff, but it was not a weapon, although it was used as such on occasions. The staff was about six feet (two metres) long and sometimes had a crook at the end of it.[9]

Since the rod is mentioned in Micah 7, the emphasis in these verses is on protection from enemies. Verse 15 compares the shepherd's work to the plagues performed in Egypt. Just as the plagues protected Israel by crippling Egypt, so God's people are here benefited by his attack on the nations. The nations are compared to the serpent. Their punishment is that they must figuratively "lick the dust," partially fulfilling the curse given to the serpent in Genesis 3:14. This verse adds to the certainty we must feel concerning the execution of final judgment on the original serpent himself.

The ultimate fulfillment of the serpent's curse is reiterated in Isaiah 65:25.

---

[8] Luder G. Whitlock, R. C. Sproul, Bruce K. Waltke and Moisés Silva, *The Reformation Study Bible: Bringing the Light of the Reformation to Scripture: New King James Version* (Nashville, TN: T. Nelson, 1995), Ps 23:4.

[9] Ralph Gower and Fred Wight, *The New Manners and Customs of Bible Times* (Chicago, IL: Moody Press, 1987).

Isaiah 65:25
"The wolf and the lamb shall graze together;
the lion shall eat straw like the ox,
    and dust shall be the serpent's food.
They shall not hurt or destroy
    in all my holy mountain," says the LORD.

Even though this is a familiar verse, I was surprised to find a clause I had overlooked before. In the middle of some beautiful statements about the wolf and lamb grazing together, the lion eating straw like an ox, and the complete lack of evil or harm, there is a statement about the serpent. Dust will be the serpent's food! This is a direct promise that the curse of Genesis 3:14 will one day fully be a reality. This verse describes future poetic justice, and there can be no doubt that justice for the serpent will come even in the food he eats.

An awareness of this theme helps us understand Matthew 23:33 on a whole new level.

Matthew 23:33 — You serpents, you brood of vipers, how are you to escape being sentenced to hell?

When Jesus called the scribes and Pharisees serpents, he was claiming they were the seed of Satan himself! This confrontation during Jesus' earthly ministry went way beyond the human level; it was one more round in the epic battle between the two serpents who had been facing off for all of history. Since Jesus was so sure of his ultimate defeat of Satan and all other serpents who cooperate with him, he was able to confidently ask, "How are you to escape being sentenced to hell?" implying that his own victory was certain. The fact that the serpents he addressed would temporarily gain the upper hand by killing him serves only to give us more confidence; no matter how bad things may seem to get in the circumstances of this life, we can know that Jesus will come out victorious! Likewise, this passage serves as a warning for us. We must guard ourselves at all cost from hypocrisy and external religion, for they are what categorized these people as descendants of the enemy; and as Jesus says, there is no hope for such people to escape the sentence dealt by the conquering serpent.

Another verse dealing with future judgment for the serpent is Isaiah 27:1.

Isaiah 27:1 — In that day the LORD with his hard and great and strong sword will punish Leviathan the fleeing serpent, Leviathan the twisting serpent, and he will slay the dragon that is in the sea.

The opening phrase of this verse ("in that day") is a key phrase used to point to the eschatological fulfillment of God's grand plan for the world. This verse uses two terms that referred in Hebrew to big and powerful creatures: *Leviathan* and *monster*. The Septuagint translates "monster" from the Greek word that sounds like "dragon," and many of our English Bibles opt for "dragon" here. The point is, it doesn't matter that the being in question is very powerful and overwhelmingly terrifying for us; God is infinitely more powerful and easily able to defeat him fully and finally in the last days.

Revelation

Isaiah didn't know many details about the serpent's defeat, but we can understand it a little more clearly because of the way it's presented in the book of Revelation. Both Revelation 12 and 20 deal with Jesus' victory over the serpent. John seizes the imagery first presented in Isaiah by calling him "the dragon" in these two chapters. Chapter 12 is about the struggle between the woman and the serpent that began in Genesis 3. We looked at it in more detail in Chapter 1 when we studied the theme of the seed, but there are a couple of details we should notice in the context of our study on the serpent. In verse 5 we are told the woman gave birth to a male child "who is to rule all the nations with a rod of iron." This is a reference to Jesus Christ, and although he isn't very prominent in this passage, it's interesting to note that his presence in this verse is described with serpent-like qualities after the pattern of Isaiah 14:29 and Micah 7:14. That is, the serpent who wields a rod is the biggest threat to the dragon of old. Even though this child does not directly attack the dragon in this passage, the implication is that Satan's days are numbered.

Another interesting detail is found in Revelation 12:14.

> **Revelation 12:14**—But the woman was given the two wings of the great eagle so that she might fly from the serpent into the wilderness, to the place where she is to be nourished for a time, and times, and half a time.

The wings given to the woman symbolically describe God's supernatural deliverance on behalf of his people. John Walvoord has interpreted it well:

> The two wings probably do not refer to modern airplanes but rather to
> God's delivering power, and are a figure of speech taken from such Old
> Testament passages as Exodus 19:4 and Deuteronomy 32:11–12.[10]

Exodus 19:4 also mentions the wings of an eagle in the context of deliverance.

> **Exodus 19:4**—You yourselves have seen what I did to the Egyptians, and
> how I bore you on eagles' wings and brought you to myself.

So the wings mentioned here give us reason to believe God will intervene in
a way at least as miraculous as what he did in the exodus from Egypt. Up to
now in the passages we have been studying, it was the ancient serpent who
was doing the flying and the fleeing (Job 26:13; Isaiah 14:29; Isaiah 27:1), but
for the first time someone else is given the ability to fly and flee from the
dragon. This obviously doesn't bode well for Satan; it's a hint that his time
is nearly over.

The most noteworthy part of Revelation 12 is that humans are key play-
ers in defeating the devil.

> **Revelation 12:10–11**—And I heard a loud voice in heaven, saying, "Now
> the salvation and the power and the kingdom of our God and the authority
> of his Christ have come, for the accuser of our brothers has been thrown
> down, who accuses them day and night before our God. And they have
> conquered him by the blood of the Lamb and by the word of their testimony,
> for they loved not their lives even unto death."

Obviously his defeat must be accomplished through God's power; we are
told that in fact it is through the blood of the Lamb. Jesus Christ is both a
gentle lamb and a threatening serpent. In fact, in his willingness to be a lamb
is where his most dangerous qualities as serpent are found. Nevertheless,
part of the means to throw the dragon down to earth is through the sacrificial death of the martyrs. We know these are people who have died for their
faith because we are told, "They loved not their lives even unto death." In-
herent in the Greek word for "martyr" is the concept that the person who
died did so proclaiming his or her testimony. In this case, the very words
these martyrs express are what end up conquering the serpent. It's interesting to note that the serpent's original victory was won in the context of a
battle of words between him and Eve. Eve allowed the serpent to twist her

---

[10] John F. Walvoord, "Revelation," *The Bible Knowledge Commentary: An Exposition
of the Scriptures*, ed. J. F. Walvoord and R. B. Zuck (Wheaton, IL: Victor Books,
1985), Re 12:13-14, Volume 2, 959.

words into a condemning analysis of God's goodness, and Adam failed to step in and correct her mistake with a true testimony of what the Lord had said. Now the final victory will be won through the correctly spoken words of God's people. It's amazing to realize that God allows us to have a significant responsibility in his battle against Satan. He gives us the potential of speaking words of truth that defeat him. There are many ways we can speak the right truth at just the right moment in a way that rescues ourselves and others from dangerous domination by the serpent. We can distinguish between right and wrong, proclaim truth, expose lies, and declare victory in Christ. As we use words in these ways, we are sharing in the gradual and culminating defeat of the serpent of old.

Revelation 12 is not the final chapter in the story; it only shows the serpent that his time is short. The final victory is found in Revelation 20. This is his end and the last we hear of him in Scripture. I find it interesting that John doesn't mention much about Christ in these verses. I would expect there to be a huge battle between him and Satan, or at least a clear mention here of Jesus gaining the victory over him. Instead, the focus is generally on the evil one, and most of what happens to him is stated simply in the passive voice. Maybe part of the reason is that Satan was really defeated at the moment of the cross and this passage simply describes his sentence being carried out. Also, it's noteworthy that the one who captures and imprisons the dragon in verses 1 to 3 is an angel. Jesus, the victorious serpent, is so powerful that all he has to do is send a mere messenger to do the task for him. This underscores for us that Christ could have chosen to consummate his final defeat of Satan whenever he wanted. The fact that Satan is currently still free to act in this world is not because our God is unable to overcome him; rather, the time simply is not yet right.

The dragon is defeated in stages. First he is thrown into the abyss and held there for a thousand years. After that he is released for a short time; God allows him to operate in order to accomplish his own divine purpose— final judgment. After the serpent unsuccessfully attempts war on the saints, he is finally thrown into the lake of fire and brimstone.

It's great to already know the final outcome for the ancient serpent. Although he seems to have a lot of influence in this world, he is already as good as dead. The only reason Satan still has any influence at all is because some people choose to continue to be his offspring. In the case of believers, the only time he has power over the choices we make is when we give him that privilege. Knowing what will happen to him gives us confidence—we can be sure that the Lord wins his victory, and we can be aware that there is no need to give in to his temptations. Additionally, anyone who chooses to follow him is obviously making a foolish choice—such a person willingly chooses to be on the losing team.

Conclusion

The serpent is an ugly image of evil. A serpent's main objective is to destroy someone else. The ancient serpent of Genesis only has designs to attack God and his people. Surprisingly, God's Word uses the same image to represent Christ in verses like Numbers 21:8–9; John 3:14; 2 Corinthians 5:21; and Isaiah 14:29. Jesus becomes a serpent so he can adopt a serpent's objective; he wants to destroy the original serpent himself. Jesus Christ defeats the serpent at his own game.

> **Hebrews 2:14**—Since therefore the children share in flesh and blood, he himself likewise partook of the same things, that through death he might destroy the one who has the power of death, that is, the devil.

Satan introduced death into this world and attempts to use it to control God's creation and maintain it under his power. The Perfect Serpent willingly placed himself temporarily under the tyranny of death in order to permanently crush the original serpent with his own weapon.

We have seen a panoramic view of the duel between these two serpents. The duel lasts a long time—all of human history so far—but not because the evil serpent is any match for the righteous one. Just like the calm, cool, collected good guy in a western movie, our Savior is taking his time because that fits best with his plan. He wants to beat the serpent at his own game because that gives him the most glory. It's definitely not what we would expect, but the Righteous Serpent knows best.

Our serpent is also a healer, and medicine is often practiced in unexpected ways. Our spiritual healer sometimes surprises us, therefore, in the way he operates. Interestingly, one of the symbols that has been used in medicine for a very long time is an image of a snake. The Rod of Asclepius is the image

Figure 3: Rod of Asclepius

of a snake wound around a stick.[11] It was supposedly wielded by the Greek god, Asclepius, a deity associated with healing and medicine.

One theory behind the origin of this image is that it comes from the snake that Moses raised in the wilderness to heal the children of Israel. The next time you see this symbol, let it remind you of spiritual realities. Our Savior uses methods that, though surprising, are wondrously effective and point to his own glory. The longer we spend in eternity seeking to comprehend them, the more we will understand how perfect they are!

Passages for further study:

Genesis 49:17

Exodus 7:15

Psalm 58:4

Psalm 140:3

Proverbs 23:32

Proverbs 30:19

Ecclesiastes 10:8–11

Jeremiah 8:17

Jeremiah 46:22

Amos 5:19

Amos 9:3

Matthew 7:10

Matthew 10:16

Mark 16:18

Luke 11:11

1 Corinthians 10:9

Revelation 9:19

---

[11] https://commons.wikimedia.org/wiki/File%3ARod_of_Asclepius2.svg, Original: CatherinMunro, Derivative work: Hazmat2 (This file was derived from: Rod of asclepius.png) [CC BY-SA 3.0 (http://creativecommons.org/licenses/by-sa/3.0)], via Wikimedia Commons, accessed 11 February 2017.

7
Discerning Good and Evil

Children don't always recognize their dependence on their parents, and this is especially true of two-year-olds. I have done a lot of painting through the years, both on our own home and contracting for others. All four of our children have enjoyed helping me with painting at different times. They seemed to like it most between about ages two and six. They were old enough to think they were helping but not really old enough to be of any help from my perspective. That wasn't too bad as long as the work was on our own house. I learned to generally relax and tell myself that imperfections were worth the experience of working alongside my children. The few times when they came with me to paint for a customer, however, I couldn't as easily let just anything go. Sometimes I could convince them to work in a less-important corner with a really small brush, where they could do less damage.

Inevitably, the attraction of the roller would become strong enough that there was no getting away from allowing them to have a little experience with it as well. The roller was almost always accompanied by my condition that we handle it together. I remember many times allowing them to hold the roller in their little hands with my hand covering and guiding theirs. Without my supervision, it was way too likely that paint would get somewhere it wasn't supposed to be. A roller is a big responsibility for a little child.

On one occasion my son David remained content with a brush. He worked long and hard on one spot and walked away proud. Unfortunately, the paint was very uneven; brush marks were visible and some paint was even running. I mistakenly thought I could smooth it over with the roller without his notice. When he came back the next day, David was very upset that I had "messed up" his work!

My children simply didn't realize how much help they needed to do quality painting. Or if they did realize it, that didn't matter as much as the independence they wanted. They wanted to do the work all by themselves and they certainly didn't want their work corrected, no matter how it looked in the end.

Needless to say, painting with my kids taught me patience. I don't think I always realized how much I was like them at that very moment, not wanting guidance and correction in the way I dealt with my children, considering my opinions as of ultimate importance. In fact, we are all a lot like children when it comes to living life. We aren't fully aware of the dependence we have on God to make the right decisions. To live life right, we need to let him place his hand over ours in guidance and correct us when we are wrong.

In this chapter we'll look at the theme of discernment in the Bible. We'll see there is only one man who is successful at choosing between good and evil. The rest of us are at best inept and will fail if we attempt to handle it on our own. Choosing between good and evil is a big responsibility for an imperfect human.

A Tree for Discernment

As you might guess, our study begins in the early chapters of Genesis. A very important part of God's provision for Adam and Eve included two special trees in the Garden of Eden.

> **Genesis 2:9** — And out of the ground the LORD God made to spring up every tree that is pleasant to the sight and good for food. The tree of life was in the midst of the garden, and the tree of the knowledge of good and evil.

God gave a special commandment regarding the second of these trees:

> **Genesis 2:17** — "But of the tree of the knowledge of good and evil you shall not eat, for in the day that you eat of it you shall surely die."

This tree became a test for Adam and Eve. Apparently there was nothing obviously evil about the tree; Adam and Eve needed God's command in order to know that it was wrong for them to eat its fruit. To say it another way, they needed God's Word to discern between their options regarding the tree. (I'll write a future chapter on the theme of word).

When Satan came along, he enticed Eve to eat the forbidden fruit partly on the basis that by doing so she and her husband would know good and evil. This was a tempting prospect to Eve because it sounded like it would result in much wisdom.

> **Genesis 3:5** — "For God knows that when you eat of it your eyes will be opened, and you will be like God, knowing good and evil."

Sadly, however, mankind's knowledge of good and evil is on a much different level from God's. God knew everything about evil even before it existed. He knows not only everything that is actual, but also everything that is potential. In his wisdom he also innately knows what is good and what is evil. Our knowledge of good and evil, on the other hand, is inherently different.

After Adam and Eve chose to disobey him, God acknowledged that they had indeed become like him in their knowledge of good and evil:

> **Genesis 3:22**—Then the LORD God said, "Behold, the man has become like one of us in knowing good and evil. Now, lest he reach out his hand and take also of the tree of life and eat, and live forever—"

Nevertheless, likeness doesn't in this case mean equality. The only way we as created beings can know evil is by experiencing it. What the Lord means is that having experienced good in its perfect state, Adam and Eve now also had a knowledge of evil, experiencing imperfection for the first time. Instead of moving toward equality with God, as Satan had led Eve to believe, they were actually now less like him than before. They had the negative experience of evil, but they were not any more adept at discerning between good and evil. For that they still needed God. Adam and Eve felt the consequences of evil but were still lacking wisdom to choose good over evil. In other words, like all of us they were dependent on God and his Word to discern between good and evil.

Let's look at how the rest of Scripture develops this theme for us. Several passages use the words *good* and *evil* to show how God has been doing a work to correct the problem that started in the Garden of Eden. All the verses I have chosen seem to refer back to the tree in Genesis 3 instead of just be coincidental appearances of the words in close proximity.

Dependence on the Lord

First we need to make a quick stop in the middle of Genesis to confirm our understanding of Genesis 3. Genesis 24 shows that, biblically, we are unable to discern on our own between good and evil. In this chapter Abraham's servant was seeking a wife for Isaac and happened upon Rebekah. Contrary to culture, Rebekah's family relinquished their right to make a decision in the matter. Look at why:

> **Genesis 24:50–51**—Then Laban and Bethuel answered and said, "The thing has come from the LORD; we cannot speak to you bad or good. Behold, Rebekah is before you; take her and go, and let her be the wife of your master's son, as the LORD has spoken."

The Hebrew words for "bad" and "good" here are the same as the ones used in chapter 3 for the tree of the knowledge of "good" and "evil," as they will be in each of the verses we examine. Laban and Bethuel recognized the Lord's obvious leading in the details of the matter at hand. The context makes it clear that God was indicating it was good for Rebekah to marry Isaac. From the very mouths of Laban and Bethuel the author communicates to us that we are unable to discern good and evil without God's help.

An Example of Discernment

Toward the end of Genesis, we see how God helps his people with the practical discernment they need. Joseph is presented as the perfect example of someone who depended on God for discernment. While Joseph was in prison, Pharaoh realized he needed Joseph to help him interpret his dreams.

> **Genesis 41:14–16**—Then Pharaoh sent and called Joseph, and they quickly brought him out of the pit. And when he had shaved himself and changed his clothes, he came in before Pharaoh. And Pharaoh said to Joseph, "I have had a dream, and there is no one who can interpret it. I have heard it said of you that when you hear a dream you can interpret it." Joseph answered Pharaoh, "It is not in me; God will give Pharaoh a favorable answer."

At this point Joseph made it really clear that what he was about to do would not be out of his own power; he was dependent on the Lord.

> **Genesis 41:17–21**—Then Pharaoh said to Joseph, "Behold, in my dream I was standing on the banks of the Nile. Seven cows, plump and attractive, came up out of the Nile and fed in the reed grass. Seven other cows came up after them, poor and very *ugly* and thin, such as I had never seen in all the land of Egypt. And the thin, *ugly* cows ate up the first seven plump cows, but when they had eaten them no one would have known that they had eaten them, for they were still as *ugly* as at the beginning. Then I awoke (emphasis added).

The word Pharaoh used to describe the ugly cows was actually the same word translated "evil" in Genesis 2 and 3. Now look at what came next in Joseph's interpretation:

> **Genesis 41:26–30**—The seven *good* cows are seven years, and the seven good ears are seven years; the dreams are one. The seven lean and *ugly* cows that came up after them are seven years, and the seven empty ears blighted by the east wind are also seven years of famine. It is as I told Pharaoh; God has shown to Pharaoh what he is about to do. There will come seven years of great plenty throughout all the land of Egypt, but after them there will arise seven years of famine, and all the plenty will be forgotten in the land of Egypt. The famine will consume the land (emphasis added),

Do you see what Joseph did? By repeating the same words used in Genesis 2 and 3, he referred to the cows in terms of good and evil, and the context shows he was discerning between the two. The author of Genesis wants us to see that, unlike Adam and Eve, Joseph was capable, with God's power, of showing discernment in regard to good and evil! This message is further highlighted by Pharaoh's analysis of the power behind Joseph's skill:

> **Genesis 41:38** — And Pharaoh said to his servants, "Can we find a man like this, in whom is the Spirit of God?"

Both Adam and Joseph needed to depend on God for their discernment;[1] one was successful, one was not. Without God's Spirit, Adam was unable to rule the garden God had entrusted him with. In contrast, Pharaoh was willing to entrust Joseph with rulership of the entire kingdom of Egypt because he exercised discernment between good and evil.

It might seem strange that this analysis of Joseph was based on his discernment regarding a seemingly insignificant thing like cows, but that is only the way it is communicated textually. Consider the more significant illustration of Joseph's discernment: he did not give in to the seduction of Potiphar's wife. His discernment in this regard is in stark contrast to the patriarchs Abraham and Isaac (Genesis chapters 12, 20, and 26). In those cases, their beautiful wives were sought after by foreign rulers. In Joseph's case, however, the handsome patriarch himself was sought after by the wife of a foreign ruler. Joseph's test was more difficult. The previous patriarchs lacked wisdom and God had to intervene to prevent disaster. In Joseph's case, God did a work with his Spirit to enable Joseph to make the right decision from the beginning. So you can see that the significance of Joseph's discernment goes a lot farther than cows, even if that's the context in which we find the textual clue.

Joseph's discernment also contrasts with Judah's immorality recounted in chapter 38. The reader is expected to notice the difference between these brothers who are literarily presented as two potential candidates for the blessing of the firstborn at the end of Genesis. (For more on this, look for a future book with a chapter on Younger Son.) Over the course of several chapters it seems Joseph would be the one to receive the greater share of his father's favor, but in the end Judah, in spite of his previous sins and failures, received the grace he didn't deserve. The big reversal climaxed in Genesis

---

[1] Sailhamer, *The Pentateuch as Narrative*, 215.

44:33 when he offered himself as a substitute for Benjamin. He showed discernment when faced with the prospect of his brother Benjamin becoming a slave. This is in contrast to what happened when he and his brothers sold Joseph into slavery. In the earlier account, it was Judah who had the idea of slavery in the first place. It seems he learned from his past failures, and Joseph received the answer to his test. Judah, instead of being instrumental in an evil choice as he was in selling Joseph, became the primary player in the good choice to save Benjamin. By the end of Genesis, Judah seems to have learned discernment the hard and slow way. Joseph, on the other hand, seems to have come by it as a gift from the Spirit when Pharaoh's cows showed up on the scene.

Judah eventually became an ancestor of Jesus. Joseph, for his part, plays the part of a type of Christ. One of the ways he represents our Lord is in his moral character. In all the numerous chapters that deal with the story of Joseph, not once is there an explicit mention of his sin. Of course Joseph sinned, as does all humankind. Leaving out any mention of his sins, however, is a literary decision that allows the author to make a statement about the future savior Joseph foreshadows. We will yet see that Jesus, more than anyone else, demonstrates discernment between good and evil.

Discernment Regarding the Promised Land
The failure to discern between good and evil is the subject of another very significant passage in the Pentateuch. As Israel approached the Promised Land, God told Moses to send spies ahead of them.

> **Numbers 13:1–2**—The LORD spoke to Moses, saying, "Send men to spy out the land of Canaan, which I am giving to the people of Israel. From each tribe of their fathers you shall send a man, every one a chief among them."

Notice God didn't give a purpose for the action of sending spies; it was probably simply as a concession based on their lack of faith. Moses' recollection of these events in Deuteronomy 1:20–23 helps clarify this verse. Probably the people first requested a chance to send spies, and then Moses permitted it because God approved it. At the very least, God's approval should not be seen as occasion to consider whether or not to enter the land; God clearly said he was giving it to them. Nevertheless, they were about to make a watershed decision about whether to conquer it as God had instructed them.

> **Numbers 13:17–19**—Moses sent them to spy out the land of Canaan and said to them, "Go up into the Negeb and go up into the hill country, and see what the land is, and whether the people who dwell in it are strong or

weak, whether they are few or many, and whether the land that they dwell in is *good* or *bad*, and whether the cities that they dwell in are camps or strongholds (emphasis added)."

Moses' words were not contrary to God's intentions for the spies; he was not giving reason to doubt God. Although he might have come close, he was not insinuating that Israel should potentially choose not to enter the land based on the outcome of the report. Rather, we can see the intentions behind Moses' statements in verse 19 with his use of the words "good" and "bad." When he asked the spies to determine whether the land was good or evil (same Hebrew words), we are intended to make a connection with the tree of the knowledge of good and evil. The correct answer from the spies clearly needed to be that the land was good, for it was a gift from God. At a deeper level, however, the reader must draw the conclusion that just as with the forbidden tree in the Garden of Eden, the Israelites had a choice to make regarding God's command. More than an evaluation of the land itself, this passage is about an evaluation of the decision the people would make about the land. Would they make the right choice and enter the good land as God had directed? Instead of repeating Adam's mistake at the beginning of Genesis, Moses was hoping the people would show the same discernment Joseph did at the end of the book. Let's see how it played out.

Did you notice that twelve spies were sent into the land—one from each tribe? In the context of discernment, we should be asking ourselves which of these tribes was most likely to succeed. We saw that at the end of Genesis, Joseph and Judah rose to the top. They were the two candidates for the favored blessing from their father. Joseph's discernment was presented as flawless and it seemed he would become the chosen one. Judah, however, matured late and made a key decision of discernment, giving him the greatest blessing from his father in Genesis 49. For that reason, we probably shouldn't be surprised that the two discerning spies in Numbers 13 and 14 turned out to be Joshua and Caleb. Caleb was a descendant of Judah and was the first to speak out with the correct decision regarding the land.

> **Numbers 13:30**—But Caleb quieted the people before Moses and said, "Let us go up at once and occupy it, for we are well able to overcome it."

Joshua represented the tribe of Ephraim. His real name was Hoshea, but the text informs us that Moses called him Joshua. Manasseh and Ephraim were the two sons of Joseph who each became the father of a tribe. Ephraim was the younger son who emerged with greater favor and, as such, became the father of the tribe that most represented the interests of Joseph himself.

Therefore, in this passage Joshua is portrayed as highly capable of following in Joseph's footsteps.

A close attention to these details shows this passage is full of echoes. We have Joshua and Caleb repeating the wise discernment of their forefathers, Joseph and Judah. At the end of Genesis, Joseph and Judah were partially successful in reversing the poor discernment Adam and Eve exercised at its beginning. Adam and Eve were on the stage at the beginning of the occupation of the land with which God had blessed his people. And now the people were once again about to occupy the land God was going to give them. Would Joshua and Caleb's discernment be sufficient to lead the people into the land? Perhaps the Promised Land would turn out to be everything Eden was intended to be!

The text begins to focus on the spies' discernment. Unfortunately, there was disagreement among them. Caleb's report was immediately rejected by the 10 other spies. The deliberation became prolonged and Joshua and Caleb stated their firm position in the next chapter. Notice their use of the word "good" to qualify the land:

> **Numbers 14:6–7** — And Joshua the son of Nun and Caleb the son of Jephunneh, who were among those who had spied out the land, tore their clothes and said to all the congregation of the people of Israel, "The land, which we passed through to spy it out, is an exceedingly *good* land (emphasis added)."

In their use of this word, it is clear they were claiming to have the correct discernment so crucially needed at the moment. Look at how the word *evil* shows up later in the chapter:

> **Numbers 14:37** — The men who brought up a *bad* report of the land — died by plague before the LORD (emphasis added).

Once again, the word for "bad" here is the same word used for "evil." The ten spies weren't brazen enough to say the land was actually evil, but here their *report* is characterized as evil. It was evil because they lacked discernment, and the result for them was death. Just as the lack of discernment in Eden resulted in death for Adam and Eve (and the whole world), now the 10 spies, and nearly all the adults of the entire nation to which they belonged, died in the wilderness before even entering the land God was offering.

Conditional Occupation

In many other Old Testament passages the issue of good and evil is associated with the land. Many times it is made clear that remaining in the land would be contingent on exercising discernment regarding good and evil. See these passages, for example:

Deuteronomy 4:21–25	Psalm 52:1–5
Deuteronomy 9:6, 18	Psalm 112
Joshua 23:14–16	Psalm 119
1 Kings 14:15	Proverbs 2
1 Kings 14:22–24	Isaiah 65
2 Chronicles 7:14	Jeremiah 6:8, 12, 16, 19
Nehemiah 9	Jeremiah 24
Job 2:3, 10	Jeremiah 42:6, 10
Psalm 34:11–16	Ezekiel 20
Psalm 37 (especially	Ezekiel 36:16–36
verses 27–29)	

I left two Deuteronomy passages off the list above because I want to deal with them more thoroughly. Conditional occupation of the land is one of the big messages of Deuteronomy. The book of Numbers recounts for us the failure to discern correctly at the first attempt to enter the land; the events of Deuteronomy occur at the time of the people's second chance. Moses was not going to be allowed to enter the Promised Land, but he wanted to ensure the people were prepared to do it right the second time. Look at how Moses reflected on God's punishment for their previous lack of discernment:

> **Deuteronomy 1:34–40** — "And the LORD heard your words and was angered, and he swore, 'Not one of these men of this evil generation shall see the good land that I swore to give to your fathers, except Caleb the son of Jephunneh. He shall see it, and to him and to his children I will give the land on which he has trodden, because he has wholly followed the LORD!' Even with me the LORD was angry on your account and said, 'You also shall not go in there. Joshua the son of Nun, who stands before you, he shall enter. Encourage him, for he shall cause Israel to inherit it. And as for your little ones, who you said would become a prey, and your children, who today have no *knowledge of good or evil*, they shall go in there. And to them I will give it, and they shall possess it. But as for you, turn, and journey into the wilderness in the direction of the Red Sea (emphasis added).'"

Moses recalls words he heard from God forty years earlier. In the middle of this quotation is a very interesting phrase. When God referred to the children who were innocent of the sin of refusing to enter the land, he said they had "no knowledge of good or evil." Obviously this phrase means the children were too young to be held accountable for the sinful decision of their parents. Besides Caleb and Joshua, those grown children were now the only Israelites who would be given a second chance. More than that, however, is communicated by the word choice here. The phrase leads us to recall the tree of the knowledge of good and evil and every subsequent test that was placed before God's people to determine their discernment. The new generation of Israelites was now, forty years after their first opportunity to enter the land, being given both another chance and another test. John H. Sailhamer first pointed me toward this understanding by noting that the Israelites were "in much the same position" as Adam and Eve. Because of their innocence they needed to depend on God's Word for knowing truth.[1] Would they make the right decision(s) as they entered the Promised Land? The question is less about their ability to choose between good and evil, and more about where they would find their resources for discernment. The clear message to this point has been that none are able to discern on their own. If the new generation learned anything of worth from the stories of Adam and Joseph, they would have learned they must depend on God to give them discernment.

This passage describes a test that in reality all of us face on a daily basis. Discernment between good and evil is a recurring need for every generation, every individual within each generation, several times every day. It's true that Adam and Eve already made the wrong decision, which results in a bent within each of us to constantly choose evil. It might seem we are in a hopeless struggle to choose good, but that is no reason to surrender. Instead our task is simply to realize where the only source of good discernment lies. If we recognize that every mistaken lack of discernment ever was due to rejecting God's help and ignoring his Word, we know the natural solution to our tendency toward evil. We all need to grow in our capacity for depending on God for our decisions. Sometimes we put a lot of weight on decisions regarding life direction, such as employment, schooling, marriage, and so on. It's true that those things are important, but we aren't always as careful as we need to be with our discernment of good and evil. We need to take this kind of decision very seriously, even more so than the former. And if it's important enough for us, we will gladly relegate the decision to Someone else, the only one who can choose correctly every time without fail! We'll further consider that soon.

---

[1] Ibid., 427.

At the end of the book of Deuteronomy, after Moses did all he could to impress the importance of his message on the nation, just before he was going to die, he summarized once again the choice that was before the people.

> **Deuteronomy 30:15–18**—"See, I have set before you today life and good, death and evil. If you obey the commandments of the LORD your God that I command you today, by loving the LORD your God, by walking in his ways, and by keeping his commandments and his statutes and his rules, then you shall live and multiply, and the LORD your God will bless you in the land that you are entering to take possession of it. But if your heart turns away, and you will not hear, but are drawn away to worship other gods and serve them, I declare to you today, that you shall surely perish. You shall not live long in the land that you are going over the Jordan to enter and possess."

Once again we see the choice between good and evil. Moses made very clear that the stakes were high. Making a good choice would result in life, and evil would bring death. He again referenced the decision made in the Garden of Eden. In verse 18 he even repeated the consequences of sin in much the same way they were described in Eden—perishing (Genesis 2:17). In his commentary on the Pentateuch John H. Sailhamer has done an excellent job of noticing the textual connections between Genesis and Deuteronomy.[2] He points out how both passages revolve around a good land. In both cases making the right choice leads to life, that is, living in the land with God's provision of either the tree of life or the fruit of the promised land. On the other hand, the wrong choice leads to death. The principle characters must depend on God's instruction for making the right choice. And in both instances the right choice would allow them to walk with God (Genesis 3:8; Deuteronomy 30:16). Thus, Moses chooses to conclude the Pentateuch in the same way that it began by portraying the Israelites as taking the same role as Adam and Eve. Compare Genesis 1:28, "Be fruitful and multiply and fill the land," with Deuteronomy 30:16, "You shall live and multiply, and the LORD your God will bless you in the land."

Circumcision of the Heart

The most beautiful part of Moses' admonition is the way we are enabled to follow it according to the context. Look at how he expected us to be able to exercise our discernment:

---

[2] Ibid., 474.

184

Deuteronomy 30:6—And the LORD your God will circumcise your heart and the heart of your offspring, so that you will love the LORD your God with all your heart and with all your soul, that you may live.

Once again we see that proper discernment does not depend on our own ability. We are able to practice it only after our hearts have been circumcised; that is, after God has done a work in us that changes us to the core. We then have his character to guide us in what would be an impossibly difficult choice on our own. The image of heart circumcision is meant to contrast with the Old Testament law. The old circumcision of the law was performed on an external organ; this new circumcision was to be performed internally. Moses is telling us that the law can never give us enough discernment to obey out of our own strength. He is pointing forward to the inner-life change that Jesus wants to do in everyone. Moses' promise is now relatively recently available since Jesus' presence here on earth made it a reality. (For more see the chapter on New Heart in a future book.)

Joshua

Just as Moses challenged the Israelites in this matter right before he died, his successor did much the same. Joshua took the nation into the land and, besides conquering what God had given them, attempted to guide them in discernment so they could remain in the land. As he came to the end of his life, he was concerned for Israel's future.

Joshua 23:11—Be very careful, therefore, to love the LORD your God.

Joshua 23:14–16—"And now I am about to go the way of all the earth, and you know in your hearts and souls, all of you, that not one word has failed of all the good things that the LORD your God promised concerning you. All have come to pass for you; not one of them has failed. But just as all the *good* things that the LORD your God promised concerning you have been fulfilled for you, so the LORD will bring upon you all the *evil* things, until he has destroyed you from off this good land that the LORD your God has given you, if you transgress the covenant of the LORD your God, which he commanded you, and go and serve other gods and bow down to them. Then the anger of the LORD will be kindled against you, and you shall perish quickly from off the good land that he has given to you (emphasis added)."

Joshua made things very clear. They could either keep the covenant with Yahweh or choose to serve other gods. Verse 15 presents the two potential results that would follow: good things or evil things. Ultimately evil would end in destruction and removal from the land. Up until now, the words "good" and "evil" have generally been used to describe the people's choice. This time the warning is so severe, an adjustment is made. "Good" and "evil" describe God's response; he will need to bring evil consequences if their choice so warrants. Once again, we are reminded by this passage that discernment of good and evil is a need that keeps repeating itself from one generation to the next. It's clear that God needs to do something to solve the issue once and for all.

Exile and Future Hope

God eventually proved his Word to be true. The warning he had repeatedly given through Moses and Joshua became reality. The Israelites had not yet been offered circumcision for their hearts, and as could be expected, they were unable to discern good and evil on their own. Remaining in the land was conditional on exercising good discernment (Deuteronomy 30:18), and as a result of their sin they were carried to exile. The story of the Garden of Eden repeated itself again. (Look for a chapter on Exile in a future book.)

While God's people were living in Babylon, the prophet Ezekiel wrote about God's future plans. Some of his message was to be fulfilled in the immediate future, but the complete fulfillment is still to come, even for us.

> Ezekiel 36:24–31 – I will take you from the nations and gather you from all the countries and bring you into your own land. I will sprinkle clean water on you, and you shall be clean from all your uncleannesses, and from all your idols I will cleanse you. And I will give you a new heart, and a new spirit I will put within you. And I will remove the heart of stone from your flesh and give you a heart of flesh. And I will put my Spirit within you, and cause you to walk in my statutes and be careful to obey my rules. You shall dwell in the land that I gave to your fathers, and you shall be my people, and I will be your God. And I will deliver you from all your uncleannesses. And I will summon the grain and make it abundant and lay no famine upon you. I will make the fruit of the tree and the increase of the field abundant, that you may never again suffer the disgrace of famine among the nations. Then you will remember your *evil* ways, and your deeds that were not *good*, and you will loathe yourselves for your iniquities and your abominations (emphasis added).

Notice the reason given in verse 31 for the exile they were experiencing: he mentions evil and good, implying a lack of discernment. The future solution referred to is once again to be a solution of the heart, replacing stone with flesh. (See the chapter on New Heart in a future book.) What's more, God promises to put his Spirit within us; that's the real secret to having discernment! We were told in Genesis that Joseph was able to make right choices for that very reason (Genesis 41:38). And now Pharaoh's question can be answered with confidence; he asked, "Can we find a man like this, in whom is the Spirit of God?" In fact yes, Pharaoh, all God's people will one day be like Joseph. Since Pentecost we all have the Holy Spirit, and the Spirit's transforming work in us will be consummated in the future. The result will be overwhelmingly good, according to verse 28: We will one day be enabled to dwell in the land without any remaining danger of being expulsed because of our lack of discernment. We will see the final fulfillment of that promise when we are able to dwell in the New Heavens and New Earth as God's people without ever again choosing evil. Land and discernment are apparently closely related; remaining in the land is conditional on wise choices. Thankfully, the condition will no longer be difficult to meet once we are completely sanctified by God's Holy Spirit.

King David

From this point forward we are going to see Scripture passages that gradually build toward the solution God offers for our discernment. Our first stop is in 2 Samuel 13–14. These two chapters offer a couple of textual clues pointing to the theme of discernment and how it relates to King David. Chapter 13 gives us a negative example and chapter 14 a positive one.

2 Samuel 13–14 is in the middle of a big drama for David's family, with high tension building between his children. Amnon and Absalom were half-brothers, both sons of King David, and they weren't getting along. Things got ugly in chapter 13 when Amnon raped Absalom's sister—a case of rape compounded by incest. Look at how Absalom responded in verse 22:

> **2 Samuel 13:22**—But Absalom spoke to Amnon neither *good* nor *bad*, for Absalom hated Amnon, because he had violated his sister Tamar (emphasis added).

Even though Absalom chose to speak to Amnon "neither good nor bad," two years later, when he had the chance, he killed Amnon (verse 28). It seems this phrase "speak neither good nor bad" probably was an idiom that meant to not do anything against someone. Compare, for example, Genesis 31:24, 29. But it seems likely to me there is more here than just the surface meaning. I believe this idiom was chosen in order to prompt the reader to question whether Absalom was discerning properly between good and evil.

The author is especially inclined to use this phrase here because of the connection it gives between Absalom and his father, David, in the next chapter. Absalom is the negative example of discernment who contrasts as a polar opposite with King David.

In the next chapter, 2 Samuel 14, we see a positive statement about David's discernment. King David had an internal conflict about how to deal with his son Absalom. He wanted to restore their relationship but apparently felt pressure to maintain a tough stance because of his position as king. Joab, his military general, sent a wise woman to encourage David to make the right choice. She counseled David to forgive Absalom and restore the relationship for the good of the nation. Her most striking words are found in verse 17:

> **2 Samuel 14:17** — "And your servant thought, 'The word of my lord the king will set me at rest,' for my lord the king is like the angel of God to *discern good and evil*. The LORD your God be with you (emphasis added)!"

The word "angel" by itself can mean either a human messenger or a supernatural angel from heaven. If she had simply said David was like an angel, that would be one thing. But she compared David to "the angel of God." This phrase is used in the Old Testament to refer to a person who is so important that he may even be an appearance of God himself. Look at how *Nelson's New Illustrated Bible Dictionary* defines this phrase:

> [The angel of God is] a mysterious messenger of God, sometimes described as the Lord Himself (Gen. 16:10–13; Ex. 3:2–6; 23:20; Judg. 6:11–18), but at other times as one sent by God. The Lord used this messenger to appear to human beings who otherwise would not be able to see Him and live (Ex. 33:20).
>
> The Angel of the Lord performed actions associated with God, such as revelation, deliverance, and destruction; but he can be spoken of as distinct from God (2 Sam. 24:16; Zech. 1:12). This special relationship has led many to conclude that the Angel of the Lord was Jesus in a pre-incarnate form.[3]

Therefore, this lady was affirming that David was nearly divine in his discerning ability. She may have been using flattery to try to push David in the direction she and Joab wanted him to go. Nevertheless, the phrase "discern good and evil" made its way to the recorded text for a reason. It seems the author allowed the praise from her lips to reflect his own evaluation of who

---

[3] Ronald F. Youngblood, F. F. Bruce, R. K. Harrison, ed., *Nelson's New Illustrated Bible Dictionary* (Nashville, TN: Thomas Nelson, Inc., 1995).

David was. King David followed in the steps of Joseph, who exercised discernment with the power of God's Spirit. King David also was the forerunner of the Messiah, and Jesus is quite possibly the Angel of the Lord incarnate. It's not that David was without his grave mistakes in discernment. Rather, the author simply wanted us to know that David humbly showed how things should be done. David, with a heart after God, depended on God for his decisions between good and evil. The speaker affirmed this by adding, "The Lord your God be with you." If the Son of David will surpass King David with respect to his eternal throne, we might also expect him to be infinitely more skillful at discernment. This passage gives us a strong indication that God has a plan for providing perfect discernment through David's descendant.

David knew something about discernment, and he shared his wisdom in Psalm 37.

> **Psalm 37:27–29**
> Turn away from *evil* and do *good*;
>   so shall you dwell forever.
> For the LORD loves justice;
>   he will not forsake his saints.
> They are preserved forever,
>   but the children of the wicked shall be cut off.
> The righteous shall inherit the land
>   and dwell upon it forever (emphasis added).

David, like few others, is qualified to exhort us to reject evil and do good. Assumed is the fact that we, like him, will depend on God for our discernment. And he shows he is fully aware of the connection between choosing good and remaining in the land. Did you notice the connection he makes with eternal life? Ultimately the most important decision we can make between good and evil concerns whether we will be children of God.

Solomon
We need to also see how this theme develops in the case of David's son, Solomon. The text holds a certain tension; we ought to read about Solomon with a question—Is he the true son of David, the fulfillment of God's promise? (See Chapter 5, "The Perfect King.") In many ways Solomon does come close to being that greater son; in a few ways he falls far short. Remember Solomon's big request from God? The Lord allowed him to request whatever he wanted, and he chose wisdom. But the key is to observe the fascinating way he worded his request:

> **1 Kings 3:9**—"Give your servant therefore an understanding mind to govern your people, that I may discern between *good* and *evil*, for who is able to govern this your great people?" (emphasis added)

Solomon wanted discernment in order to follow in Joseph and David's footprints. He wanted to choose well between good and evil. For this reason it seems he could be a likely candidate to be Messiah. The next chapters even show us how good he was at discernment, but later we learn of the problems. Later we learn that even in this area he fell far short, making poor decisions regarding good and evil. He was close and yet so far from perfection.

Immanuel

As we move closer to seeing God's mighty work through Jesus, we need to see one passage in the prophets. King Ahaz, king of Judah, was facing a big military challenge. He was concerned about possibly losing his kingdom in a battle with Syria. The king of Syria had convinced Israel, Judah's brotherly northern kingdom, to join as allies against Judah. Besides being a great military threat, theologically this should be understood as a fight between brothers and even a rejection of the God-ordained king from the tribe of Judah. Even though Ahaz was a terrible king, he was, nevertheless, a king in the line of David. God showed what was important to him by what he did in response; he gave a promise for protection. It's not that Judah was safe from all military threats; the Lord would eventually choose to punish her in this very way. But it would not be by the hand of Israel. Through the prophet Isaiah God assured Ahaz that the perceived threat was not an actual threat at all. He gave a message to Ahaz:

> **Isaiah 7:14–16**—Therefore the Lord himself will give you a sign. Behold, the virgin shall conceive and bear a son, and shall call his name Immanuel. He shall eat curds and honey when he knows how to refuse the *evil* and choose the *good*. For before the boy knows how to refuse the *evil* and choose the *good*, the land whose two kings you dread will be deserted (emphasis added).

This prophecy probably has two referents—one that was fulfilled in the following months and years in Ahaz's day, and an even bigger fulfillment when Jesus Christ came to earth. God was, on the one hand, referring to a young lady who was still a virgin when Ahaz heard these words, but later ceased to be a virgin when she conceived. He was also referring to Mary's conception of Jesus while she remained a virgin.

Immanuel means "God with us." It was an appropriate name for the boy who was born in Ahaz's day, for he was a reminder of God's protective presence. The name is even more appropriately applied to Jesus, who was actually God himself dwelling with humanity. The curds and honey might seem to point in a positive way to a bountiful supply of food, but the context shows us why it would be abundant—the land would be deserted and uncultivated, a negative consequence of the people's exile. The Lord referred to this boy reaching an age of accountability at which he would know how to choose between good and evil. The point in the immediate context was that it wouldn't be very long before these things would happen.

When Matthew applied this prophecy to Christ in Matthew 1:23, refusing evil and choosing good took on a whole new level of meaning. When Jesus reached the level of accountability, one could also say he had learned to refuse evil and choose good. The tremendous significance behind that statement is that he learned discernment infinitely better than any other human ever has. Jesus has never sinned; that means in every single instance of his life, from the age of accountability, he has always chosen the good! Down through all the centuries and all the millennia from Genesis 3 onward, discerning between good and evil has always been an issue. In fact, more than an issue, it has been an impossible challenge! But now through the words of Isaiah, the Lord made known he had a plan for God himself (Immanuel) to dwell with us and show us how to flawlessly choose between good and evil.

Jesus Passes the Test
Now let's move to the New Testament and see an example of how Jesus Christ demonstrated his discernment for us. The gospel writers recorded Jesus' temptation in the wilderness in a way that shows they understood it to connect to the theme we are studying (Matthew 4:1–11; Mark 1:12–13; Luke 4:1–13).

> **Matthew 4:1–4**—Then Jesus was led up by the Spirit into the wilderness to be tempted by the devil. And after fasting forty days and forty nights, he was hungry. And the tempter came and said to him, "If you are the Son of God, command these stones to become loaves of bread." But he answered, "It is written, " 'Man shall not live by bread alone, but by every word that comes from the mouth of God.' "

Have you ever wondered why Jesus fasted for 40 days before his testing? Remember our study of the Pentateuch earlier in this chapter. Adam and Eve failed to discern properly, but Joseph showed it could be done with God's help. On a small scale he reversed their earlier failure. Nevertheless,

Israel as a whole failed to discern properly when it was time to enter the Promised Land. They had to wander 40 years in the desert as punishment. After those 40 years they were given another chance in which they more or less succeeded by at least entering the land and starting to get things right. In Matthew, Jesus entered the scene with a chance to reverse the failure of Adam and Eve on a much larger scale. He also played the role of the second generation of Israelites who successfully entered the land. Jesus' 40 days of fasting in the wilderness correspond to their 40 years of wandering in the wilderness. Jesus would be God's provision for the second chance of all second chances, and he would achieve it with full perfection!

The tests Jesus faced were very similar in nature and circumstance to the tests Adam and Eve failed. If their test was difficult to pass, Jesus' test was humanly impossible, for the text paints his as even more challenging. Look at the parallels and contrasts we are given:[4]

Adam and Eve	Jesus
Tested by the serpent	Tested by the tempter
Temptation regarding food	Temptation regarding food
Eve repeated God's command, but with imprecision.	Jesus quoted Scripture.
Both were tested not in "obedience to an eternal moral principle rooted in the character of God, [but in a matter] of pure obedience to God's specific directive" (Grudem, 536)	
Fellowship with each other and God	No human fellowship
Abundance of all kinds of food	No food
Death did not exist until after they sinned.	Jesus nearly reached physical death before his temptation.
Adam and Eve failed the test in spite of every advantage.	Jesus succeeded against all odds.

[4] Wayne A. Grudem, *Systematic Theology* (Leicester, England: Inter-Varsity Press, 1994), 536.

Our Rest

Because Jesus is perfectly able to choose good over evil, he offers us an in-dispensable blessing. Hebrews 3:7–4:16 teaches an extremely significant concept in this regard. We could study the whole passage in depth, but let's just look at some highlights here. (For a deeper study, see the chapter on Rest in a future book.) The author of Hebrews wants to show us that we all have an opportunity similar to the one the Israelites had in Deuteronomy just before entering the Promised Land. The Promised Land was meant to be a place of rest for Israel. When they finished conquering it in the book of Joshua, we are told in two verses that they had received their rest (Joshua 22:4; 23:1). Now, however, Hebrews teaches us that a greater and more com-plete rest is offered to us all. It is also rest in the sense that the work to achieve it is completely done.

We still need to discern between good and evil, but now the discernment happens on a different level. Look at the warning the author gives about discernment:

> **Hebrews 3:12**—Take care, brothers, lest there be in any of you an evil, un-believing heart, leading you to fall away from the living God.

The warning is quite a bit different than what we saw in the Old Testament. Now, instead of choosing between good and evil actions, we need to discern the condition of our hearts. We need to observe whether our hearts have faith or unbelief. Basically, we need to consider whether God has circum-cised our hearts with a resulting change to the core of our being (see the future chapter on New Heart). The responsibility to discern between good and evil actions has already been taken care of by Jesus' perfect life lived on our behalf. Now we rest from our works:

> **Hebrews 4:10**—For whoever has entered God's rest has also rested from his works as God did from his.

It's not that works are unimportant. It's not that the difference between good and evil no longer matters. The rest Jesus offers still requires discernment between good and evil, but the work of discernment has already been com-pleted by him! Jesus exercised discernment in a way that reminds us of Jo-seph. The difference is that Joseph only *appears* in Scripture to be sinless, whereas Jesus truly was without sin. In every moment of his life he has al-ways chosen good and rejected evil.

Hebrews 4:15—For we do not have a high priest who is unable to sympathize with our weaknesses, but one who in every respect has been tempted as we are, yet without sin.

We have the benefit of Jesus' completed work of discernment, and he completed it perfectly! He died to take the penalty of every evil choice ever made, and he lived to perfectly choose the good in our place (see Romans 5:18–20). After we enter our rest, there's no more work to be done. That is, he offers the work to achieve salvation, then it's a done deal.

Our Privilege

These truths from Hebrews need to be balanced by something the apostle John teaches us. Even though Hebrews rightly teaches us that the work of discernment is completely done, John shows us we still get to be involved. We still have the privilege of choosing between right and wrong; it's just not work anymore. It's not work because it's not required in order to receive our salvation. Instead of work, our discernment has now become the centerpiece of a loving relationship.

John 14:15–17—"If you love me, you will keep my commandments. And I will ask the Father, and he will give you another Helper, to be with you forever, even the Spirit of truth, whom the world cannot receive, because it neither sees him nor knows him. You know him, for he dwells with you and will be in you."

Our relationship with Jesus our Savior compels us to keep his commandments. Obeying him isn't a requirement for our salvation. Rather, it's a natural product of our salvation. That is, if we claim to follow Jesus, the only human who ever perfectly exercised discernment, we will want to emulate him in the application of that same skill. The really good news is that Christ gives us another Helper, a paraclete—the Holy Spirit. Notice he says *another* Helper. Jesus can and does help us choose between good and evil, but currently the greatest source of our help is the Holy Spirit, someone who is equal to Christ in his ability to discern. Remember how Joseph accomplished righteousness in Genesis 41:38? His discernment was given to him because he had the presence of the Spirit. That was a privilege not everyone had in that age, but the story is different for us. Jesus' promise in verse 17 is that all his followers have the Spirit—not only with us, but *in* us. There's no doubt about his efficacy to help us choose between good and evil in every moment!

Future Completion

Our future hope includes a work that God will do in us to give us his flaw-less discernment. When we are with him in New Jerusalem, his work in us will be so complete that it will actually be impossible for us to choose incorrectly.

> **Revelation 21:27**—But nothing unclean will ever enter it, nor anyone who does what is detestable or false, but only those who are written in the Lamb's book of life.

In heaven we will be reintroduced to the tree of life from the Garden of Eden (Revelation 2:7; 22:2, 14), but there won't be a tree of the knowledge of good and evil. It won't be needed. We already know evil; God is working in his people to help them know good. In that final state, the knowledge will be complete and there will never again be a danger of making the wrong choice. I'm excited about that!

Conclusion

A five-year-old boy loves to paint with a roller. He loves to get his hands on the painting equipment and control where it goes. Probably more than any-thing else, he loves the satisfaction of stepping back and seeing the results of what he has done—be it constructive or damaging! We're all like that, really. We all want the satisfaction of seeing our choices result in something big. Thankfully we have a God who is more than willing to put his hand over ours and guide our choices. Because he's working in my life, I have full confidence that my choices are painting something really constructive. Are you letting him be the source of your discernment? If so, the results will probably be more beautiful than you can even conceive!

Passages for further study:

Genesis 31:24, 29
Leviticus 27:9–14
1 Samuel 16:23
2 Samuel 19:35
Psalm 34:11–16
Psalm 36:1–4
Psalm 52:1–5
Ecclesiastes 12:14

Isaiah 5:20
Amos 5:14–15
Malachi 2:17
Matthew 12:33–37
Matthew 13:47–50
Luke 6:43–45
1 Thessalonians 5:21–24

I would love to hear from you with your
feedback, additions, corrections, criticism or praise.

Write to me at:

scott.edgren@gmail.com

If you appreciate this book, considering posting a review on
Amazon.com

Bibliography

Alexander, T. Desmond and Brian S. Rosner, ed. *New Dictionary of Biblical Theology*, electronic ed. Downers Grove, IL: InterVarsity Press, 2000.

Alexander, T. Desmond. *From Eden to the New Jerusalem: An Introduction to Biblical Theology*. Grand Rapids, MI: Kregel, 2008.

Alter, Robert. *The Art of Biblical Narrative*. United States of America: Harper Collins, 1981.

Alter, Robert. *The Five Books of Moses: A Translation with Commentary*. New York: W. W. Norton & Company, 2004.

Anderson, Don. *A Gift Too Wonderful for Words*. Neptune, New Jersey: Loizeaux Brothers, 1987.

Arnold, Bill T. *Genesis*. Cambridge, UK: Cambridge University Press, 2009.

Beale, G. K. and D. A. Carson, ed. *Commentary on the New Testament Use of the Old Testament*. Grand Rapids: Baker Academic, 2007.

Brown, Francis, Samuel Rolles Driver and Charles Augustus Briggs. *Enhanced Brown-Driver-Briggs Hebrew and English Lexicon*, electronic ed. Oak Harbor, WA: Logos Research Systems, 2000.

Budd, Phillip J. *Numbers*, Word Biblical Commentary. Dallas, TX: Word, Incorporated, 1998.

Carson, D. A. 'Introduction to Biblical Theology.' *The Gospel Coalition*. The Gospel Coalition's 2014 National Women's Conference. Audio. 29 June 2014. Web. http://resources.thegospelcoalition.org/library/introduction-to-biblical-theology. Accessed 28 July 2015.

Christensen, Duane L. *Deuteronomy 21:10–34:12*, Word Biblical Commentary. Dallas: Word, Incorporated, 2002.

Deliriumsrealm.com. 'Seraphim: Fiery Serpent Demons.' N.p., 2015. Web. Accessed 7 December 2014. http://www.deliriumsrealm.com/seraphim/.

Dempster, Stephen G. *Dominion and Dynasty: A Biblical Theology of the Hebrew Bible*. Downers Grove, IL: Intervarsity Press, 2003.

DeYoung, Kevin and Greg Gilbert. *What is the Mission of the Church? Making Sense of Social Justice, Shalom and the Great Commission*, audiobook. Wheaton, IL: Crossway, 2011.

Gage, Warren Austin. *Gospel Typology in Joshua and Revelation: A Whore and Her Scarlet, Seven Trumpets Sound, A Great City Falls*. Fort Lauderdale, FL: St. Andrews House, 2013.

Gentry, Peter John and Stephen J. Wellum. *Kingdom Through Covenant: A Biblical-Theological Understanding of the Covenants*, Kindle version. Wheaton, IL: Crossway, 2012.

GotQuestions.org. *'Who Was the Joshua In Zechariah 3:1–10?'* N.p., 2015. Web. Accessed 6 June 2015. http://www.gotquestions.org/Joshua-in-Zechariah.html.

Gower, Ralph and Fred Wight, *The New Manners and Customs of Bible Times*. Chicago, IL: Moody Press, 1987.

Greatriverspartnership.org "Mississippi River Basin." N.p., 2012. Web. Accessed 17 May 2016. http://www.greatriverspartnership.org/en-us/northamerica/mississippi/pages/default.aspx.

Green Prophet: Sustainable News for the Middle East. '2000-Year-Old Date Pit Sprouts In Israel.' N.p., 25 March 2012. Web. Accessed 13 May 2016. http://www.greenprophet.com/2012/03/2000-year-old-date-pit-sprouts-in-israel/.

Grudem, Wayne A. *Systematic Theology*. Leicester, England: Inter-Varsity Press, 1994.

Hagopian, David G., ed. *The Genesis Debate: Three Views On the Days of Creation*. Mission Viejo, CA: Crux Press, Inc. 2001.

Halpern, Baruch. "Kenites," *The Anchor Yale Bible Dictionary*, ed. David Noel Freedman. New York, NY: Doubleday, 1992.

Holladay, William Lee and Ludwig Köhler. *A Concise Hebrew and Aramaic Lexicon of the Old Testament*. Leiden, Netherlands: Brill, 2000.

Ingalls Wilder, Laura and Garth Williams. *Little House On The Prairie*. New York, NY: Harper & Bros., 1971.

Jeansonne, Sharon Pace. "Jeshurun." Ed. David Noel Freedman. *The Anchor Yale Bible Dictionary*, 1992: Volume 3. London, UK: Yale University Press, 1992.

Koehler, Ludwig, Walter Baumgartner, et al. *The Hebrew and Aramaic Lexicon of the Old Testament*. Leiden, Netherlands: Brill, 1994–2000.

Kinzel, Len. Sermon. English Fellowship Church, 24 March 2013.

Lewis, C. S. *The Lion, The Witch, And The Wardrobe*. New York: Collier Books, 1970.

Lewis, W. H. *The Splendid Century: Life in the France of Louis XIV*. Garden City, N.Y.: Doubleday, 1957.

Longman III, Tremper. *Literary Approaches to Biblical Interpretation*. Foundations of Contemporary Interpretation, Moisés Silva, Series Editor, Volume 3. Grand Rapids: Zondervan Publishing House, 1987.

MacDonald, William. *Believer's Bible Commentary: Old and New Testaments*, ed. Arthur Farstad. Nashville, TN: Thomas Nelson, 1995.

McLatchie, Jonathan. '*Jesus Foreshadowed by Joshua the High Priest.*' CrossExamined.org. 25 November 2011. Web. http://crossexamined.org/jesus-foreshadowed-by-joshua-the-high-priest/ Accessed 5 June 2015.

National Geographic. '2,000-Year-Old Seed Sprouts, Sapling Is Thriving.' N.p., 22 November 2005. Web. Accessed 13 May 2016. http://news.nationalgeographic.com/news/051122-old-plant-seed-food/.

Nelson, Michael. *Guide to the Presidency*. New York, NY: Routledge, 2015.

Newman, Jr., Barclay M. *A Concise Greek-English Dictionary of the New Testament*. Stuttgart, Germany: Deutsche Bibelgesellschaft; United Bible Societies, 1993.

Packard, Laurence Bradford. *The Age of Louis XIV*. New York: Hold, Rinehart and Winston, 1957.

Ross, Allen P. "Genesis", *The Bible Knowledge Commentary: An Exposition of the Scriptures*, ed. J. F. Walvoord and R. B. Zuck. Wheaton, IL: Victor Books, 1985.

Ross, Allen P. "Psalms," *The Bible Knowledge Commentary: An Exposition of the Scriptures*, ed. J. F. Walvoord and R. B. Zuck. Wheaton, IL: Victor Books, 1985.

Rubin, David Lee. *The Sun King: the ascendancy of French culture during the reign of Louis XIV*. Washington: Folger Shakespeare Library; London: Associated University Presses, 1992.

Ryken, Leland. *How To Read the Bible as Literature*. Grand Rapids: Zondervan Publishing House, 1984.

Sailhamer, John H. *Introduction to Old Testament Theology: A Canonical Approach*. Grand Rapids: Zondervan Publishing House, 1995.

———. *The Meaning of the Pentateuch: Revelation, Composition and Interpretation*. Downers Grove, IL: InterVarsity Press, 2009.

———. *The Pentateuch as Narrative: A Biblical-Theological Commentary*. Grand Rapids, MI: Zondervan Publishing House, 1992.

Sandom, Carrie. *The Gospel Coalition Podcast*, February 13, 2015.

Swanson, James. *Dictionary of Biblical Languages With Semantic Domains: Hebrew (Old Testament)*, electronic ed. Oak Harbor, WA: Logos Research Systems, Inc., 1997.

Thielman, Frank. *Theology of the New Testament: A Canonical and Synthetic Approach*. Grand Rapids: Zondervan Publishing House, 2005.

Walvoord, John F. "Revelation," *The Bible Knowledge Commentary: An Exposition of the Scriptures*, Volume 2, ed. J. F. Walvoord and R. B. Zuck. Wheaton, IL: Victor Books, 1985.

Wenham, Gordon J. "Sanctuary Symbolism in the Garden of Eden Story," in *I Studied Inscriptions from before the Flood: Ancient Near Eastern, Literary, and Linguistic Approaches to Genesis 1–11*, ed. R. S. Hess and D. T. Tsumura, Sources for Biblical and Theological Study 4. Winona Lake, IN: Eisenbrauns, 1994. http://www.godawa.com/chronicles_of_the_nephilim/Articles_By_Others/Wenham-Sanctuary_Symbolism_Garden_of_Eden.pdf

Wenham, Gordon J. *Genesis 1–15*. Word Biblical Commentary, Vol. 1. Dallas: Word, Incorporated, 1998.

Whitlock, Luder G. R. C. Sproul, Bruce K. Waltke and Moisés Silva, *The Reformation Study Bible: Bringing the Light of the Reformation to Scripture: New King James Version*. Nashville, TN: T. Nelson, 1995.

Wight, Fred Hartley. *Devotional Studies of Old Testament Types*. Chicago, IL: Moody Press, 1956.

Youngblood, Ronald F., F. F. Bruce, and R. K. Harrison, ed. *Nelson's New Illustrated Bible Dictionary*. Nashville, TN: Thomas Nelson, Inc., 1995.

Scripture Index

Made in the USA
San Bernardino, CA
01 May 2018